AWS CodeBuild User Guide

A catalogue record for this book is available from the Hong Kong Public Libraries.

Published in Hong Kong by Samurai Media Limited.

Email: info@samuraimedia.org

ISBN 9789888407859

Contents

What Is AWS CodeBuild?

AWS CodeBuild is a fully managed build service in the cloud. AWS CodeBuild compiles your source code, runs unit tests, and produces artifacts that are ready to deploy. AWS CodeBuild eliminates the need to provision, manage, and scale your own build servers. It provides prepackaged build environments for the most popular programming languages and build tools such as Apache Maven, Gradle, and more. You can also customize build environments in AWS CodeBuild to use your own build tools. AWS CodeBuild scales automatically to meet peak build requests.

AWS CodeBuild provides these benefits:

- **Fully managed** – AWS CodeBuild eliminates the need to set up, patch, update, and manage your own build servers.
- **On demand** – AWS CodeBuild scales on demand to meet your build needs. You pay only for the number of build minutes you consume.
- **Out of the box** – AWS CodeBuild provides preconfigured build environments for the most popular programming languages. All you need to do is point to your build script to start your first build.

For more information, see AWS CodeBuild.

Topics

- How to Run AWS CodeBuild
- Pricing for AWS CodeBuild
- How Do I Get Started with AWS CodeBuild?
- AWS CodeBuild Concepts

How to Run AWS CodeBuild

You can run AWS CodeBuild by using the AWS CodeBuild or AWS CodePipeline console. You can also automate the running of AWS CodeBuild by using the AWS Command Line Interface (AWS CLI) or the AWS SDKs.

To run AWS CodeBuild by using the AWS CodeBuild console, AWS CLI, AWS SDKs, see Run AWS CodeBuild Directly.

As the following diagram shows, you can add AWS CodeBuild as a build or test action to the build or test stage of a pipeline in AWS CodePipeline. AWS CodePipeline is a continuous delivery service that enables you to model, visualize, and automate the steps required to release your code. This includes building your code. A *pipeline* is a workflow construct that describes how code changes go through a release process.

To use AWS CodePipeline to create a pipeline and then add an AWS CodeBuild build or test action, see Use AWS CodePipeline with AWS CodeBuild. For more information about AWS CodePipeline, see the AWS CodePipeline User Guide.

Pricing for AWS CodeBuild

For information, see AWS CodeBuild Pricing.

How Do I Get Started with AWS CodeBuild?

We recommend that you complete the following steps:

1. **Learn** more about AWS CodeBuild by reading the information in Concepts.
2. **Experiment** with AWS CodeBuild in an example scenario by following the instructions in Getting Started.
3. **Use** AWS CodeBuild in your own scenarios by following the instructions in Plan a Build.

AWS CodeBuild Concepts

The following concepts are important for understanding how AWS CodeBuild works.

Topics

- How AWS CodeBuild Works
- Next Steps

How AWS CodeBuild Works

The following diagram shows what happens when you run a build with AWS CodeBuild:

1. As input, you must provide AWS CodeBuild with a build project. A *build project* defines how AWS CodeBuild will run a build. It includes information such as where to get the source code, the build environment to use, the build commands to run, and where to store the build output. A *build environment* represents a combination of operating system, programming language runtime, and tools that AWS CodeBuild uses to run a build. For more information, see:
   - Create a Build Project
   - Build Environment Reference

2. AWS CodeBuild uses the build project to create the build environment.

3. AWS CodeBuild downloads the source code into the build environment and then uses the build specification (build spec), as defined in the build project or included directly in the source code. A *build spec* is a collection of build commands and related settings, in YAML format, that AWS CodeBuild uses to run a build. For more information, see the Build Spec Reference.

4. If there is any build output, the build environment uploads its output to an Amazon S3 bucket. The build environment can also perform tasks that you specify in the build spec (for example, sending build notifications to an Amazon SNS topic). For an example, see Build Notifications Sample.

5. While the build is running, the build environment sends information to AWS CodeBuild and Amazon CloudWatch Logs.

6. While the build is running, you can use the AWS CodeBuild console, AWS CLI, or AWS SDKs, to get summarized build information from AWS CodeBuild and detailed build information from Amazon CloudWatch Logs. If you use AWS CodePipeline to run builds, you can get limited build information from AWS CodePipeline.

Next Steps

Now that you know more about AWS CodeBuild, we recommend that you complete the following steps:

1. **Experiment** with AWS CodeBuild in an example scenario by following the instructions in Getting Started.

2. **Use** AWS CodeBuild in your own scenarios by following the instructions in Plan a Build.

Getting Started with AWS CodeBuild

In this walkthrough, you will use AWS CodeBuild to build a collection of sample source code input files (which we call *build input artifacts* or *build input*) into a deployable version of the source code (which we call *build output artifact* or *build output*). Specifically, you will instruct AWS CodeBuild to use Apache Maven, a common build tool, to build a set of Java class files into a Java Archive (JAR) file. You do not need to be familiar with Apache Maven or Java to complete this walkthrough.

Important
Completing this walkthrough may result in charges to your AWS account. These include possible charges for AWS CodeBuild and for AWS resources and actions related to Amazon S3, AWS KMS, and CloudWatch Logs. For more information, see AWS CodeBuild Pricing, Amazon S3 Pricing, AWS Key Management Service Pricing, and Amazon CloudWatch Pricing.

Topics
- Step 1: Create or Use Amazon S3 Buckets to Store the Build Input and Output
- Step 2: Create the Source Code to Build
- Step 3: Create the Build Spec
- Step 4: Add the Source Code and the Build Spec to the Input Bucket
- Step 5: Create the Build Project
- Step 6: Run the Build
- Step 7: View Summarized Build Information
- Step 8: View Detailed Build Information
- Step 9: Get the Build Output Artifact
- Step 10: Clean Up
- Next Steps

Step 1: Create or Use Amazon S3 Buckets to Store the Build Input and Output

To complete this walkthrough, you will need two Amazon S3 buckets:
- One of these buckets will store the build input (which we call the *input bucket*). In this walkthrough, we will name this input bucket `codebuild-region-ID-account-ID-input-bucket`, where *region-ID* represents the AWS region of the bucket, and *account-ID* represents your AWS account ID.
- The other bucket will store the build output (which we call the *output bucket*). In this walkthrough, we will name this output bucket `codebuild-region-ID-account-ID-output-bucket`.

If you chose a different name for either of these buckets, substitute it throughout this walkthrough.

These two buckets must be in the same AWS region as your builds. For example, if you instruct AWS CodeBuild to run a build in the US East (Ohio) region, then these buckets must also be in the US East (Ohio) region.

To create a bucket, see Creating a Bucket in the *Amazon Simple Storage Service User Guide*.

Note
You could use a single bucket for this walkthrough. However, using two buckets can make it easier to see where the build input is coming from and where the build output is going.
Although AWS CodeBuild also supports build input stored in AWS CodeCommit, GitHub, and Bitbucket repositories, this walkthrough does not show you how to use them. For more information, see Plan a Build.

Step 2: Create the Source Code to Build

In this step, you will create the source code that you want AWS CodeBuild to build to the output bucket. This source code consists of two Java class files and an Apache Maven Project Object Model (POM) file.

1. In an empty directory on your local computer or instance, create this directory structure.

```
1 (root directory name)
2     `-- src
3         |-- main
4         |     `-- java
5         `-- test
6               `-- java
```

2. Using a text editor of your choice, create this file, name it `MessageUtil.java`, and then save it in the `src/main/java` directory.

```
1 public class MessageUtil {
2   private String message;
3
4   public MessageUtil(String message) {
5     this.message = message;
6   }
7
8   public String printMessage() {
9     System.out.println(message);
10    return message;
11  }
12
13  public String salutationMessage() {
14    message = "Hi!" + message;
15    System.out.println(message);
16    return message;
17  }
18 }
```

This class file creates as output the string of characters passed into it. The `MessageUtil` constructor sets the string of characters. The `printMessage` method creates the output. The `salutationMessage` method outputs `Hi!` followed by the string of characters.

3. Create this file, name it `TestMessageUtil.java`, and then save it in the `/src/test/java` directory.

```
1 import org.junit.Test;
2 import org.junit.Ignore;
3 import static org.junit.Assert.assertEquals;
4
5 public class TestMessageUtil {
6
7   String message = "Robert";
8   MessageUtil messageUtil = new MessageUtil(message);
9
10  @Test
11  public void testPrintMessage() {
12    System.out.println("Inside testPrintMessage()");
13    assertEquals(message,messageUtil.printMessage());
14  }
15
16  @Test
17  public void testSalutationMessage() {
18    System.out.println("Inside testSalutationMessage()");
19    message = "Hi!" + "Robert";
20    assertEquals(message,messageUtil.salutationMessage());
21  }
22 }
```

14

This class file sets the `message` variable in the `MessageUtil` class to `Robert`. It then tests to see if the `message` variable was successfully set by checking whether the strings `Robert` and `Hi!Robert` appear in the output.

4. Create this file, name it `pom.xml`, and then save it in the root (top level) directory.

```
1  <project xmlns="http://maven.apache.org/POM/4.0.0"
2      xmlns:xsi="http://www.w3.org/2001/XMLSchema-instance"
3      xsi:schemaLocation="http://maven.apache.org/POM/4.0.0 http://maven.apache.org/maven-
          v4_0_0.xsd">
4    <modelVersion>4.0.0</modelVersion>
5    <groupId>org.example</groupId>
6    <artifactId>messageUtil</artifactId>
7    <version>1.0</version>
8    <packaging>jar</packaging>
9    <name>Message Utility Java Sample App</name>
10   <dependencies>
11     <dependency>
12       <groupId>junit</groupId>
13       <artifactId>junit</artifactId>
14       <version>4.11</version>
15       <scope>test</scope>
16     </dependency>
17   </dependencies>
18 </project>
```

Apache Maven will use the instructions in this file to convert the `MessageUtil.java` and `TestMessageUtil.java` files into a file named `messageUtil-1.0.jar` and then run the specified tests.

At this point, your directory structure should look like this.

```
1  (root directory name)
2      |-- pom.xml
3      `-- src
4          |-- main
5          |     `-- java
6          |             `-- MessageUtil.java
7          `-- test
8                `-- java
9                        `-- TestMessageUtil.java
```

Step 3: Create the Build Spec

In this step, you will create a build specification (build spec) file. A *build spec* is a collection of build commands and related settings, in YAML format, that AWS CodeBuild uses to run a build. Without a build spec, AWS CodeBuild will not be able to successfully convert your build input into build output, nor will it be able to locate the build output artifact in the build environment to upload to your output bucket.

Create this file, name it `buildspec.yml`, and then save it in the root (top level) directory.

```
1  version: 0.2
2
3  phases:
4    install:
5      commands:
6        - echo Nothing to do in the install phase...
```

```
 7    pre_build:
 8      commands:
 9        - echo Nothing to do in the pre_build phase...
10    build:
11      commands:
12        - echo Build started on `date`
13        - mvn install
14    post_build:
15      commands:
16        - echo Build completed on `date`
17 artifacts:
18   files:
19     - target/messageUtil-1.0.jar
```

Important

Because a build spec declaration must be valid YAML, the spacing in a build spec declaration is important. If the number of spaces in your build spec declaration does not match this one, the build might fail immediately. You can use a YAML validator to test whether your build spec declaration is valid YAML.

Note

Instead of including a build spec file in your source code, you can declare build commands separately when you create a build project. This is helpful if you want to build your source code with different build commands without updating your source code's repository each time. For more information, see Build Spec Syntax.

In this build spec declaration:

- **version** represents the version of the build spec standard being used. This build spec declaration uses the latest version, 0.2.

- **phases** represents the build phases during which you can instruct AWS CodeBuild to run commands. These build phases are listed here as **install**, **pre_build**, **build**, and **post_build**. You cannot change the spelling of these build phase names, and you cannot create additional build phase names.

  In this example, during the **build** phase, AWS CodeBuild runs the **mvn install** command. This command instructs Apache Maven to compile, test, and package the compiled Java class files into a build output artifact. For completeness, a few **echo** commands are placed in each build phase in this example. When you view detailed build information later in this walkthrough, the output of these **echo** commands can help you better understand how AWS CodeBuild runs commands and in which order. (Although all build phases are included in this example, you are not required to include an build phase if you do not plan to run any commands during that phase.) For each build phase included, AWS CodeBuild runs each specified command, one at a time, in the order listed, from beginning to end.

- **artifacts** represents the set of build output artifacts that AWS CodeBuild will upload to the output bucket. **files** represents the files to include in the build output. AWS CodeBuild will upload the single **messageUtil-1.0.jar** file found in the **target** relative directory in the build environment. The file name **messageUtil-1.0.jar** and the directory name **target** are based on the way Apache Maven creates and stores build output artifacts for this example only. In your own builds, these file names and directories will be different.

For more information, see the Build Spec Reference.

At this point, your directory structure should look like this.

```
1 (root directory name)
2      |-- pom.xml
3      |-- buildspec.yml
4      `-- src
5          |-- main
6          |      `-- java
```

```
7           |               `-- MessageUtil.java
8           `-- test
9                   `-- java
10                          `-- TestMessageUtil.java
```

Step 4: Add the Source Code and the Build Spec to the Input Bucket

In this step, you will add the source code and build spec file to the input bucket.

Using your operating system's zip utility, create a file named `MessageUtil.zip` that includes `MessageUtil.java`, `TestMessageUtil.java`, `pom.xml`, and `buildspec.yml`.

The `MessageUtil.zip` file's directory structure must look like this.

```
1  MessageUtil.zip
2       |-- pom.xml
3       |-- buildspec.yml
4       `-- src
5           |-- main
6           |       `-- java
7           |               `-- MessageUtil.java
8           `-- test
9                   `-- java
10                          `-- TestMessageUtil.java
```

Important
Do not include the (`root directory name`) directory, only the directories and files contained in the (`root directory name`) directory.

Upload the `MessageUtil.zip` file to the input bucket named `codebuild-region-ID-account-ID-input-bucket`.

Important
For AWS CodeCommit, GitHub, and Bitbucket repositories, by convention, you must store a build spec file named `buildspec.yml` in the root (top level) of each repository or include the build spec declaration as part of the build project definition. Do not create a ZIP file that contains the repository's source code and build spec file.
For build input stored in Amazon S3 buckets only, you must create a ZIP file that contains the source code and, by convention, a build spec file named `buildspec.yml` at the root (top level) or include the build spec declaration as part of the build project definition.
If you want to use a different name for your build spec file, or you want to reference a build spec in a location other than the root, you can specify a build spec override as part of the build project definition. For more information, see Build Spec File Name and Storage Location.

Step 5: Create the Build Project

In this step, you will create a build project that AWS CodeBuild will use to run the build. A *build project* defines how AWS CodeBuild will run a build. It includes information such as where to get the source code, the build environment to use, the build commands to run, and where to store the build output. A *build environment* represents a combination of operating system, programming language runtime, and tools that AWS CodeBuild uses to run a build. The build environment is expressed as a Docker image. (For more information, see the Docker Overview topic on the Docker Docs website.) For this build environment, you'll instruct AWS CodeBuild to use a Docker image that contains a version of the Java Development Kit (JDK) and Apache Maven.

You can complete this step with the AWS CodeBuild console or with the AWS CLI.

17

Note

You can work with AWS CodeBuild in several ways: through the AWS CodeBuild console, AWS CodePipeline, the AWS CLI, or the AWS SDKs. This walkthrough demonstrates how to use the AWS CodeBuild console and the AWS CLI. To learn how to use AWS CodePipeline, see Use AWS CodePipeline with AWS CodeBuild. To learn how to use the AWS SDKs, see Run AWS CodeBuild Directly.

To create the build project (console)

1. Sign in to the AWS Management Console and open the AWS CodeBuild console at https://console.aws. amazon.com/codebuild/.

2. In the AWS region selector, choose a region that supports AWS CodeBuild. For more information, see AWS CodeBuild in the "Regions and Endpoints" topic in the *Amazon Web Services General Reference*.

3. If a welcome page is displayed, choose **Get started**.

   If a welcome page is not displayed, then on the navigation pane, choose **Build projects**, and then choose **Create project**.

4. On the **Configure your project** page, for **Project name**, type a name for this build project (in this example, `codebuild-demo-project`). Build project names must be unique across each AWS account. If you use a different name, substitute it throughout this walkthrough. **Note**
   On the **Configure project** page, you may see an error message similar to the following: **User: *user-ARN* is not authorized to perform: codebuild:ListProjects**. This is most likely because you signed in to the AWS Management Console as an IAM user that does not have sufficient permissions to use AWS CodeBuild in the console. To fix this, sign out of the AWS Management Console, and then sign back in with credentials belonging to one of the following IAM entities:
   Your AWS root account. This is not recommended. For more information, see The Account Root User in the *IAM User Guide*. An administrator IAM user in your AWS account. For more information, see Creating Your First IAM Admin User and Group in the *IAM User Guide*. An IAM user in your AWS account with the AWS managed policies named **AWSCodeBuildAdminAccess**, **AmazonS3ReadOnlyAccess**, and **IAMFullAccess** attached to that IAM user or to an IAM group that the IAM user belongs to. If you do not have an IAM user or group in your AWS account with these permission, and you are not able to add these permissions to your IAM user or group, contact your AWS account administrator for assistance. For more information, see AWS Managed (Predefined) Policies for AWS CodeBuild.

5. In **Source: What to build**, for **Source provider**, choose **Amazon S3**.

6. For **Bucket**, choose **codebuild-*region-ID-account-ID*-input-bucket**.

7. For **S3 object key**, type `MessageUtil.zip`.

8. In **Environment: How to build**, for **Environment image**, leave **Use an image managed by AWS CodeBuild** selected.

9. For **Operating system**, choose **Ubuntu**.

10. For **Runtime**, choose **Java**.

11. For **Version**, choose **aws/codebuild/java:openjdk-8**.

12. For **Build specification**, leave **Use the buildspec.yml in the source code root directory** selected.

13. In **Artifacts: Where to put the artifacts from this build project**, for **Artifacts type**, choose **Amazon S3**.

14. Leave **Artifacts name** blank.

15. For **Bucket name**, choose **codebuild-*region-ID-account-ID*-output-bucket**.

16. In **Service role**, leave **Create a service role in your account** selected, and leave **Role name** unchanged.

17. Choose **Continue**.

18. On the **Review** page, choose **Save**.

Skip ahead to Step 6: Run the Build.

To create the build project (AWS CLI)

1. Use the AWS CLI to run the `create-project` command, as follows:

```
1 aws codebuild create-project --generate-cli-skeleton
```

JSON-formatted data appears in the output. Copy the data to a file named `create-project.json` in a location on the local computer or instance where the AWS CLI is installed. If you choose to use a different file name, be sure to substitute it for `create-project.json` throughout this walkthrough.

Modify the copied data to follow this format, and then save your results:

```
1 {
2   "name": "codebuild-demo-project",
3   "source": {
4     "type": "S3",
5     "location": "codebuild-region-ID-account-ID-input-bucket/MessageUtil.zip"
6   },
7   "artifacts": {
8     "type": "S3",
9     "location": "codebuild-region-ID-account-ID-output-bucket"
10   },
11   "environment": {
12     "type": "LINUX_CONTAINER",
13     "image": "aws/codebuild/java:openjdk-8",
14     "computeType": "BUILD_GENERAL1_SMALL"
15   },
16   "serviceRole": "serviceIAMRole"
17 }
```

Replace *serviceIAMRole* with the Amazon Resource Name (ARN) of an AWS CodeBuild service role (for example, `arn:aws:iam::account-ID:role/role-name`). To create one, see Create an AWS CodeBuild Service Role.

In this data:

- `name` represents a required identifier for this build project (in this example, `codebuild-demo-project`). If you use a different name, substitute it throughout this procedure. Build project names must be unique across all build projects in your account.

- For `source`, `type` is a required value that represents the source code's repository type (in this example, S3 for an Amazon S3 bucket).

- For `source`, `location` represents the path to the source code (in this example, the input bucket name followed by the ZIP file name).

- For `artifacts`, `type` is a required value that represents the build output artifact's repository type (in this example, S3 for an Amazon S3 bucket).

- For `artifacts`, `location` represents the name of the output bucket you created or identified earlier (in this example, `codebuild-region-ID-account-ID-output-bucket`).

- For `environment`, `type` is a required value that represents the type of build environment (`LINUX_CONTAINER` is currently the only allowed value).

- For `environment`, `image` is a required value that represents the Docker image name and tag combination this build project will use, as specified by the Docker image repository type (in this example, `aws/codebuild/java:openjdk-8` for a Docker image in the AWS CodeBuild Docker images repository). `aws/codebuild/java` is the name of the Docker image. `openjdk-8` is the tag of the Docker image.

To find more Docker images you can use in your scenarios, see the Build Environment Reference.

- For `environment`, `computeType` is a required value that represents the computing resources AWS CodeBuild will use (in this example, `BUILD_GENERAL1_SMALL`). **Note**
Other available values in the original JSON-formatted data, such as `description`, `buildspec`, `auth` (including `type` and `resource`), `path`, `namespaceType`, `name` (for `artifacts`), `packaging`, `environmentVariables` (including `name` and `value`), `timeoutInMinutes`, `encryptionKey`, and `tags` (including `key` and `value`) are optional. They are not used in this walkthrough, so they are not shown here. For more information, see Create a Build Project (AWS CLI).

2. Switch to the directory that contains the file you just saved, and then run the `create-project` command again.

```
1 aws codebuild create-project --cli-input-json file://create-project.json
```

If successful, data similar to this will appear in the output.

```
1 {
2   "project": {
3     "name": "codebuild-demo-project",
4     "serviceRole": "serviceIAMRole",
5     "tags": [],
6     "artifacts": {
7       "packaging": "NONE",
8       "type": "S3",
9       "location": "codebuild-region-ID-account-ID-output-bucket",
10      "name": "message-util.zip"
11    },
12    "lastModified": 1472661575.244,
13    "timeoutInMinutes": 60,
14    "created": 1472661575.244,
15    "environment": {
16      "computeType": "BUILD_GENERAL1_SMALL",
17      "image": "aws/codebuild/java:openjdk-8",
18      "type": "LINUX_CONTAINER",
19      "environmentVariables": []
20    },
21    "source": {
22      "type": "S3",
23      "location": "codebuild-region-ID-account-ID-input-bucket/MessageUtil.zip"
24    },
25    "encryptionKey": "arn:aws:kms:region-ID:account-ID:alias/aws/s3",
26    "arn": "arn:aws:codebuild:region-ID:account-ID:project/codebuild-demo-project"
27  }
28 }
```

- `project` represents information about this build project.
  - `tags` represents any tags that were declared.
  - `packaging` represents how the build output artifact will be stored in the output bucket. `NONE` means that a folder will be created inside of the output bucket and then the build output artifact will be stored inside of that folder.
  - `lastModified` represents the time, in Unix time format, when information about the build project was last changed.

- `timeoutInMinutes` represents the number of minutes after which AWS CodeBuild will stop the build if the build has not been completed. (The default is 60 minutes.)
- `created` represents the time, in Unix time format, when the build project was created.
- `environmentVariables` represents any environment variables that were declared and are available for AWS CodeBuild to use during the build.
- `encryptionKey` represents the Amazon Resource Name (ARN) of the AWS KMS customer master key (CMK) that AWS CodeBuild used to encrypt the build output artifact.
- `arn` represents the ARN of the build project.

Note

After you run the create-project command, an error message similar to the following may be output: **User: user-ARN is not authorized to perform: codebuild:CreateProject**. This is most likely because you configured the AWS CLI with the credentials of an IAM user that does not have sufficient permissions to use AWS CodeBuild to create build projects. To fix this, configure the AWS CLI with credentials belonging to one of the following IAM entities:

Your AWS root account. This is not recommended. For more information, see The Account Root User in the *IAM User Guide*. An administrator IAM user in your AWS account. For more information, see Creating Your First IAM Admin User and Group in the *IAM User Guide*. An IAM user in your AWS account with the AWS managed policies named **AWSCodeBuildAdminAccess**, **AmazonS3ReadOnlyAccess**, and **IAMFullAccess** attached to that IAM user or to an IAM group that the IAM user belongs to. If you do not have an IAM user or group in your AWS account with these permission, and you are not able to add these permissions to your IAM user or group, contact your AWS account administrator for assistance. For more information, see AWS Managed (Predefined) Policies for AWS CodeBuild.

Step 6: Run the Build

In this step, you will instruct AWS CodeBuild to run the build with the settings in the build project.

You can complete this step with the AWS CodeBuild console or the AWS CLI.

To run the build (console)

1. If the **Build projects** page is not displayed, then in the navigation pane, choose **Build projects**.

2. In the list of build projects, choose **codebuild-demo-project**, and then choose **Start build**.

3. On the **Start new build** page, choose **Start build**.

4. Skip ahead to Step 7: View Summarized Build Information.

To run the build (AWS CLI)

1. Use the AWS CLI to run the `start-build` command:

```
1 aws codebuild start-build --project-name project-name
```

Replace *project-name* with your build project name from the previous step (for example, `codebuild-demo -project`).

2. If successful, data similar to the following will appear in the output:

```
1 {
2   "build": {
3     "buildComplete": false,
4     "initiator": "user-name",
5     "artifacts": {
6       "location": "arn:aws:s3:::codebuild-region-ID-account-ID-output-bucket/message-util.
          zip"
7     },
8     "projectName": "codebuild-demo-project",
```

```
 9        "timeoutInMinutes": 60,
10        "buildStatus": "IN_PROGRESS",
11        "environment": {
12          "computeType": "BUILD_GENERAL1_SMALL",
13          "image": "aws/codebuild/java:openjdk-8",
14          "type": "LINUX_CONTAINER",
15          "environmentVariables": []
16        },
17        "source": {
18          "type": "S3",
19          "location": "codebuild-region-ID-account-ID-input-bucket/MessageUtil.zip"
20        },
21        "currentPhase": "SUBMITTED",
22        "startTime": 1472848787.882,
23        "id": "codebuild-demo-project:0cfbb6ec-3db9-4e8c-992b-1ab28EXAMPLE",
24        "arn": "arn:aws:codebuild:region-ID:account-ID:build/codebuild-demo-project:0cfbb6ec-3
             db9-4e8c-992b-1ab28EXAMPLE"
25      }
26    }
```

- `build` represents information about this build.
  - `buildComplete` represents whether the build was completed (`true`); otherwise, `false`.
  - `initiator` represents the entity that started the build.
  - `artifacts` represents information about the build output, including its location.
  - `projectName` represents the name of the build project.
  - `buildStatus` represents the current build status when the `start-build` command was run.
  - `currentPhase` represents the current build phase when the `start-build` command was run.
  - `startTime` represents the time, in Unix time format, when the build process started.
  - `id` represents the ID of the build.
  - `arn` represents the Amazon Resource Name (ARN) of the build.

Make a note of the `id` value. You will need it in the next step.

Step 7: View Summarized Build Information

In this step, you will view summarized information about the status of your build.

You can complete this step with the AWS CodeBuild console or the AWS CLI.

To view summarized build information (console)

1. If the **codebuild-demo-project:***build-ID* page is not displayed, then in the navigation bar, choose **Build history**. Next, in the list of build projects, choose the **Build run** link that corresponds to **codebuild-demo-project** for **Project**. There should be only one matching link. (If you have completed this walkthrough before, choose the link that corresponds to the most recent value in the **Completed** column.)

2. On the build details page, in **Phase details**, the following list of build phases should be displayed, with **Succeeded** in the **Status** column:

   - **SUBMITTED**
   - **PROVISIONING**
   - **DOWNLOAD_SOURCE**
   - **INSTALL**
   - **PRE_BUILD**

- BUILD
- POST_BUILD
- UPLOAD_ARTIFACTS
- FINALIZING
- COMPLETED

In the page title area, a green box with **Succeeded** should be displayed.

If you see a blue box with **In Progress** instead, choose the refresh button to see the latest progress.

3. Next to each build phase, the **Duration** value indicates how long that build phase lasted. The **Completed** value indicates when that build phase ended.

If you expand a build phase, the phase's start and end times are displayed.

Skip ahead to Step 8: View Detailed Build Information.

To view summarized build information (AWS CLI)

Use the AWS CLI to run the `batch-get-builds` command.

```
1 aws codebuild batch-get-builds --ids id
```

Replace *id* with the `id` value that appeared in the output of the previous step.

If successful, data similar to this will appear in the output.

```
1  {
2    "buildsNotFound": [],
3    "builds": [
4      {
5        "buildComplete": true,
6        "phases": [
7          {
8            "phaseStatus": "SUCCEEDED",
9            "endTime": 1472848788.525,
10           "phaseType": "SUBMITTED",
11           "durationInSeconds": 0,
12           "startTime": 1472848787.882
13         },
14         ... The full list of build phases has been omitted for brevity ...
15         {
16           "phaseType": "COMPLETED",
17           "startTime": 1472848878.079
18         }
19       ],
20       "logs": {
21         "groupName": "/aws/codebuild/codebuild-demo-project",
22         "deepLink": "https://console.aws.amazon.com/cloudwatch/home?region=region-ID#logEvent:
                group=/aws/codebuild/codebuild-demo-project;stream=38ca1c4a-e9ca-4dbc-bef1-
                d52bfEXAMPLE",
23         "streamName": "38ca1c4a-e9ca-4dbc-bef1-d52bfEXAMPLE"
24       },
25       "artifacts": {
26         "md5sum": "MD5-hash",
27         "location": "arn:aws:s3:::codebuild-region-ID-account-ID-output-bucket/message-util.zip
                ",
28         "sha256sum": "SHA-256-hash"
```

```
29        },
30        "projectName": "codebuild-demo-project",
31        "timeoutInMinutes": 60,
32        "initiator": "user-name",
33        "buildStatus": "SUCCEEDED",
34        "environment": {
35          "computeType": "BUILD_GENERAL1_SMALL",
36          "image": "aws/codebuild/java:openjdk-8",
37          "type": "LINUX_CONTAINER",
38          "environmentVariables": []
39        },
40        "source": {
41          "type": "S3",
42          "location": "codebuild-region-ID-account-ID-input-bucket/MessageUtil.zip"
43        },
44        "currentPhase": "COMPLETED",
45        "startTime": 1472848787.882,
46        "endTime": 1472848878.079,
47        "id": "codebuild-demo-project:38ca1c4a-e9ca-4dbc-bef1-d52bfEXAMPLE",
48        "arn": "arn:aws:codebuild:region-ID:account-ID:build/codebuild-demo-project:38ca1c4a-e9ca
           -4dbc-bef1-d52bfEXAMPLE"
49      }
50    ]
51 }
```

- buildsNotFound represents the build IDs for any builds where information is not available. In this example, it should be empty.
- builds represents information about each build where information is available. In this example, information about only one build appears in the output.
  - phases represents the set of build phases AWS CodeBuild runs during the build process. Information about each build phase is listed separately as startTime, endTime, and durationInSeconds (when the build phase started and ended, expressed in Unix time format, and how long it lasted, in seconds), as well as phaseType such as (SUBMITTED, PROVISIONING, DOWNLOAD_SOURCE, INSTALL, PRE_BUILD, BUILD, POST_BUILD, UPLOAD_ARTIFACTS, FINALIZING, or COMPLETED) and phaseStatus (such as SUCCEEDED, FAILED, FAULT, TIMED_OUT, IN_PROGRESS, or STOPPED). The first time you run the batch-get-builds command, there might not be many (or any) phases. After subsequent runs of the batch-get-builds command with the same build ID, more build phases should appear in the output.
  - logs represents information in Amazon CloudWatch Logs about the build's logs.
  - md5sum and sha256sum represent MD5 and SHA-256 hashes of the build's output artifact. These appear in the output only if the related build project's packaging value is set to ZIP (which you did not set in this walkthrough) . You can use these hashes along with a checksum tool to confirm both file integrity and authenticity. **Note**
    You can also use the Amazon S3 console to view these hashes. Select the box next to the build output artifact, and then choose **Actions, Properties**. In the **Properties** pane, expand **Metadata**, and view the values for **x-amz-meta-codebuild-content-md5** and **x-amz-meta-codebuild-content-sha256**. (In the Amazon S3 console, the build output artifact's **ETag** value should not be interpreted to be either the MD5 or SHA-256 hash.)
    If you use the AWS SDKs to get these hashes, the values are named codebuild-content-md5 and codebuild-content-sha256.
  - endTime represents the time, in Unix time format, when the build process ended.

24

Step 8: View Detailed Build Information

In this step, you will view detailed information about your build in CloudWatch Logs.

You can complete this step with the AWS CodeBuild console or the AWS CLI.

To view detailed build information (console)

1. With the build details page still displayed from the previous step, the last 10,000 lines of the build log are displayed in **Build logs**. To see the entire build log in CloudWatch Logs, choose the **View entire log** link.

2. In the CloudWatch Logs log stream, you can browse the log events. By default, only the last set of log events is displayed. To see earlier log events, scroll to the beginning of the list.

3. In this walkthrough, most of the log events contain verbose information about AWS CodeBuild downloading and installing build dependency files into its build environment, which you probably don't care about. You can use the **Filter events** box to reduce the information displayed. For example, if you type "[INFO]" in the **Filter events** box and then press Enter, only those events containing the characters [INFO] will be displayed. For more information, see Filter and Pattern Syntax in the *Amazon CloudWatch User Guide*.

Skip ahead to Step 9: Get the Build Output Artifact.

To view detailed build information (AWS CLI)

1. Use your web browser to go to the deepLink location that appeared in the output in the previous step (for example, https://console.aws.amazon.com/cloudwatch/home?region=region-ID#logEvent:group=/aws/codebuild/codebuild-demo-project;stream=38ca1c4a-e9ca-4dbc-bef1-d52bfEXAMPLE).

2. In the CloudWatch Logs log stream, you can browse the log events. By default, only the last set of log events is displayed. To see earlier log events, scroll to the beginning of the list.

3. In this walkthrough, most of the log events contain verbose information about AWS CodeBuild downloading and installing build dependency files into its build environment, which you probably don't care about. You can use the **Filter events** box to reduce the information displayed. For example, if you type "[INFO]" in the **Filter events** box and then press Enter, only those events containing the characters [INFO] will be displayed. For more information, see Filter and Pattern Syntax in the *Amazon CloudWatch User Guide*.

These portions of a CloudWatch Logs log stream pertain to this walkthrough.

```
 1  ...
 2  [Container] 2016/04/15 17:49:42 Entering phase PRE_BUILD
 3  [Container] 2016/04/15 17:49:42 Running command echo Entering pre_build phase...
 4  [Container] 2016/04/15 17:49:42 Entering pre_build phase...
 5  [Container] 2016/04/15 17:49:42 Phase complete: PRE_BUILD Success: true
 6  [Container] 2016/04/15 17:49:42 Entering phase BUILD
 7  [Container] 2016/04/15 17:49:42 Running command echo Entering build phase...
 8  [Container] 2016/04/15 17:49:42 Entering build phase...
 9  [Container] 2016/04/15 17:49:42 Running command mvn install
10  [Container] 2016/04/15 17:49:44 [INFO] Scanning for projects...
11  [Container] 2016/04/15 17:49:44 [INFO]
12  [Container] 2016/04/15 17:49:44 [INFO]
        ------------------------------------------------------------------
13  [Container] 2016/04/15 17:49:44 [INFO] Building Message Utility Java Sample App 1.0
14  [Container] 2016/04/15 17:49:44 [INFO]
        ------------------------------------------------------------------
15  ...
16  [Container] 2016/04/15 17:49:55 ------------------------------------------------------------
17  [Container] 2016/04/15 17:49:55  T E S T S
18  [Container] 2016/04/15 17:49:55 ------------------------------------------------------------
19  [Container] 2016/04/15 17:49:55 Running TestMessageUtil
```

```
20 [Container] 2016/04/15 17:49:55 Inside testSalutationMessage()
21 [Container] 2016/04/15 17:49:55 Hi!Robert
22 [Container] 2016/04/15 17:49:55 Inside testPrintMessage()
23 [Container] 2016/04/15 17:49:55 Robert
24 [Container] 2016/04/15 17:49:55 Tests run: 2, Failures: 0, Errors: 0, Skipped: 0, Time elapsed:
     0.018 sec
25 [Container] 2016/04/15 17:49:55
26 [Container] 2016/04/15 17:49:55 Results :
27 [Container] 2016/04/15 17:49:55
28 [Container] 2016/04/15 17:49:55 Tests run: 2, Failures: 0, Errors: 0, Skipped: 0
29 ...
30 [Container] 2016/04/15 17:49:56 [INFO]
     ------------------------------------------------------------------------
31 [Container] 2016/04/15 17:49:56 [INFO] BUILD SUCCESS
32 [Container] 2016/04/15 17:49:56 [INFO]
     ------------------------------------------------------------------------
33 [Container] 2016/04/15 17:49:56 [INFO] Total time: 11.845 s
34 [Container] 2016/04/15 17:49:56 [INFO] Finished at: 2016-04-15T17:49:56+00:00
35 [Container] 2016/04/15 17:49:56 [INFO] Final Memory: 18M/216M
36 [Container] 2016/04/15 17:49:56 [INFO]
     ------------------------------------------------------------------------
37 [Container] 2016/04/15 17:49:56 Phase complete: BUILD Success: true
38 [Container] 2016/04/15 17:49:56 Entering phase POST_BUILD
39 [Container] 2016/04/15 17:49:56 Running command echo Entering post_build phase...
40 [Container] 2016/04/15 17:49:56 Entering post_build phase...
41 [Container] 2016/04/15 17:49:56 Phase complete: POST_BUILD Success: true
42 [Container] 2016/04/15 17:49:57 Preparing to copy artifacts
43 [Container] 2016/04/15 17:49:57 Assembling file list
44 [Container] 2016/04/15 17:49:57 Expanding target/messageUtil-1.0.jar
45 [Container] 2016/04/15 17:49:57 Found target/messageUtil-1.0.jar
46 [Container] 2016/04/15 17:49:57 Creating zip artifact
```

In this example, AWS CodeBuild successfully completed the pre-build, build, and post-build build phases. It ran the unit tests and successfully built the `messageUtil-1.0.jar` file.

Step 9: Get the Build Output Artifact

In this step, you will get the `messageUtil-1.0.jar` file that AWS CodeBuild built and then uploaded to the output bucket.

You can complete this step with the AWS CodeBuild console or the Amazon S3 console.

To get the build output artifact (AWS CodeBuild console)

1. With the AWS CodeBuild console still open and the build details page still displayed from the previous step, expand **Build details**, and then choose the **Build artifacts** link. This opens the folder in Amazon S3 for the build output artifact. (If the build details page is not displayed, in the navigation bar, choose **Build history**, and then choose the **Build run** link.)

2. Open the folder named `target`, where you will find the build output artifact file named `messageUtil -1.0.jar`.

   Skip ahead to Step 10: Clean Up.

To get the build output artifact (Amazon S3 console)

1. Open the Amazon S3 console at https://console.aws.amazon.com/s3/.

2. Open the bucket named `codebuild-region-ID-account-ID-output-bucket`.

3. Open the folder named `codebuild-demo-project`.

4. Open the folder named `target`, where you will find the build output artifact file named `messageUtil -1.0.jar`.

Step 10: Clean Up

To prevent ongoing charges to your AWS account, you can delete the input bucket used in this walkthrough. For instructions, see Deleting or Emptying a Bucket in the *Amazon Simple Storage Service Developer Guide*.

If you are using the IAM user to delete this bucket instead of an AWS root account or an administrator IAM user, then the user must have additional access permissions. (Using an AWS root account is not recommended.) Add the statement between the markers (*### BEGIN ADDING STATEMENT HERE ###* and *### END ADDING STATEMENTS HERE ###*) to an existing access policy for the user. Ellipses (...) are used for brevity and to help you locate where to add the statement. Do not remove any statements in the existing access policy, and do not type these ellipses into the existing policy.

```
1  {
2    "Version": "2012-10-17",
3    "Id": "...",
4    "Statement": [
5      ### BEGIN ADDING STATEMENT HERE ###
6      {
7        "Effect": "Allow",
8        "Action": [
9          "s3:DeleteBucket",
10         "s3:DeleteObject"
11       ],
12       "Resource": "*"
13     }
14     ### END ADDING STATEMENT HERE ###
15   ]
16 }
```

Next Steps

In this walkthrough, you used AWS CodeBuild to build a set of Java class files into a JAR file. You then viewed the build's results.

You can now try using AWS CodeBuild in your own scenarios by following the instructions in Plan a Build. If you don't feel ready yet, you might want to try building some of our samples. For more information, see Samples.

AWS CodeBuild Samples

These use case-based samples can be used to experiment with AWS CodeBuild:

Name	Description
Amazon ECR Sample	Uses a Docker image in an Amazon ECR repository to use Apache Maven to produce a single JAR file.
Docker Sample	Uses a build image provided by AWS Code-Build with Docker support to produce a Docker image with Apache Maven. Pushes the Docker image to a repository in Amazon ECR. You can adapt this sample to push the Docker image to Docker Hub.
GitHub Enterprise Sample	Uses AWS CodeBuild with GitHub Enterprise as the source repository, with certificates installed and webhooks enabled, to rebuild the source code every time a code change is pushed to the repository.
GitHub Pull Request Sample	Uses AWS CodeBuild with GitHub as the source repository, and webhooks enabled, to rebuild the source code every time a code change is pushed to the repository.
Use AWS Config with AWS CodeBuild Sample	Shows how to set up AWS Config. Lists which AWS CodeBuild resources are tracked and describes how to look up AWS CodeBuild projects in AWS Config.
Build Badges Sample	Shows how to set up AWS CodeBuild with build badges.
Build Notifications Sample	Uses Apache Maven to produce a single JAR file. Sends a build notification to subscribers of an Amazon SNS topic.
Docker in Custom Image Sample	Uses a custom Docker image to produce a Docker image.
AWS CodeDeploy Sample	Uses Apache Maven to produce a single JAR file. Uses AWS CodeDeploy to deploy the JAR file to an Amazon Linux instance. You can also use AWS CodePipeline to build and deploy the sample.
AWS Lambda Sample	Uses AWS CodeBuild along with Lambda, AWS CloudFormation, and AWS Code-Pipeline to build and deploy a serverless application that follows the AWS Serverless Application Model (AWS SAM) standard.
Elastic Beanstalk Sample	Uses Apache Maven to produce a single WAR file. Uses Elastic Beanstalk to deploy the WAR file to an Elastic Beanstalk instance.

You can use these code-based samples to experiment with AWS CodeBuild:

Name	Description
C++ Sample	Uses C++ to output a single .out file.
Go Sample	Uses Go to output a single binary file.
Maven Sample	Uses Apache Maven to produce a single JAR file.
Node.js Sample	Uses Mocha to test whether an internal variable in code contains a specific string value. Produces a single .js file.
Python Sample	Uses Python to test whether an internal variable in code is set to a specific string value. Produces a single .py file.
Ruby Sample	Uses RSpec to test whether an internal variable in code is set to a specific string value. Produces a single .rb file.
Scala Sample	Uses sbt to produce a single JAR file.
Java Sample	Uses Apache Maven to produce a single WAR file.
Windows Samples	Uses the Microsoft .NET Framework or .NET Core to build an executable file from C#, F#, or Visual Basic code.
.NET Core in Linux Sample	Uses .NET Core to build an executable file out of code written in C#.

Microsoft Windows Samples for AWS CodeBuild

These samples use an AWS CodeBuild build environment running Microsoft Windows Server 2016, the Microsoft .NET Framework, and the .NET Core SDK to build executables file out of code written in C#, F#, and Visual Basic.

Important
Running these samples may result in charges to your AWS account. These include possible charges for AWS CodeBuild and for AWS resources and actions related to Amazon S3, AWS KMS, and CloudWatch Logs. For more information, see AWS CodeBuild Pricing, Amazon S3 Pricing, AWS Key Management Service Pricing, and Amazon CloudWatch Pricing.

Running the Samples

To run these samples:

1. Create the files as described in the Directory Structure and Files sections of this topic, and then upload them to an Amazon S3 input bucket or an AWS CodeCommit or GitHub repository. **Important**
   Do not upload (root directory name), just the files inside of (root directory name).
   If you are using an Amazon S3 input bucket, be sure to create a ZIP file that contains the files, and then upload it to the input bucket. Do not add (root directory name) to the ZIP file, just the files inside of (root directory name).

2. Create a build project, run the build, and follow the steps in Run AWS CodeBuild Directly.

   If you use the AWS CLI to create the build project, the JSON-formatted input to the create-project command might look similar to this. (Replace the placeholders with your own values.)

```
{
  "name": "sample-windows-build-project",
  "source": {
    "type": "S3",
    "location": "codebuild-region-ID-account-ID-input-bucket/windows-build-input-artifact.
      zip"
  },
  "artifacts": {
    "type": "S3",
    "location": "codebuild-region-ID-account-ID-output-bucket",
    "packaging": "ZIP",
    "name": "windows-build-output-artifact.zip"
  },
  "environment": {
    "type": "WINDOWS_CONTAINER",
    "image": "aws/codebuild/windows-base:1.0",
    "computeType": "BUILD_GENERAL1_MEDIUM"
  },
  "serviceRole": "arn:aws:iam::account-ID:role/role-name",
  "encryptionKey": "arn:aws:kms:region-ID:account-ID:key/key-ID"
}
```

3. To get the build output artifact, in your Amazon S3 output bucket, download the `windows-build-output -artifact.zip` file to your local computer or instance. Extract the contents to get to the executable and other files.

   - The executable file for the C# sample using the Microsoft .NET Framework, `CSharpHelloWorld.exe`, can be found in the `CSharpHelloWorld\bin\Debug` directory.

- The executable file for the F# sample using the Microsoft .NET Framework, `FSharpHelloWorld.exe`, can be found in the `FSharpHelloWorld\bin\Debug` directory.
- The executable file for the Visual Basic sample using the Microsoft .NET Framework, `VBHelloWorld` `.exe`, can be found in the `VBHelloWorld\bin\Debug` directory.
- The executable file for the C# sample using .NET Core, `HelloWorldSample.dll`, can be found in the `bin\Debug\netcoreapp1.0` directory.

Directory Structure

These samples assume the following directory structures.

C# and the Microsoft .NET Framework

```
1  (root directory name)
2   |-- buildspec.yml
3   |-- CSharpHelloWorld.sln
4   `-- CSharpHelloWorld
5       |-- App.config
6       |-- CSharpHelloWorld.csproj
7       |-- Program.cs
8       `-- Properties
9             `-- AssemblyInfo.cs
```

F# and the Microsoft .NET Framework

```
1  (root directory name)
2   |-- buildspec.yml
3   |-- FSharpHelloWorld.sln
4   `-- FSharpHelloWorld
5       |-- App.config
6       |-- AssemblyInfo.fs
7       |-- FSharpHelloWorld.fsproj
8       `-- Program.fs
```

Visual Basic and the Microsoft .NET Framework

```
1   (root directory name)
2    |-- buildspec.yml
3    |-- VBHelloWorld.sln
4    `-- VBHelloWorld
5        |-- App.config
6        |-- HelloWorld.vb
7        |-- VBHelloWorld.vbproj
8        `-- My Project
9            |-- Application.Designer.vb
10           |-- Application.myapp
11           |-- AssemblyInfo.vb
12           |-- Resources.Designer.vb
13           |-- Resources.resx
14           |-- Settings.Designer.vb
15           `-- Settings.settings
```

C# and .NET Core

```
1 (root directory name)
2   |-- buildspec.yml
3   |-- HelloWorldSample.csproj
4   `-- Program.cs
```

Files

These samples use the following files:

C# and the Microsoft .NET Framework

buildspec.yml (in (root directory name)):

```
 1 version: 0.2
 2
 3 env:
 4   variables:
 5     SOLUTION: .\CSharpHelloWorld.sln
 6     PACKAGE_DIRECTORY: .\packages
 7     DOTNET_FRAMEWORK: 4.6.2
 8
 9 phases:
10   build:
11     commands:
12       - '& "C:\ProgramData\chocolatey\bin\NuGet.exe" restore $env:SOLUTION -PackagesDirectory
           $env:PACKAGE_DIRECTORY'
13       - '& "C:\Program Files (x86)\MSBuild\14.0\Bin\MSBuild.exe" -p:FrameworkPathOverride="C:\
           Program Files (x86)\Reference Assemblies\Microsoft\Framework\.NETFramework\v$env:
           DOTNET_FRAMEWORK" $env:SOLUTION'
14 artifacts:
15   files:
16     - .\CSharpHelloWorld\bin\Debug\*
```

CSharpHelloWorld.sln (in (root directory name)):

```
 1 Microsoft Visual Studio Solution File, Format Version 12.00
 2 # Visual Studio 14
 3 VisualStudioVersion = 14.0.25420.1
 4 MinimumVisualStudioVersion = 10.0.40219.1
 5 Project("{FAE04EC0-301F-11D3-BF4B-00C04F79EFBC}") = "CSharpHelloWorld", "CSharpHelloWorld\
     CSharpHelloWorld.csproj", "{2F8752D5-E628-4A38-AA7E-BC4B4E697CBB}"
 6 EndProject
 7 Global
 8   GlobalSection(SolutionConfigurationPlatforms) = preSolution
 9     Debug|Any CPU = Debug|Any CPU
10     Release|Any CPU = Release|Any CPU
11   EndGlobalSection
12   GlobalSection(ProjectConfigurationPlatforms) = postSolution
13     {2F8752D5-E628-4A38-AA7E-BC4B4E697CBB}.Debug|Any CPU.ActiveCfg = Debug|Any CPU
14     {2F8752D5-E628-4A38-AA7E-BC4B4E697CBB}.Debug|Any CPU.Build.0 = Debug|Any CPU
15     {2F8752D5-E628-4A38-AA7E-BC4B4E697CBB}.Release|Any CPU.ActiveCfg = Release|Any CPU
16     {2F8752D5-E628-4A38-AA7E-BC4B4E697CBB}.Release|Any CPU.Build.0 = Release|Any CPU
17   EndGlobalSection
18   GlobalSection(SolutionProperties) = preSolution
19     HideSolutionNode = FALSE
```

```
20   EndGlobalSection
21 EndGlobal
```

App.config (in (root directory name)\CSharpHelloWorld):

```
1 <?xml version="1.0" encoding="utf-8" ?>
2 <configuration>
3   <startup>
4     <supportedRuntime version="v4.0" sku=".NETFramework,Version=v4.6.2" />
5   </startup>
6 </configuration>
```

CSharpHelloWorld.csproj (in (root directory name)\CSharpHelloWorld):

```
1 <?xml version="1.0" encoding="utf-8"?>
2 <Project ToolsVersion="14.0" DefaultTargets="Build" xmlns="http://schemas.microsoft.com/
      developer/msbuild/2003">
3   <Import Project="$(MSBuildExtensionsPath)\$(MSBuildToolsVersion)\Microsoft.Common.props"
        Condition="Exists('$(MSBuildExtensionsPath)\$(MSBuildToolsVersion)\Microsoft.Common.props
        ')" />
4   <PropertyGroup>
5     <Configuration Condition=" '$(Configuration)' == '' ">Debug</Configuration>
6     <Platform Condition=" '$(Platform)' == '' ">AnyCPU</Platform>
7     <ProjectGuid>{2F8752D5-E628-4A38-AA7E-BC4B4E697CBB}</ProjectGuid>
8     <OutputType>Exe</OutputType>
9     <AppDesignerFolder>Properties</AppDesignerFolder>
10    <RootNamespace>CSharpHelloWorld</RootNamespace>
11    <AssemblyName>CSharpHelloWorld</AssemblyName>
12    <TargetFrameworkVersion>v4.6.2</TargetFrameworkVersion>
13    <FileAlignment>512</FileAlignment>
14    <AutoGenerateBindingRedirects>true</AutoGenerateBindingRedirects>
15  </PropertyGroup>
16  <PropertyGroup Condition=" '$(Configuration)|$(Platform)' == 'Debug|AnyCPU' ">
17    <PlatformTarget>AnyCPU</PlatformTarget>
18    <DebugSymbols>true</DebugSymbols>
19    <DebugType>full</DebugType>
20    <Optimize>false</Optimize>
21    <OutputPath>bin\Debug\</OutputPath>
22    <DefineConstants>DEBUG;TRACE</DefineConstants>
23    <ErrorReport>prompt</ErrorReport>
24    <WarningLevel>4</WarningLevel>
25  </PropertyGroup>
26  <PropertyGroup Condition=" '$(Configuration)|$(Platform)' == 'Release|AnyCPU' ">
27    <PlatformTarget>AnyCPU</PlatformTarget>
28    <DebugType>pdbonly</DebugType>
29    <Optimize>true</Optimize>
30    <OutputPath>bin\Release\</OutputPath>
31    <DefineConstants>TRACE</DefineConstants>
32    <ErrorReport>prompt</ErrorReport>
33    <WarningLevel>4</WarningLevel>
34  </PropertyGroup>
35  <ItemGroup>
36    <Reference Include="System" />
37    <Reference Include="System.Core" />
38    <Reference Include="System.Xml.Linq" />
39    <Reference Include="System.Data.DataSetExtensions" />
```

```
40     <Reference Include="Microsoft.CSharp" />
41     <Reference Include="System.Data" />
42     <Reference Include="System.Net.Http" />
43     <Reference Include="System.Xml" />
44   </ItemGroup>
45   <ItemGroup>
46     <Compile Include="Program.cs" />
47     <Compile Include="Properties\AssemblyInfo.cs" />
48   </ItemGroup>
49   <ItemGroup>
50     <None Include="App.config" />
51   </ItemGroup>
52   <Import Project="$(MSBuildToolsPath)\Microsoft.CSharp.targets" />
53   <!-- To modify your build process, add your task inside one of the targets below and uncomment
         it.
54       Other similar extension points exist, see Microsoft.Common.targets.
55   <Target Name="BeforeBuild">
56   </Target>
57   <Target Name="AfterBuild">
58   </Target>
59   -->
60 </Project>
```

Program.cs (in (root directory name)\CSharpHelloWorld):

```
1 using System;
2 using System.Collections.Generic;
3 using System.Linq;
4 using System.Text;
5 using System.Threading.Tasks;
6
7 namespace CSharpHelloWorld
8 {
9   class Program
10   {
11     static void Main(string[] args)
12     {
13       System.Console.WriteLine("Hello World");
14       System.Threading.Thread.Sleep(10);
15     }
16   }
17 }
```

AssemblyInfo.cs (in (root directory name)\CSharpHelloWorld\Properties):

```
1 using System.Reflection;
2 using System.Runtime.CompilerServices;
3 using System.Runtime.InteropServices;
4
5 // General Information about an assembly is controlled through the following
6 // set of attributes. Change these attribute values to modify the information
7 // associated with an assembly.
8 [assembly: AssemblyTitle("CSharpHelloWorld")]
9 [assembly: AssemblyDescription("")]
10 [assembly: AssemblyConfiguration("")]
11 [assembly: AssemblyCompany("")]
```

```
12 [assembly: AssemblyProduct("CSharpHelloWorld")]
13 [assembly: AssemblyCopyright("Copyright ©  2017")]
14 [assembly: AssemblyTrademark("")]
15 [assembly: AssemblyCulture("")]
16
17 // Setting ComVisible to false makes the types in this assembly not visible
18 // to COM components.  If you need to access a type in this assembly from
19 // COM, set the ComVisible attribute to true on that type.
20 [assembly: ComVisible(false)]
21
22 // The following GUID is for the ID of the typelib if this project is exposed to COM
23 [assembly: Guid("2f8752d5-e628-4a38-aa7e-bc4b4e697cbb")]
24
25 // Version information for an assembly consists of the following four values:
26 //
27 // Major Version
28 // Minor Version
29 // Build Number
30 // Revision
31 //
32 // You can specify all the values or you can default the Build and Revision Numbers
33 // by using the '*' as shown below:
34 // [assembly: AssemblyVersion("1.0.*")]
35 [assembly: AssemblyVersion("1.0.0.0")]
36 [assembly: AssemblyFileVersion("1.0.0.0")]
```

F# and the Microsoft .NET Framework

buildspec.yml (in (root directory name)):

```
1 version: 0.2
2
3 env:
4   variables:
5     SOLUTION: .\FSharpHelloWorld.sln
6     PACKAGE_DIRECTORY: .\packages
7     DOTNET_FRAMEWORK: 4.6.2
8
9 phases:
10   build:
11     commands:
12       - '& "C:\ProgramData\chocolatey\bin\NuGet.exe" restore $env:SOLUTION -PackagesDirectory
             $env:PACKAGE_DIRECTORY'
13      - '& "C:\Program Files (x86)\MSBuild\14.0\Bin\MSBuild.exe" -p:FrameworkPathOverride="C:\
             Program Files (x86)\Reference Assemblies\Microsoft\Framework\.NETFramework\v$env:
             DOTNET_FRAMEWORK" $env:SOLUTION'
14 artifacts:
15   files:
16     - .\FSharpHelloWorld\bin\Debug\*
```

FSharpHelloWorld.sln (in (root directory name)):

```
1 Microsoft Visual Studio Solution File, Format Version 12.00
2 # Visual Studio 14
3 VisualStudioVersion = 14.0.25420.1
```

```
 4 MinimumVisualStudioVersion = 10.0.40219.1
 5 Project("{F2A71F9B-5D33-465A-A702-920D77279786}") = "FSharpHelloWorld", "FSharpHelloWorld\
     FSharpHelloWorld.fsproj", "{D60939B6-526D-43F4-9A89-577B2980DF62}"
 6 EndProject
 7 Global
 8   GlobalSection(SolutionConfigurationPlatforms) = preSolution
 9     Debug|Any CPU = Debug|Any CPU
10     Release|Any CPU = Release|Any CPU
11   EndGlobalSection
12   GlobalSection(ProjectConfigurationPlatforms) = postSolution
13     {D60939B6-526D-43F4-9A89-577B2980DF62}.Debug|Any CPU.ActiveCfg = Debug|Any CPU
14     {D60939B6-526D-43F4-9A89-577B2980DF62}.Debug|Any CPU.Build.0 = Debug|Any CPU
15     {D60939B6-526D-43F4-9A89-577B2980DF62}.Release|Any CPU.ActiveCfg = Release|Any CPU
16     {D60939B6-526D-43F4-9A89-577B2980DF62}.Release|Any CPU.Build.0 = Release|Any CPU
17   EndGlobalSection
18   GlobalSection(SolutionProperties) = preSolution
19     HideSolutionNode = FALSE
20   EndGlobalSection
21 EndGlobal
```

App.config (in (root directory name)\FSharpHelloWorld):

```
 1 <?xml version="1.0" encoding="utf-8" ?>
 2 <configuration>
 3   <startup>
 4     <supportedRuntime version="v4.0" sku=".NETFramework,Version=v4.6.2" />
 5   </startup>
 6 </configuration>
```

AssemblyInfo.fs (in (root directory name)\FSharpHelloWorld):

```
 1 namespace FSharpHelloWorld.AssemblyInfo
 2
 3 open System.Reflection
 4 open System.Runtime.CompilerServices
 5 open System.Runtime.InteropServices
 6
 7 // General Information about an assembly is controlled through the following
 8 // set of attributes. Change these attribute values to modify the information
 9 // associated with an assembly.
10 [<assembly: AssemblyTitle("FSharpHelloWorld")>]
11 [<assembly: AssemblyDescription("")>]
12 [<assembly: AssemblyConfiguration("")>]
13 [<assembly: AssemblyCompany("")>]
14 [<assembly: AssemblyProduct("FSharpHelloWorld")>]
15 [<assembly: AssemblyCopyright("Copyright © 2017")>]
16 [<assembly: AssemblyTrademark("")>]
17 [<assembly: AssemblyCulture("")>]
18
19 // Setting ComVisible to false makes the types in this assembly not visible
20 // to COM components.  If you need to access a type in this assembly from
21 // COM, set the ComVisible attribute to true on that type.
22 [<assembly: ComVisible(false)>]
23
24 // The following GUID is for the ID of the typelib if this project is exposed to COM
25 [<assembly: Guid("d60939b6-526d-43f4-9a89-577b2980df62")>]
```

```
26
27  // Version information for an assembly consists of the following four values:
28  //
29  // Major Version
30  // Minor Version
31  // Build Number
32  // Revision
33  //
34  // You can specify all the values or you can default the Build and Revision Numbers
35  // by using the '*' as shown below:
36  // [<assembly: AssemblyVersion("1.0.*")>]
37  [<assembly: AssemblyVersion("1.0.0.0")>]
38  [<assembly: AssemblyFileVersion("1.0.0.0")>]
39
40  do
41      ()
```

FSharpHelloWorld.fsproj (in (root directory name)\FSharpHelloWorld):

```
1   <?xml version="1.0" encoding="utf-8"?>
2   <Project ToolsVersion="14.0" DefaultTargets="Build" xmlns="http://schemas.microsoft.com/
        developer/msbuild/2003">
3     <Import Project="$(MSBuildExtensionsPath)\$(MSBuildToolsVersion)\Microsoft.Common.props"
          Condition="Exists('$(MSBuildExtensionsPath)\$(MSBuildToolsVersion)\Microsoft.Common.props
          ')" />
4     <PropertyGroup>
5       <Configuration Condition=" '$(Configuration)' == '' ">Debug</Configuration>
6       <Platform Condition=" '$(Platform)' == '' ">AnyCPU</Platform>
7       <SchemaVersion>2.0</SchemaVersion>
8       <ProjectGuid>d60939b6-526d-43f4-9a89-577b2980df62</ProjectGuid>
9       <OutputType>Exe</OutputType>
10      <RootNamespace>FSharpHelloWorld</RootNamespace>
11      <AssemblyName>FSharpHelloWorld</AssemblyName>
12      <TargetFrameworkVersion>v4.6.2</TargetFrameworkVersion>
13      <AutoGenerateBindingRedirects>true</AutoGenerateBindingRedirects>
14      <TargetFSharpCoreVersion>4.4.0.0</TargetFSharpCoreVersion>
15      <Name>FSharpHelloWorld</Name>
16    </PropertyGroup>
17    <PropertyGroup Condition=" '$(Configuration)|$(Platform)' == 'Debug|AnyCPU' ">
18      <DebugSymbols>true</DebugSymbols>
19      <DebugType>full</DebugType>
20      <Optimize>false</Optimize>
21      <Tailcalls>false</Tailcalls>
22      <OutputPath>bin\Debug\</OutputPath>
23      <DefineConstants>DEBUG;TRACE</DefineConstants>
24      <WarningLevel>3</WarningLevel>
25      <PlatformTarget>AnyCPU</PlatformTarget>
26      <DocumentationFile>bin\Debug\FSharpHelloWorld.XML</DocumentationFile>
27      <Prefer32Bit>true</Prefer32Bit>
28    </PropertyGroup>
29    <PropertyGroup Condition=" '$(Configuration)|$(Platform)' == 'Release|AnyCPU' ">
30      <DebugType>pdbonly</DebugType>
31      <Optimize>true</Optimize>
32      <Tailcalls>true</Tailcalls>
33      <OutputPath>bin\Release\</OutputPath>
```

```
34    <DefineConstants>TRACE</DefineConstants>
35    <WarningLevel>3</WarningLevel>
36    <PlatformTarget>AnyCPU</PlatformTarget>
37    <DocumentationFile>bin\Release\FSharpHelloWorld.XML</DocumentationFile>
38    <Prefer32Bit>true</Prefer32Bit>
39  </PropertyGroup>
40  <ItemGroup>
41    <Reference Include="mscorlib" />
42    <Reference Include="FSharp.Core, Version=$(TargetFSharpCoreVersion), Culture=neutral,
          PublicKeyToken=b03f5f7f11d50a3a">
43      <Private>True</Private>
44    </Reference>
45    <Reference Include="System" />
46    <Reference Include="System.Core" />
47    <Reference Include="System.Numerics" />
48  </ItemGroup>
49  <ItemGroup>
50    <Compile Include="AssemblyInfo.fs" />
51    <Compile Include="Program.fs" />
52    <None Include="App.config" />
53  </ItemGroup>
54  <PropertyGroup>
55    <MinimumVisualStudioVersion Condition="'$(MinimumVisualStudioVersion)' == ''">11</
          MinimumVisualStudioVersion>
56  </PropertyGroup>
57  <Choose>
58    <When Condition="'$(VisualStudioVersion)' == '11.0'">
59      <PropertyGroup Condition="Exists('$(MSBuildExtensionsPath32)\..\Microsoft SDKs\F#\3.0\
          Framework\v4.0\Microsoft.FSharp.Targets')">
60        <FSharpTargetsPath>$(MSBuildExtensionsPath32)\..\Microsoft SDKs\F#\3.0\Framework\v4.0\
          Microsoft.FSharp.Targets</FSharpTargetsPath>
61      </PropertyGroup>
62    </When>
63    <Otherwise>
64      <PropertyGroup Condition="Exists('$(MSBuildExtensionsPath32)\Microsoft\VisualStudio\v$(
          VisualStudioVersion)\FSharp\Microsoft.FSharp.Targets')">
65        <FSharpTargetsPath>$(MSBuildExtensionsPath32)\Microsoft\VisualStudio\v$(
          VisualStudioVersion)\FSharp\Microsoft.FSharp.Targets</FSharpTargetsPath>
66      </PropertyGroup>
67    </Otherwise>
68  </Choose>
69  <Import Project="$(FSharpTargetsPath)" />
70  <!-- To modify your build process, add your task inside one of the targets below and uncomment
          it.
71       Other similar extension points exist, see Microsoft.Common.targets.
72  <Target Name="BeforeBuild">
73  </Target>
74  <Target Name="AfterBuild">
75  </Target>
76  -->
77 </Project>
```

Program.fs (in (root directory name)\FSharpHelloWorld):

```
1 // Learn more about F# at http://fsharp.org
```

```
2 // See the 'F# Tutorial' project for more help.
3
4 [<EntryPoint>]
5 let main argv =
6   printfn "Hello World"
7   0 // return an integer exit code
```

Visual Basic and the Microsoft .NET Framework

buildspec.yml (in (root directory name)):

```
1 version: 0.2
2
3 env:
4   variables:
5     SOLUTION: .\VBHelloWorld.sln
6     PACKAGE_DIRECTORY: .\packages
7     DOTNET_FRAMEWORK: 4.6.2
8
9 phases:
10   build:
11     commands:
12       - '& "C:\ProgramData\chocolatey\bin\NuGet.exe" restore $env:SOLUTION -PackagesDirectory
            $env:PACKAGE_DIRECTORY'
13      - '& "C:\Program Files (x86)\MSBuild\14.0\Bin\MSBuild.exe" -p:FrameworkPathOverride="C:\
            Program Files (x86)\Reference Assemblies\Microsoft\Framework\.NETFramework\v$env:
            DOTNET_FRAMEWORK" $env:SOLUTION'.2
14 artifacts:
15   files:
16     - .\VBHelloWorld\bin\Debug\*
```

VBHelloWorld.sln (in (root directory name)):

```
1 Microsoft Visual Studio Solution File, Format Version 12.00
2 # Visual Studio 14
3 VisualStudioVersion = 14.0.25420.1
4 MinimumVisualStudioVersion = 10.0.40219.1
5 Project("{F184B08F-C81C-45F6-A57F-5ABD9991F28F}") = "VBHelloWorld", "VBHelloWorld\VBHelloWorld.
     vbproj", "{4DCEC446-7156-4FE6-8CCC-219E34DD409D}"
6 EndProject
7 Global
8   GlobalSection(SolutionConfigurationPlatforms) = preSolution
9     Debug|Any CPU = Debug|Any CPU
10    Release|Any CPU = Release|Any CPU
11   EndGlobalSection
12   GlobalSection(ProjectConfigurationPlatforms) = postSolution
13    {4DCEC446-7156-4FE6-8CCC-219E34DD409D}.Debug|Any CPU.ActiveCfg = Debug|Any CPU
14    {4DCEC446-7156-4FE6-8CCC-219E34DD409D}.Debug|Any CPU.Build.0 = Debug|Any CPU
15    {4DCEC446-7156-4FE6-8CCC-219E34DD409D}.Release|Any CPU.ActiveCfg = Release|Any CPU
16    {4DCEC446-7156-4FE6-8CCC-219E34DD409D}.Release|Any CPU.Build.0 = Release|Any CPU
17   EndGlobalSection
18   GlobalSection(SolutionProperties) = preSolution
19     HideSolutionNode = FALSE
20   EndGlobalSection
21 EndGlobal
```

App.config (in (root directory name)\VBHelloWorld):

```
1  <?xml version="1.0" encoding="utf-8" ?>
2  <configuration>
3    <startup>
4      <supportedRuntime version="v4.0" sku=".NETFramework,Version=v4.6.2" />
5    </startup>
6  </configuration>
```

HelloWorld.vb (in (root directory name)\VBHelloWorld):

```
1  Module HelloWorld
2
3    Sub Main()
4      MsgBox("Hello World")
5    End Sub
6
7  End Module
```

VBHelloWorld.vbproj (in (root directory name)\VBHelloWorld):

```
1  <?xml version="1.0" encoding="utf-8"?>
2  <Project ToolsVersion="14.0" DefaultTargets="Build" xmlns="http://schemas.microsoft.com/
       developer/msbuild/2003">
3    <Import Project="$(MSBuildExtensionsPath)\$(MSBuildToolsVersion)\Microsoft.Common.props"
        Condition="Exists('$(MSBuildExtensionsPath)\$(MSBuildToolsVersion)\Microsoft.Common.props
        ')" />
4    <PropertyGroup>
5      <Configuration Condition=" '$(Configuration)' == '' ">Debug</Configuration>
6      <Platform Condition=" '$(Platform)' == '' ">AnyCPU</Platform>
7      <ProjectGuid>{4DCEC446-7156-4FE6-8CCC-219E34DD409D}</ProjectGuid>
8      <OutputType>Exe</OutputType>
9      <StartupObject>VBHelloWorld.HelloWorld</StartupObject>
10     <RootNamespace>VBHelloWorld</RootNamespace>
11     <AssemblyName>VBHelloWorld</AssemblyName>
12     <FileAlignment>512</FileAlignment>
13     <MyType>Console</MyType>
14     <TargetFrameworkVersion>v4.6.2</TargetFrameworkVersion>
15     <AutoGenerateBindingRedirects>true</AutoGenerateBindingRedirects>
16   </PropertyGroup>
17   <PropertyGroup Condition=" '$(Configuration)|$(Platform)' == 'Debug|AnyCPU' ">
18     <PlatformTarget>AnyCPU</PlatformTarget>
19     <DebugSymbols>true</DebugSymbols>
20     <DebugType>full</DebugType>
21     <DefineDebug>true</DefineDebug>
22     <DefineTrace>true</DefineTrace>
23     <OutputPath>bin\Debug\</OutputPath>
24     <DocumentationFile>VBHelloWorld.xml</DocumentationFile>
25     <NoWarn>42016,41999,42017,42018,42019,42032,42036,42020,42021,42022</NoWarn>
26   </PropertyGroup>
27   <PropertyGroup Condition=" '$(Configuration)|$(Platform)' == 'Release|AnyCPU' ">
28     <PlatformTarget>AnyCPU</PlatformTarget>
29     <DebugType>pdbonly</DebugType>
30     <DefineDebug>false</DefineDebug>
31     <DefineTrace>true</DefineTrace>
32     <Optimize>true</Optimize>
```

```
33    <OutputPath>bin\Release\</OutputPath>
34    <DocumentationFile>VBHelloWorld.xml</DocumentationFile>
35    <NoWarn>42016,41999,42017,42018,42019,42032,42036,42020,42021,42022</NoWarn>
36  </PropertyGroup>
37  <PropertyGroup>
38    <OptionExplicit>On</OptionExplicit>
39  </PropertyGroup>
40  <PropertyGroup>
41    <OptionCompare>Binary</OptionCompare>
42  </PropertyGroup>
43  <PropertyGroup>
44    <OptionStrict>Off</OptionStrict>
45  </PropertyGroup>
46  <PropertyGroup>
47    <OptionInfer>On</OptionInfer>
48  </PropertyGroup>
49  <ItemGroup>
50    <Reference Include="System" />
51    <Reference Include="System.Data" />
52    <Reference Include="System.Deployment" />
53    <Reference Include="System.Xml" />
54    <Reference Include="System.Core" />
55    <Reference Include="System.Xml.Linq" />
56    <Reference Include="System.Data.DataSetExtensions" />
57    <Reference Include="System.Net.Http" />
58  </ItemGroup>
59  <ItemGroup>
60    <Import Include="Microsoft.VisualBasic" />
61    <Import Include="System" />
62    <Import Include="System.Collections" />
63    <Import Include="System.Collections.Generic" />
64    <Import Include="System.Data" />
65    <Import Include="System.Diagnostics" />
66    <Import Include="System.Linq" />
67    <Import Include="System.Xml.Linq" />
68    <Import Include="System.Threading.Tasks" />
69  </ItemGroup>
70  <ItemGroup>
71    <Compile Include="HelloWorld.vb" />
72    <Compile Include="My Project\AssemblyInfo.vb" />
73    <Compile Include="My Project\Application.Designer.vb">
74      <AutoGen>True</AutoGen>
75      <DependentUpon>Application.myapp</DependentUpon>
76    </Compile>
77    <Compile Include="My Project\Resources.Designer.vb">
78      <AutoGen>True</AutoGen>
79      <DesignTime>True</DesignTime>
80      <DependentUpon>Resources.resx</DependentUpon>
81    </Compile>
82    <Compile Include="My Project\Settings.Designer.vb">
83      <AutoGen>True</AutoGen>
84      <DependentUpon>Settings.settings</DependentUpon>
85      <DesignTimeSharedInput>True</DesignTimeSharedInput>
86    </Compile>
```

```
87   </ItemGroup>
88   <ItemGroup>
89     <EmbeddedResource Include="My Project\Resources.resx">
90       <Generator>VbMyResourcesResXFileCodeGenerator</Generator>
91       <LastGenOutput>Resources.Designer.vb</LastGenOutput>
92       <CustomToolNamespace>My.Resources</CustomToolNamespace>
93       <SubType>Designer</SubType>
94     </EmbeddedResource>
95   </ItemGroup>
96   <ItemGroup>
97     <None Include="My Project\Application.myapp">
98       <Generator>MyApplicationCodeGenerator</Generator>
99       <LastGenOutput>Application.Designer.vb</LastGenOutput>
100    </None>
101    <None Include="My Project\Settings.settings">
102      <Generator>SettingsSingleFileGenerator</Generator>
103      <CustomToolNamespace>My</CustomToolNamespace>
104      <LastGenOutput>Settings.Designer.vb</LastGenOutput>
105    </None>
106    <None Include="App.config" />
107  </ItemGroup>
108  <Import Project="$(MSBuildToolsPath)\Microsoft.VisualBasic.targets" />
109  <!-- To modify your build process, add your task inside one of the targets below and uncomment
        it.
110      Other similar extension points exist, see Microsoft.Common.targets.
111  <Target Name="BeforeBuild">
112  </Target>
113  <Target Name="AfterBuild">
114  </Target>
115  -->
116 </Project>
```

Application.Designer.vb (in (root directory name)\VBHelloWorld\My Project):

```
1  '------------------------------------------------------------------------------
2  ' <auto-generated>
3  '     This code was generated by a tool.
4  '     Runtime Version:4.0.30319.42000
5  '
6  '     Changes to this file may cause incorrect behavior and will be lost if
7  '     the code is regenerated.
8  ' </auto-generated>
9  '------------------------------------------------------------------------------
10
11 Option Strict On
12 Option Explicit On
```

Application.myapp (in (root directory name)\VBHelloWorld\My Project):

```
1 <?xml version="1.0" encoding="utf-8"?>
2 <MyApplicationData xmlns:xsi="http://www.w3.org/2001/XMLSchema-instance" xmlns:xsd="http://www.
    w3.org/2001/XMLSchema">
3   <MySubMain>false</MySubMain>
4   <SingleInstance>false</SingleInstance>
5   <ShutdownMode>0</ShutdownMode>
6   <EnableVisualStyles>true</EnableVisualStyles>
```

```
7    <AuthenticationMode>0</AuthenticationMode>
8    <ApplicationType>2</ApplicationType>
9    <SaveMySettingsOnExit>true</SaveMySettingsOnExit>
10 </MyApplicationData>
```

AssemblyInfo.vb (in (root directory name)\VBHelloWorld\My Project):

```
1  Imports System
2  Imports System.Reflection
3  Imports System.Runtime.InteropServices
4
5  ' General Information about an assembly is controlled through the following
6  ' set of attributes. Change these attribute values to modify the information
7  ' associated with an assembly.
8
9  ' Review the values of the assembly attributes
10
11 <Assembly: AssemblyTitle("VBHelloWorld")>
12 <Assembly: AssemblyDescription("")>
13 <Assembly: AssemblyCompany("")>
14 <Assembly: AssemblyProduct("VBHelloWorld")>
15 <Assembly: AssemblyCopyright("Copyright ©  2017")>
16 <Assembly: AssemblyTrademark("")>
17
18 <Assembly: ComVisible(False)>
19
20 'The following GUID is for the ID of the typelib if this project is exposed to COM
21 <Assembly: Guid("137c362b-36ef-4c3e-84ab-f95082487a5a")>
22
23 ' Version information for an assembly consists of the following four values:
24 '
25 ' Major Version
26 ' Minor Version
27 ' Build Number
28 ' Revision
29 '
30 ' You can specify all the values or you can default the Build and Revision Numbers
31 ' by using the '*' as shown below:
32 ' <Assembly: AssemblyVersion("1.0.*")>
33
34 <Assembly: AssemblyVersion("1.0.0.0")>
35 <Assembly: AssemblyFileVersion("1.0.0.0")>
```

Resources.Designer.vb (in (root directory name)\VBHelloWorld\My Project):

```
1  '------------------------------------------------------------------------------
2  ' <auto-generated>
3  '    This code was generated by a tool.
4  '    Runtime Version:4.0.30319.42000
5  '
6  '    Changes to this file may cause incorrect behavior and will be lost if
7  '    the code is regenerated.
8  ' </auto-generated>
9  '------------------------------------------------------------------------------
10
11 Option Strict On
```

```vb
12 Option Explicit On
13
14 Namespace My.Resources
15
16    'This class was auto-generated by the StronglyTypedResourceBuilder
17    'class via a tool like ResGen or Visual Studio.
18    'To add or remove a member, edit your .ResX file then rerun ResGen
19    'with the /str option, or rebuild your VS project.
20    '''<summary>
21    '''  A strongly-typed resource class, for looking up localized strings, etc.
22    '''</summary>
23    <Global.System.CodeDom.Compiler.GeneratedCodeAttribute("System.Resources.Tools.
         StronglyTypedResourceBuilder", "4.0.0.0"), _
24    Global.System.Diagnostics.DebuggerNonUserCodeAttribute(), _
25    Global.System.Runtime.CompilerServices.CompilerGeneratedAttribute(), _
26    Global.Microsoft.VisualBasic.HideModuleNameAttribute()> _
27    Friend Module Resources
28
29      Private resourceMan As Global.System.Resources.ResourceManager
30
31      Private resourceCulture As Global.System.Globalization.CultureInfo
32
33      '''<summary>
34      '''  Returns the cached ResourceManager instance used by this class.
35      '''</summary>
36      <Global.System.ComponentModel.EditorBrowsableAttribute(Global.System.ComponentModel.
           EditorBrowsableState.Advanced)> _
37      Friend ReadOnly Property ResourceManager() As Global.System.Resources.ResourceManager
38        Get
39          If Object.ReferenceEquals(resourceMan, Nothing) Then
40            Dim temp As Global.System.Resources.ResourceManager = New Global.System.Resources.
                 ResourceManager("VBHelloWorld.Resources", GetType(Resources).Assembly)
41            resourceMan = temp
42          End If
43          Return resourceMan
44        End Get
45      End Property
46
47      '''<summary>
48      '''  Overrides the current thread's CurrentUICulture property for all
49      '''  resource lookups using this strongly typed resource class.
50      '''</summary>
51      <Global.System.ComponentModel.EditorBrowsableAttribute(Global.System.ComponentModel.
           EditorBrowsableState.Advanced)> _
52      Friend Property Culture() As Global.System.Globalization.CultureInfo
53        Get
54          Return resourceCulture
55        End Get
56        Set(ByVal value As Global.System.Globalization.CultureInfo)
57          resourceCulture = value
58        End Set
59      End Property
60    End Module
61 End Namespace
```

Resources.resx (in (root directory name)\VBHelloWorld\My Project):

```
1  <?xml version="1.0" encoding="utf-8"?>
2  <root>
3    <!--
4      Microsoft ResX Schema
5
6      Version 2.0
7
8      The primary goals of this format is to allow a simple XML format
9      that is mostly human readable. The generation and parsing of the
10     various data types are done through the TypeConverter classes
11     associated with the data types.
12
13     Example:
14
15     ... ado.net/XML headers & schema ...
16     <resheader name="resmimetype">text/microsoft-resx</resheader>
17     <resheader name="version">2.0</resheader>
18     <resheader name="reader">System.Resources.ResXResourceReader, System.Windows.Forms, ...</
           resheader>
19     <resheader name="writer">System.Resources.ResXResourceWriter, System.Windows.Forms, ...</
           resheader>
20     <data name="Name1"><value>this is my long string</value><comment>this is a comment</comment
           ></data>
21     <data name="Color1" type="System.Drawing.Color, System.Drawing">Blue</data>
22     <data name="Bitmap1" mimetype="application/x-microsoft.net.object.binary.base64">
23       <value>[base64 mime encoded serialized .NET Framework object]</value>
24     </data>
25     <data name="Icon1" type="System.Drawing.Icon, System.Drawing" mimetype="application/x-
           microsoft.net.object.bytearray.base64">
26       <value>[base64 mime encoded string representing a byte array form of the .NET Framework
               object]</value>
27       <comment>This is a comment</comment>
28     </data>
29
30     There are any number of "resheader" rows that contain simple
31     name/value pairs.
32
33     Each data row contains a name, and value. The row also contains a
34     type or mimetype. Type corresponds to a .NET class that support
35     text/value conversion through the TypeConverter architecture.
36     Classes that don't support this are serialized and stored with the
37     mimetype set.
38
39     The mimetype is used for serialized objects, and tells the
40     ResXResourceReader how to depersist the object. This is currently not
41     extensible. For a given mimetype the value must be set accordingly:
42
43     Note - application/x-microsoft.net.object.binary.base64 is the format
44     that the ResXResourceWriter will generate, however the reader can
45     read any of the formats listed below.
46
47     mimetype: application/x-microsoft.net.object.binary.base64
48     value    : The object must be serialized with
```

```
49              : System.Serialization.Formatters.Binary.BinaryFormatter
50              : and then encoded with base64 encoding.
51
52      mimetype: application/x-microsoft.net.object.soap.base64
53      value   : The object must be serialized with
54              : System.Runtime.Serialization.Formatters.Soap.SoapFormatter
55              : and then encoded with base64 encoding.
56
57      mimetype: application/x-microsoft.net.object.bytearray.base64
58      value   : The object must be serialized into a byte array
59              : using a System.ComponentModel.TypeConverter
60              : and then encoded with base64 encoding.
61  -->
62  <xsd:schema id="root" xmlns="" xmlns:xsd="http://www.w3.org/2001/XMLSchema" xmlns:msdata="urn:
       schemas-microsoft-com:xml-msdata">
63    <xsd:element name="root" msdata:IsDataSet="true">
64      <xsd:complexType>
65        <xsd:choice maxOccurs="unbounded">
66          <xsd:element name="metadata">
67            <xsd:complexType>
68              <xsd:sequence>
69                <xsd:element name="value" type="xsd:string" minOccurs="0" />
70              </xsd:sequence>
71              <xsd:attribute name="name" type="xsd:string" />
72              <xsd:attribute name="type" type="xsd:string" />
73              <xsd:attribute name="mimetype" type="xsd:string" />
74            </xsd:complexType>
75          </xsd:element>
76          <xsd:element name="assembly">
77            <xsd:complexType>
78              <xsd:attribute name="alias" type="xsd:string" />
79              <xsd:attribute name="name" type="xsd:string" />
80            </xsd:complexType>
81          </xsd:element>
82          <xsd:element name="data">
83            <xsd:complexType>
84              <xsd:sequence>
85                <xsd:element name="value" type="xsd:string" minOccurs="0" msdata:Ordinal="1" />
86                <xsd:element name="comment" type="xsd:string" minOccurs="0" msdata:Ordinal="2"
                     />
87              </xsd:sequence>
88              <xsd:attribute name="name" type="xsd:string" msdata:Ordinal="1" />
89              <xsd:attribute name="type" type="xsd:string" msdata:Ordinal="3" />
90              <xsd:attribute name="mimetype" type="xsd:string" msdata:Ordinal="4" />
91            </xsd:complexType>
92          </xsd:element>
93          <xsd:element name="resheader">
94            <xsd:complexType>
95              <xsd:sequence>
96                <xsd:element name="value" type="xsd:string" minOccurs="0" msdata:Ordinal="1" />
97              </xsd:sequence>
98              <xsd:attribute name="name" type="xsd:string" use="required" />
99            </xsd:complexType>
100         </xsd:element>
```

```
101        </xsd:choice>
102      </xsd:complexType>
103    </xsd:element>
104  </xsd:schema>
105  <resheader name="resmimetype">
106    <value>text/microsoft-resx</value>
107  </resheader>
108  <resheader name="version">
109    <value>2.0</value>
110  </resheader>
111  <resheader name="reader">
112    <value>System.Resources.ResXResourceReader, System.Windows.Forms, Version=2.0.0.0, Culture=
           neutral, PublicKeyToken=b77a5c561934e089</value>
113  </resheader>
114  <resheader name="writer">
115    <value>System.Resources.ResXResourceWriter, System.Windows.Forms, Version=2.0.0.0, Culture=
           neutral, PublicKeyToken=b77a5c561934e089</value>
116  </resheader>
117  </root>
```

Settings.Designer.vb (in (root directory name)\VBHelloWorld\My Project):

```
1  '------------------------------------------------------------------------------
2  ' <auto-generated>
3  '     This code was generated by a tool.
4  '     Runtime Version:4.0.30319.42000
5  '
6  '     Changes to this file may cause incorrect behavior and will be lost if
7  '     the code is regenerated.
8  ' </auto-generated>
9  '------------------------------------------------------------------------------
10
11 Option Strict On
12 Option Explicit On
13
14 Namespace My
15
16    <Global.System.Runtime.CompilerServices.CompilerGeneratedAttribute(), _
17    Global.System.CodeDom.Compiler.GeneratedCodeAttribute("Microsoft.VisualStudio.Editors.
           SettingsDesigner.SettingsSingleFileGenerator", "11.0.0.0"), _
18    Global.System.ComponentModel.EditorBrowsableAttribute(Global.System.ComponentModel.
           EditorBrowsableState.Advanced)> _
19    Partial Friend NotInheritable Class MySettings
20       Inherits Global.System.Configuration.ApplicationSettingsBase
21
22       Private Shared defaultInstance As MySettings = CType(Global.System.Configuration.
              ApplicationSettingsBase.Synchronized(New MySettings), MySettings)
23
24       #Region "My.Settings Auto-Save Functionality"
25         #If _MyType = "WindowsForms" Then
26           Private Shared addedHandler As Boolean
27
28           Private Shared addedHandlerLockObject As New Object
29
30           <Global.System.Diagnostics.DebuggerNonUserCodeAttribute(), Global.System.ComponentModel.
```

47

```vbnet
                    EditorBrowsableAttribute(Global.System.ComponentModel.EditorBrowsableState.Advanced)
                    > _
31      Private Shared Sub AutoSaveSettings(ByVal sender As Global.System.Object, ByVal e As
                    Global.System.EventArgs)
32          If My.Application.SaveMySettingsOnExit Then
33              My.Settings.Save()
34          End If
35      End Sub
36    #End If
37  #End Region

39  Public Shared ReadOnly Property [Default]() As MySettings
40      Get

42        #If _MyType = "WindowsForms" Then
43          If Not addedHandler Then
44            SyncLock addedHandlerLockObject
45              If Not addedHandler Then
46                AddHandler My.Application.Shutdown, AddressOf AutoSaveSettings
47                addedHandler = True
48              End If
49            End SyncLock
50          End If
51        #End If
52        Return defaultInstance
53      End Get
54  End Property
55  End Class
56 End Namespace

58 Namespace My

60    <Global.Microsoft.VisualBasic.HideModuleNameAttribute(), _
61    Global.System.Diagnostics.DebuggerNonUserCodeAttribute(), _
62    Global.System.Runtime.CompilerServices.CompilerGeneratedAttribute()> _
63    Friend Module MySettingsProperty

65      <Global.System.ComponentModel.Design.HelpKeywordAttribute("My.Settings")> _
66      Friend ReadOnly Property Settings() As Global.VBHelloWorld.My.MySettings
67        Get
68          Return Global.VBHelloWorld.My.MySettings.Default
69        End Get
70      End Property
71    End Module
72 End Namespace
```

Settings.settings (in (root directory name)\VBHelloWorld\My Project):

```xml
1 <?xml version='1.0' encoding='utf-8'?>
2 <SettingsFile xmlns="http://schemas.microsoft.com/VisualStudio/2004/01/settings" CurrentProfile
      ="(Default)" UseMySettingsClassName="true">
3   <Profiles>
4     <Profile Name="(Default)" />
5   </Profiles>
6   <Settings />
```

```
7 </SettingsFile>
```

C# and .NET Core

buildspec.yml (in (root directory name)

```
1 version: 0.2
2
3 phases:
4   build:
5     commands:
6       - dotnet restore
7       - dotnet build
8 artifacts:
9   files:
10      - .\bin\Debug\netcoreapp1.0\*
```

HelloWorldSample.csproj (in (root directory name)

```
1 <Project Sdk="Microsoft.NET.Sdk">
2   <PropertyGroup>
3     <OutputType>Exe</OutputType>
4     <TargetFramework>netcoreapp1.0</TargetFramework>
5   </PropertyGroup>
6 </Project>
```

Program.cs (in (root directory name)

```
1 using System;
2
3 namespace HelloWorldSample
4 {
5   public static class Program
6   {
7     public static void Main()
8     {
9       Console.WriteLine("Hello World!");
10     }
11   }
12 }
```

AWS CodeBuild Use Case-Based Samples

You can use these use case-based samples to experiment with AWS CodeBuild:

Name	Description
Amazon ECR Sample	Uses a Docker image in an Amazon ECR repository to use Apache Maven to produce a single JAR file.
Docker Sample	Uses a build image provided by AWS CodeBuild with Docker support to produce a Docker image with Apache Maven. Pushes the Docker image to a repository in Amazon ECR. You can also adapt this sample to push the Docker image to Docker Hub.
GitHub Enterprise Sample	Uses AWS CodeBuild with GitHub Enterprise as the source repository, with certificates installed and webhooks enabled, to rebuild the source code every time a code change is pushed to the repository.
GitHub Pull Request Sample	Uses AWS CodeBuild with GitHub as the source repository, and webhooks enabled, to rebuild the source code every time a code change is pushed to the repository.
Use AWS Config with AWS CodeBuild Sample	Shows how to set up AWS Config. Lists which AWS CodeBuild resources are tracked and describes how to look up AWS CodeBuild projects in AWS Config.
Build Badges Sample	Shows how to set up AWS CodeBuild with build badges.
Build Notifications Sample	Uses Apache Maven to produce a single JAR file. Sends a build notification to subscribers of an Amazon SNS topic.
Docker in Custom Image Sample	Uses a custom Docker image to produce a Docker image.
AWS CodeDeploy Sample	Uses Apache Maven to produce a single JAR file. Uses AWS CodeDeploy to deploy the JAR file to an Amazon Linux instance. You can also use AWS CodePipeline to build and deploy the sample.
AWS Lambda Sample	Uses AWS CodeBuild along with Lambda, AWS CloudFormation, and AWS CodePipeline to build and deploy a serverless application that follows the AWS Serverless Application Model (AWS SAM) standard.
Elastic Beanstalk Sample	Uses Apache Maven to produce a single WAR file. Uses Elastic Beanstalk to deploy the WAR file to an Elastic Beanstalk instance.

Amazon ECR Sample for AWS CodeBuild

This sample uses a Docker image in an Amazon Elastic Container Registry (Amazon ECR) image repository to build the Go Sample for AWS CodeBuild.

Important
Running this sample may result in charges to your AWS account. These include possible charges for AWS CodeBuild and for AWS resources and actions related to Amazon S3, AWS KMS, CloudWatch Logs, and Amazon ECR. For more information, see AWS CodeBuild Pricing, Amazon S3 Pricing, AWS Key Management Service Pricing, Amazon CloudWatch Pricing, and Amazon Elastic Container Registry Pricing.

Running the Sample

To run this sample:

1. To create and push the Docker image to your image repository in Amazon ECR, complete the steps in the Running the Sample section of the Docker Sample.

2. To create and upload the source code to be built, complete steps 1 through 4 of the Running the Sample section of the Go Sample.

3. Assign permissions to your image repository in Amazon ECR so that AWS CodeBuild can pull the repository's Docker image into the build environment:

    1. If you are using an IAM user instead of an AWS root account or an administrator IAM user to work with Amazon ECR, add the statement (between *### BEGIN ADDING STATEMENT HERE ###* and *### END ADDING STATEMENT HERE ###*) to the user (or IAM group the user is associated with). (Using an AWS root account is not recommended.) This statement enables access to managing permissions for Amazon ECR repositories. Ellipses (...) are used for brevity and to help you locate where to add the statement. Do not remove any statements, and do not type these ellipses into the policy. For more information, see Working with Inline Policies Using the AWS Management Console in the *IAM User Guide*.

```
1  {
2    "Statement": [
3      ### BEGIN ADDING STATEMENT HERE ###
4      {
5        "Action": [
6          "ecr:GetRepositoryPolicy",
7          "ecr:SetRepositoryPolicy"
8        ],
9        "Resource": "*",
10       "Effect": "Allow"
11     },
12     ### END ADDING STATEMENT HERE ###
13     ...
14   ],
15   "Version": "2012-10-17"
16 }
```

Note
The IAM entity that modifies this policy must have permission in IAM to modify policies.

    1. Open the Amazon ECS console at https://console.aws.amazon.com/ecs/.

    2. Choose **Repositories**.

    3. In the list of repository names, choose the name of the repository you created or selected.

4. Choose the **Permissions** tab, choose **Add**, and then create a statement.

5. For **Sid**, type an identifier (for example, **CodeBuildAccess**).

6. For **Effect**, leave **Allow** selected because you want to allow access to AWS CodeBuild.

7. For **Principal**, type **codebuild.amazonaws.com**. Leave **Everybody** cleared because you want to allow access to AWS CodeBuild only.

8. Skip the **All IAM entities** list.

9. For **Action**, select **Pull only actions**.

   All of the pull-only actions (**ecr:GetDownloadUrlForLayer**, **ecr:BatchGetImage**, and **ecr:BatchCheckLayerAvailability**) will be selected.

10. Choose **Save all**.

    This policy will be displayed in **Policy document**.

```
1  {
2    "Version": "2012-10-17",
3    "Statement": [
4      {
5        "Sid": "CodeBuildAccess",
6        "Effect": "Allow",
7        "Principal": {
8          "Service": "codebuild.amazonaws.com"
9        },
10       "Action": [
11         "ecr:GetDownloadUrlForLayer",
12         "ecr:BatchGetImage",
13         "ecr:BatchCheckLayerAvailability"
14       ]
15     }
16   ]
17 }
```

11. Create a build project, run the build, and view build information by following the steps in Run AWS CodeBuild Directly.

    If you use the AWS CLI to create the build project, the JSON-formatted input to the `create-project` command might look similar to this. (Replace the placeholders with your own values.)

```
1  {
2    "name": "amazon-ecr-sample-project",
3    "source": {
4      "type": "S3",
5      "location": "codebuild-region-ID-account-ID-input-bucket/GoSample.zip"
6    },
7    "artifacts": {
8      "type": "S3",
9      "location": "codebuild-region-ID-account-ID-output-bucket",
10     "packaging": "ZIP",
11     "name": "GoOutputArtifact.zip"
12   },
13   "environment": {
14     "type": "LINUX_CONTAINER",
15     "image": "account-ID.dkr.ecr.region-ID.amazonaws.com/your-Amazon-ECR-repo-name:latest",
16     "computeType": "BUILD_GENERAL1_SMALL"
```

```
17    },
18    "serviceRole": "arn:aws:iam::account-ID:role/role-name",
19    "encryptionKey": "arn:aws:kms:region-ID:account-ID:key/key-ID"
20  }
```

12. To get the build output artifact, open your Amazon S3 output bucket.

13. Download the `GoOutputArtifact.zip` file to your local computer or instance, and then extract the contents of the `GoOutputArtifact.zip` file. In the extracted contents, get the `hello` file.

Related Resources

- For more information about getting started with AWS CodeBuild, see Getting Started with AWS CodeBuild.
- For more information about troubleshooting problems with AWS CodeBuild, see Troubleshooting AWS CodeBuild.
- For more information about limits in AWS CodeBuild, see Limits for AWS CodeBuild.

Docker Sample for AWS CodeBuild

This sample produces as build output a Docker image and then pushes the Docker image to an Amazon Elastic Container Registry (Amazon ECR) image repository. You can adapt this sample to push the Docker image to Docker Hub. For more information, see Adapting the Sample to Push the Image to Docker Hub.

To learn how to build a Docker image by using a custom Docker build image instead (`docker:dind` in Docker Hub), see our Docker in Custom Image Sample.

This sample was tested referencing `golang:1.9`

This sample uses the new multi-stage Docker builds feature, which produces a Docker image as build output. It then pushes the Docker image to an Amazon ECR image repository. Multi-stage Docker image builds help to reduce the size of the final Docker image. For more information, see Use multi-stage builds with Docker.

Important

Running this sample may result in charges to your AWS account. These include possible charges for AWS CodeBuild and for AWS resources and actions related to Amazon S3, AWS KMS, CloudWatch Logs, and Amazon ECR. For more information, see AWS CodeBuild Pricing, Amazon S3 Pricing, AWS Key Management Service Pricing, Amazon CloudWatch Pricing, and Amazon Elastic Container Registry Pricing.

Topics

- Running the Sample
- Directory Structure
- Files
- Adapting the Sample to Push the Image to Docker Hub
- Related Resources

Running the Sample

To run this sample:

1. If you already have an image repository in Amazon ECR you want to use, skip to step 3. Otherwise, if you are using an IAM user instead of an AWS root account or an administrator IAM user to work with Amazon ECR, add this statement (between *### BEGIN ADDING STATEMENT HERE ###* and *### END ADDING STATEMENT HERE ###*) to the user (or IAM group the user is associated with). (Using an AWS root account is not recommended.) This statement enables creating Amazon ECR repositories for storing Docker images. Ellipses (. . .) are used for brevity and to help you locate where to add the statement. Do not remove any statements, and do not type these ellipses into the policy. For more information, see Working with Inline Policies Using the AWS Management Console in the *IAM User Guide*.

```
1  {
2    "Statement": [
3      ### BEGIN ADDING STATEMENT HERE ###
4      {
5        "Action": [
6          "ecr:CreateRepository"
7        ],
8        "Resource": "*",
9        "Effect": "Allow"
10     },
11     ### END ADDING STATEMENT HERE ###
12     ...
13   ],
14   "Version": "2012-10-17"
15 }
```

Note

The IAM entity that modifies this policy must have permission in IAM to modify policies.

1. Create an image repository in Amazon ECR. Be sure to create the repository in the same AWS region where you will be creating your build environment and running your build. For more information, see Creating a Repository in the *Amazon ECR User Guide*. This repository's name must match the repository name you will specify later in this procedure, represented by the `IMAGE_REPO_NAME` environment variable.

2. Add this statement (between *### BEGIN ADDING STATEMENT HERE ###* and *### END ADDING STATEMENT HERE ###*) to the policy you attached to your AWS CodeBuild service role. This statement enables AWS CodeBuild to upload Docker images to Amazon ECR repositories. Ellipses (...) are used for brevity and to help you locate where to add the statement. Do not remove any statements, and do not type these ellipses into the policy.

```
1  {
2    "Statement": [
3      ### BEGIN ADDING STATEMENT HERE ###
4      {
5        "Action": [
6          "ecr:BatchCheckLayerAvailability",
7          "ecr:CompleteLayerUpload",
8          "ecr:GetAuthorizationToken",
9          "ecr:InitiateLayerUpload",
10         "ecr:PutImage",
11         "ecr:UploadLayerPart"
12       ],
13       "Resource": "*",
14       "Effect": "Allow"
15     },
16     ### END ADDING STATEMENT HERE ###
17     ...
18   ],
19   "Version": "2012-10-17"
20 }
```

Note

The IAM entity that modifies this policy must have permission in IAM to modify policies.

1. Create the files as described in the Directory Structure and Files sections of this topic, and then upload them to an Amazon S3 input bucket or an AWS CodeCommit, GitHub, or Bitbucket repository. **Important** Do not upload (`root directory name`), just the files inside of (`root directory name`).
   If you are using an Amazon S3 input bucket, be sure to create a ZIP file that contains the files, and then upload it to the input bucket. Do not add (`root directory name`) to the ZIP file, just the files inside of (`root directory name`).

2. Create a build project, run the build, and view related build information by following the steps in Run AWS CodeBuild Directly.

   If you use the AWS CLI to create the build project, the JSON-formatted input to the `create-project` command might look similar to this. (Replace the placeholders with your own values.)

```
1  {
2    "name": "sample-docker-project",
3    "source": {
4      "type": "S3",
5      "location": "codebuild-region-ID-account-ID-input-bucket/DockerSample.zip"
6    },
7    "artifacts": {
```

```
 8      "type": "NO_ARTIFACTS"
 9    },
10    "environment": {
11      "type": "LINUX_CONTAINER",
12      "image": "aws/codebuild/docker:17.09.0",
13      "computeType": "BUILD_GENERAL1_SMALL",
14      "environmentVariables": [
15        {
16          "name": "AWS_DEFAULT_REGION",
17          "value": "region-ID"
18        },
19        {
20          "name": "AWS_ACCOUNT_ID",
21          "value": "account-ID"
22        },
23        {
24          "name": "IMAGE_REPO_NAME",
25          "value": "Amazon-ECR-repo-name"
26        },
27        {
28          "name": "IMAGE_TAG",
29          "value": "latest"
30        }
31      ]
32    },
33    "serviceRole": "arn:aws:iam::account-ID:role/role-name",
34    "encryptionKey": "arn:aws:kms:region-ID:account-ID:key/key-ID"
35 }
```

3. Confirm that AWS CodeBuild successfully pushed the Docker image to the repository:

    1. Open the Amazon ECS console at https://console.aws.amazon.com/ecs/.

    2. Choose **Repositories**.

    3. Choose the repository name. The image should be listed on the **Images** tab.

Directory Structure

This sample assumes this directory structure.

```
1 (root directory name)
2     |-- buildspec.yml
3     `-- Dockerfile
```

Files

This sample uses these files.

buildspec.yml (in (root directory name))

Note
If you are using Docker prior to version 17.06, remove the --no-include-email option.

```
1 version: 0.2
2
```

```
3  phases:
4    pre_build:
5      commands:
6        - echo Logging in to Amazon ECR...
7        - $(aws ecr get-login --no-include-email --region $AWS_DEFAULT_REGION)
8    build:
9      commands:
10       - echo Build started on `date`
11       - echo Building the Docker image...
12       - docker build -t $IMAGE_REPO_NAME:$IMAGE_TAG .
13       - docker tag $IMAGE_REPO_NAME:$IMAGE_TAG $AWS_ACCOUNT_ID.dkr.ecr.$AWS_DEFAULT_REGION.
              amazonaws.com/$IMAGE_REPO_NAME:$IMAGE_TAG
14   post_build:
15     commands:
16       - echo Build completed on `date`
17       - echo Pushing the Docker image...
18       - docker push $AWS_ACCOUNT_ID.dkr.ecr.$AWS_DEFAULT_REGION.amazonaws.com/$IMAGE_REPO_NAME:
              $IMAGE_TAG
```

Dockerfile (in (root directory name))

```
1  FROM golang:1.9 as builder
2  RUN go get -d -v golang.org/x/net/html
3  RUN go get -d -v github.com/alexellis/href-counter/
4  WORKDIR /go/src/github.com/alexellis/href-counter/.
5  RUN CGO_ENABLED=0 GOOS=linux go build -a -installsuffix cgo -o app .
6
7  FROM alpine:latest
8  RUN apk --no-cache add ca-certificates
9  WORKDIR /root/
10 COPY --from=builder /go/src/github.com/alexellis/href-counter/app .
11 CMD ["./app"]
```

Adapting the Sample to Push the Image to Docker Hub

To push the Docker image to Docker Hub instead of Amazon ECR, modify this sample's code.

1. Replace these Amazon ECR-specific lines of code in the buildspec.yml file: **Note**
   If you are using Docker prior to version 17.06, remove the --no-include-email option.

```
1  ...
2    pre_build:
3      commands:
4        - echo Logging in to Amazon ECR...
5        - $(aws ecr get-login --no-include-email --region $AWS_DEFAULT_REGION)
6    build:
7      commands:
8        - echo Build started on `date`
9        - echo Building the Docker image...
10       - docker build -t $IMAGE_REPO_NAME:$IMAGE_TAG .
11       - docker tag $IMAGE_REPO_NAME:$IMAGE_TAG $AWS_ACCOUNT_ID.dkr.ecr.$AWS_DEFAULT_REGION.
              amazonaws.com/$IMAGE_REPO_NAME:$IMAGE_TAG
12   post_build:
13     commands:
14       - echo Build completed on `date`
```

```
15        - echo Pushing the Docker image...
16        - docker push $AWS_ACCOUNT_ID.dkr.ecr.$AWS_DEFAULT_REGION.amazonaws.com/
              $IMAGE_REPO_NAME:$IMAGE_TAG
17    ...
```

With these Docker Hub-specific lines of code.

```
1     ...
2     pre_build:
3       commands:
4         - echo Logging in to Docker Hub...
5         # Type the command to log in to your Docker Hub account here.
6     build:
7       commands:
8         - echo Build started on `date`
9         - echo Building the Docker image...
10        - docker build -t $IMAGE_REPO_NAME:$IMAGE_TAG .
11        - docker tag $IMAGE_REPO_NAME:$IMAGE_TAG $IMAGE_REPO_NAME:$IMAGE_TAG
12    post_build:
13      commands:
14        - echo Build completed on `date`
15        - echo Pushing the Docker image...
16        - docker push $IMAGE_REPO_NAME:$IMAGE_TAG
17    ...
```

2. Upload the modified code to an Amazon S3 input bucket or an AWS CodeCommit, GitHub, or Bitbucket repository. **Important**
Do not upload (root directory name), just the files inside of (root directory name).
If you are using an Amazon S3 input bucket, be sure to create a ZIP file that contains the files, and then upload it to the input bucket. Do not add (root directory name) to the ZIP file, just the files inside of (root directory name).

3. Replace these lines of code from the JSON-formatted input to the `create-project` command:

```
1     ...
2       "environmentVariables": [
3         {
4           "name": "AWS_DEFAULT_REGION",
5           "value": "region-ID"
6         },
7         {
8           "name": "AWS_ACCOUNT_ID",
9           "value": "account-ID"
10        },
11        {
12          "name": "IMAGE_REPO_NAME",
13          "value": "Amazon-ECR-repo-name"
14        },
15        {
16          "name": "IMAGE_TAG",
17          "value": "latest"
18        }
19      ]
20    ...
```

With these lines of code.

```
1  ...
2    "environmentVariables": [
3      {
4        "name": "IMAGE_REPO_NAME",
5        "value": "your-Docker-Hub-repo-name"
6      },
7      {
8        "name": "IMAGE_TAG",
9        "value": "latest"
10     }
11   ]
12 ...
```

4. Follow the steps in Run AWS CodeBuild Directly to create a build environment, run the build, and view related build information.

5. Confirm that AWS CodeBuild successfully pushed the Docker image to the repository. Sign in to Docker Hub, go to the repository, and choose the **Tags** tab. The `latest` tag should contain a very recent **Last Updated** value.

Related Resources

- For more information about getting started with AWS CodeBuild, see Getting Started with AWS CodeBuild.
- For more information about troubleshooting problems with AWS CodeBuild, see Troubleshooting AWS CodeBuild.
- For more information about limits in AWS CodeBuild, see Limits for AWS CodeBuild.

GitHub Enterprise Sample for AWS CodeBuild

AWS CodeBuild now supports GitHub Enterprise as a source repository. This sample describes how to set up your AWS CodeBuild projects when your GitHub Enterprise repository has a certificate installed. It also explains how to enable webhooks so that AWS CodeBuild rebuilds the source code every time a code change is pushed to your private GitHub Enterprise repository.

Prerequisites

1. Generate a personal access token that will be entered into your AWS CodeBuild project. We recommend that you create a new GitHub Enterprise user and generate a personal access token for this user. Copy it to your clipboard so that it can be used when you create your AWS CodeBuild project. For more information, see Creating a Personal Access Token in GitHub Enterprise on the GitHub Help website.

   When you create the personal access token, include the repo scope in the definition.

2. Download your certificate from GitHub Enterprise. AWS CodeBuild uses the certificate to make a trusted SSL connection to the repository.

   Linux/macOS clients:

   From a terminal window, run the following command:

   ```
   1 echo -n | openssl s_client -connect HOST:PORTNUMBER \
   2     | sed -ne '/-BEGIN CERTIFICATE-/,/-END CERTIFICATE-/p' > /folder/filename.pem
   ```

   Replace the placeholders in the command with the following values:

   HOST. The IP address of your GitHub Enterprise repository.

   PORTNUMBER. The port number you are using to connect (for example, 443).

   folder. The folder where you downloaded your certificate.

   filename. The file name of your certificate file. **Important**
   Save the certificate as a .pem file.

   Windows clients:

   Download your certificate from GitHub Enterprise using your browser. To see the site's certificate details, choose the padlock icon. For information about how to export the certificate, see your browser documentation. **Important**
   Save the certificate as a .pem file.

3. Upload your certificate file to an Amazon S3 bucket. For information about how to create an Amazon S3 bucket, see How Do I Create an Amazon S3 Bucket? For information about how to upload objects to an Amazon S3 bucket, see How Do I Upload Files and Folders to a Bucket? **Note**
   This bucket must be in the same AWS region as your builds. For example, if you instruct AWS CodeBuild to run a build in the US East (Ohio) region, the bucket must be in the US East (Ohio) region.

Create a Build Project with GitHub Enterprise as the Source Repository and Enable Webhooks (Console)

1. Open the AWS CodeBuild console at https://console.aws.amazon.com/codebuild/.

2. If a welcome page is displayed, choose **Get started**. If a welcome page is not displayed, on the navigation pane, choose **Build projects**, and then choose **Create project**.

3. On the **Configure your project** page, for **Project name**, type a name for this build project. Build project names must be unique across each AWS account.

4. In **Source: What to build**, for **Source provider**, choose **GitHub Enterprise**.

   - For **Personal Access Token**, paste the token you copied to your clipboard and choose **Save Token**. In **Repository URL**, enter the URL for your GitHub Enterprise repository. **Note** You only need to enter and save the personal access token once. All future AWS CodeBuild projects will use this token.
   - Select **Webhook** to rebuild every time a code change is pushed to this repository.
   - Select **Insecure SSL** to ignore SSL warnings while connecting to your GitHub Enterprise project repository. **Note** We recommend that you use **Insecure SSL** for testing only. It should not be used in a production environment.

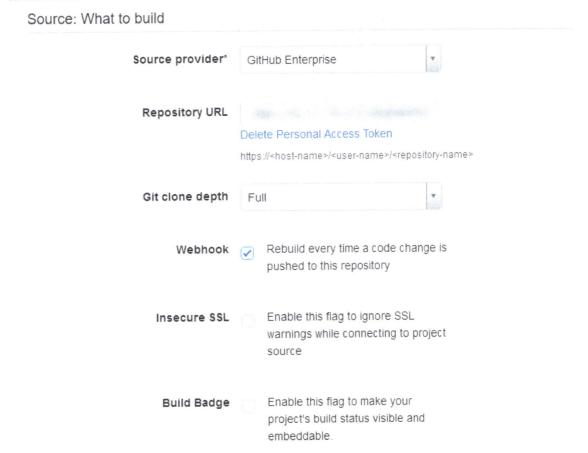

5. In **Environment: How to build**:

   For **Environment image**, do one of the following:

   - To use a Docker image managed by AWS CodeBuild, choose **Use an image managed by AWS CodeBuild**, and then make selections from **Operating system**, **Runtime**, and **Version**.

- To use another Docker image, choose **Specify a Docker image**. For **Custom image type**, choose **Other** or **Amazon ECR**. If you choose **Other**, then for **Custom image ID**, type the name and tag of the Docker image in Docker Hub, using the format `repository-name/image-name:image-tag`. If you choose **Amazon ECR**, then use **Amazon ECR repository** and **Amazon ECR image** to choose the Docker image in your AWS account.

For **Build specification**, do one of the following:

- Use the buildspec.yml file in the source code root directory.
- Override the build specification by inserting the build commands.

For more information, see the Build Spec Reference.

For **Certificate**, choose **Install certificate from your S3**. For **Bucket of certificate**, choose the S3 bucket where your SSL certificate is stored. For **Object key of certificate**, type the name of your S3 object key.

6. In **Artifacts: Where to put the artifacts from this build project**, for **Artifacts type**, do one of the following:

- If you do not want to create any build output artifacts, choose **No artifacts**.
- To store the build output in an Amazon S3 bucket, choose **Amazon S3**, and then do the following:
  - If you want to use your project name for the build output ZIP file or folder, leave **Artifacts name** blank. Otherwise, type the name in the **Artifacts name** box. By default, the artifact name is the project name. If you want to specify a different name, type it in the artifacts name box. If you want to output a ZIP file, then include the zip extension.
  - For **Bucket name**, choose the name of the output bucket.
  - If you chose **Insert build commands** earlier in this procedure, then for **Output files**, type the locations of the files from the build that you want to put into the build output ZIP file or folder. For multiple locations, separate each location with a comma (for example, `appspec.yml`, `target/my-app.jar`). For more information, see the description of `files` in Build Spec Syntax.

7. In **Cache**, do one of the following:

- If you do not want to use a cache, choose **No cache**.
- To use a cache, choose **Amazon S3**, and then do the following:
  - For **Bucket**, choose the name of the Amazon S3 bucket where the cache is stored.
  - (Optional) For **Path prefix**, type an Amazon S3 path prefix. The **Path prefix** value is similar to a directory name that enables you to store the cache under the same directory in a bucket. **Important**
    Do not append "/" to the end of **Path prefix**.

Using a cache saves considerable build time because reusable pieces of the build environment are stored in the cache and used across builds.

8. In **Service role**, do one of the following:

- If you do not have an AWS CodeBuild service role, choose **Create a service role in your account**. In **Role name**, accept the default name or type your own.
- If you have an AWS CodeBuild service role, choose **Choose an service existing role from your account**. In **Role name**, choose the service role. **Note**
  When you use the console to create or update a build project, you can create an AWS CodeBuild service role at the same time. By default, the role works with that build project only. If you use the console to associate this service role with another build project, the role is updated to work with the other build project. A service role can work with up to 10 build projects.

9. In **VPC**, do one of the following:

- If you are not using a VPC for your project, choose **No VPC**.
- If you are using want AWS CodeBuild to work with your VPC:

- For **VPC**, choose the VPC ID that AWS CodeBuild uses.
- For **Subnets**, choose the subnets that include resources that AWS CodeBuild uses.
- For **Security Groups**, choose the security groups that AWS CodeBuild uses to allow access to resources in the VPCs.

For more information, see Use AWS CodeBuild with Amazon Virtual Private Cloud.

10. Expand **Show advanced settings** and set them as appropriate.

11. Choose **Continue**. On the **Review** page, choose **Save and build** or, to run the build later, choose **Save**.

12. If you enabled webhooks in **Source: What to Build**, then a **Create webhook** dialog box appears with values displayed for **Payload URL** and **Secret**. **Important**
The **Create webhook** dialog box appears only once. Copy the payload URL and secret key. You need them when you add a webhook in GitHub Enterprise.
If you need to generate a payload URL and secret key again, you must first delete the webhook from your GitHub Enterprise repository. In your AWS CodeBuild project, clear the **Webhook** check box and then choose **Save**. You can then create or update an AWS CodeBuild project with the **Webhook** check box selected. The **Create webhook** dialog box appears again.

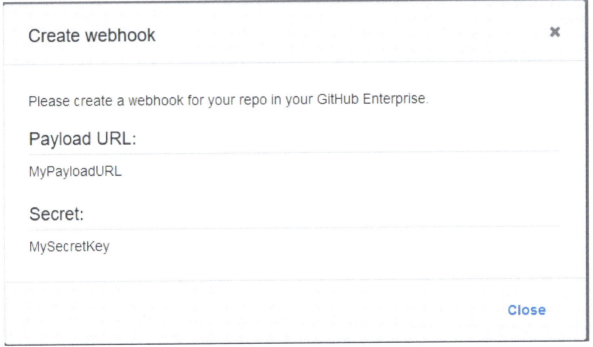

13. In GitHub Enterprise, choose the repository where your AWS CodeBuild project is stored, choose **Settings**, choose **Hooks & services **, and then choose **Add webhook**. Enter the payload URL and secret key, accept the defaults for the other fields, and choose **Add webhook**.

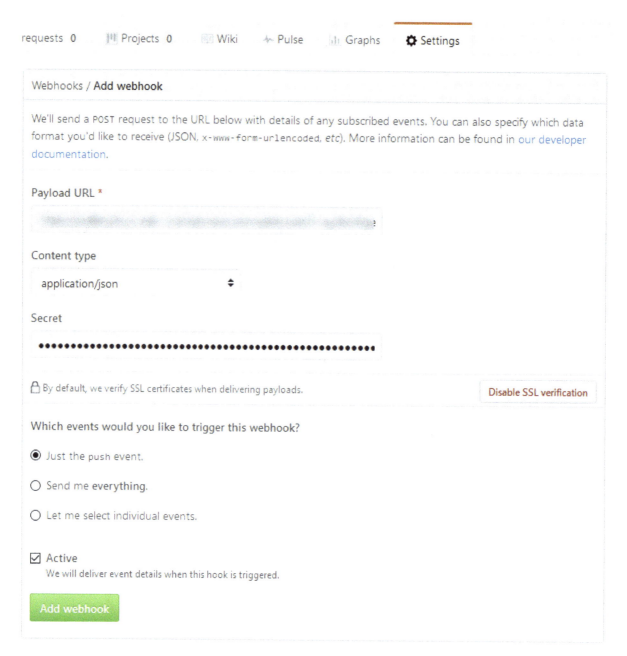

Webhooks / **Add webhook**

We'll send a POST request to the URL below with details of any subscribed events. You can also specify which data format you'd like to receive (JSON, x-www-form-urlencoded, *etc*). More information can be found in our developer documentation.

Payload URL *

Content type

application/json ⬍

Secret

●●●

🔒 By default, we verify SSL certificates when delivering payloads.

Disable SSL verification

Which events would you like to trigger this webhook?

⦿ Just the push event.

◯ Send me **everything**.

◯ Let me select individual events.

☑ Active
We will deliver event details when this hook is triggered.

Add webhook

14. Return to your AWS CodeBuild project. Close the **Create webhook** dialog box and choose **Start build**.

GitHub Pull Request Sample for AWS CodeBuild

AWS CodeBuild now supports webhooks, when the source repository is GitHub. This means that for an AWS CodeBuild build project that has its source code stored in a private GitHub repository, webhooks enables AWS CodeBuild to begin automatically rebuilding the source code every time a code change is pushed to the private repository.

Create a Build Project with GitHub as the Source Repository and Enable Webhooks (Console)

1. Open the AWS CodeBuild console at https://console.aws.amazon.com/codebuild/.

2. If a welcome page is displayed, choose **Get started**. If a welcome page is not displayed, on the navigation pane, choose **Build projects**, and then choose **Create project**.

3. On the **Configure your project** page, for **Project name**, type a name for this build project. Build project names must be unique across each AWS account.

4. In **Source: What to build**, for **Source provider**, choose **GitHub**. Follow the instructions to connect (or reconnect) with GitHub and choose **Authorize**.

   For **Webhook**, select the **Rebuild every time a code change is pushed to this repository** check box. You can select this check box only if, under** Repository**, you chose **Use a repository in my account**.

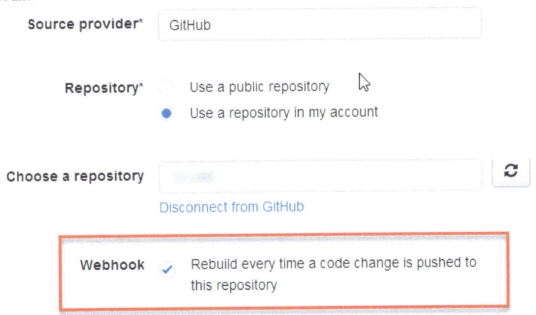

5. In **Environment: How to build**:

   For **Environment image**, do one of the following:

   - To use a Docker image managed by AWS CodeBuild, choose **Use an image managed by AWS CodeBuild**, and then make selections from **Operating system, Runtime, and Version**.
   - To use another Docker image, choose **Specify a Docker image**. For **Custom image type**, choose **Other** or **Amazon ECR**. If you choose **Other**, then for **Custom image ID**, type the name and tag of the Docker image in Docker Hub, using the format `repository-name/image-name:image-tag`. If you choose **Amazon ECR**, then use **Amazon ECR repository** and **Amazon ECR image** to choose the Docker image in your AWS account.

For **Build specification**, do one of the following:

- Use the buildspec.yml file in the source code root directory.
- Override the build specification by inserting the build commands.

For more information, see the Build Spec Reference.

6. In **Artifacts: Where to put the artifacts from this build project**, for **Artifacts type**, do one of the following:

- If you do not want to create any build output artifacts, choose **No artifacts**.
- To store the build output in an Amazon S3 bucket, choose **Amazon S3**, and then do the following:
  - If you want to use your project name for the build output ZIP file or folder, leave **Artifacts name** blank. Otherwise, type the name in the **Artifacts name** box. (By default, the artifact name is the project name. If you want to specify a different name, type it in the artifacts name box. If you want to output a ZIP file, then include the zip extension.
  - For **Bucket name**, choose the name of the output bucket.
  - If you chose **Insert build commands** earlier in this procedure, then for **Output files**, type the locations of the files from the build that you want to put into the build output ZIP file or folder. For multiple locations, separate each location with a comma (for example, `appspec.yml`, `target/my-app.jar`). For more information, see the description of `files` in Build Spec Syntax.

7. In **Service role**, do one of the following:

- If you do not have an AWS CodeBuild service role, choose **Create a service role in your account**. In **Role name**, accept the default name or type your own.
- If you have an AWS CodeBuild service role, choose **Choose an service existing role from your account**. In **Role name**, choose the service role. **Note**
  When you use the console to create or update a build project, you can create an AWS CodeBuild service role at the same time. By default, the role works with that build project only. If you use the console to associate this service role with another build project, the role is updated to work with the other build project. A service role can work with up to 10 build projects.

8. Expand **Show advanced settings** and set them as appropriate.

9. Choose **Continue**. On the **Review** page, choose **Save and build** or, to run the build later, choose **Save**.

Verification Checks

1. On your **AWS CodeBuild project ** page, do the following:

- Choose **Project Details** and then choose the **Webhook** URL link. In your GitHub repository, on the **Settings** page, under **Webhooks**, verify that **Pull Request** and **Push** are both selected.

2. In GitHub, under **Accounts, Settings, Authorized OAuth Apps**, you should see the AWS CodeBuild region that has been authorized.

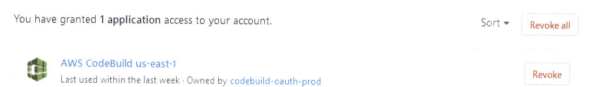

Use AWS Config with AWS CodeBuild Sample

AWS Config provides an inventory of your AWS resources and a history of configuration changes to these resources. AWS Config now supports AWS CodeBuild as an AWS resource, which means the service can track your AWS CodeBuild projects. For more information about AWS Config, see What Is AWS Config? in the *AWS Config Developer Guide*.

You can see the following information about AWS CodeBuild resources on the **Resource Inventory** page in the AWS Config console:

- A timeline of your AWS CodeBuild configuration changes.
- Configuration details for each AWS CodeBuild project.
- Relationships with other AWS resources.
- A list of changes to your AWS CodeBuild projects.

The procedures in this topic show you how to set up AWS Config and look up and view AWS CodeBuild projects.

Topics

- Prerequisites
- Set Up AWS Config
- Look Up AWS CodeBuild Projects
- Viewing AWS CodeBuild Configuration Details in the AWS Config Console

Prerequisites

Create your AWS CodeBuild project(s). For more information, see Create a Build Project.

Set Up AWS Config

- Setting up AWS Config (Console)
- Setting up AWS Config (AWS CLI)

Note
It can take up to 10 minutes before a user is able to see AWS CodeBuild projects in the AWS Config console.

Look Up AWS CodeBuild Projects

1. Sign in to the AWS Management Console and open the AWS Config console at https://console.aws.amazon.com/config.

2. On the **Resource inventory** page, choose **Resources**. Scroll down and select the **CodeBuild project** check box.

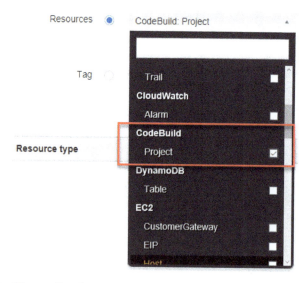

3. Choose **Look up**.

4. After the list of AWS CodeBuild projects is added, choose the AWS CodeBuild project name link in the **Config timeline** column.

Viewing AWS CodeBuild Configuration Details in the AWS Config Console

When you look up resources on the **Resource inventory** page, you can choose the AWS Config timeline to view details about your AWS CodeBuild project. The details page for a resource provides information about the configuration, relationships, and number of changes made to that resource.

The blocks at the top of the page are collectively called the timeline. The timeline shows the date and time that the recording was made.

For more information, see Viewing Configuration Details in the AWS Config Console in the *AWS Config Developer Guide*.

Example of a AWS CodeBuild Project in AWS Config:

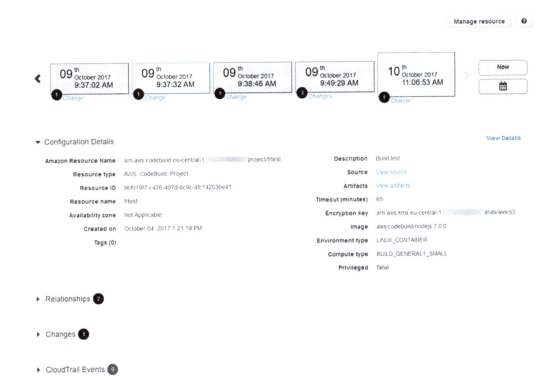

Manage resource   ❓

09th October 2017 9:37:02 AM	09th October 2017 9:37:32 AM	09th October 2017 9:38:46 AM	09th October 2017 9:49:29 AM	10th October 2017 11:06:53 AM
① Change	① Change	① Change	③ Changes	① Change

Now

📅

▼ Configuration Details   View Details

Amazon Resource Name	arn:aws:codebuild:eu-central-1::::::::::::::::::::::project/frtest	**Description**	Build test
Resource type	AWS::CodeBuild::Project	**Source**	View source
Resource ID	b6f019f7-c476-497d-8c9c-4fc14203be41	**Artifacts**	View artifacts
Resource name	frtest	**Timeout (minutes)**	65
Availability zone	Not Applicable	**Encryption key**	arn:aws:kms:eu-central-1::::::::::::::::::::alias/aws/s3
Created on	October 04, 2017 1:21:19 PM	**Image**	aws/codebuild/nodejs:7.0.0
Tags (0)		**Environment type**	LINUX_CONTAINER
		Compute type	BUILD_GENERAL1_SMALL
		Privileged	false

▸ Relationships ②

▸ Changes ①

▸ CloudTrail Events ⓪

Build Badges Sample with AWS CodeBuild

AWS CodeBuild now supports the use of build badges, which provide an embeddable, dynamically generated image (*badge*) that displays the status of the latest build for a project. This image is accessible through a publicly available URL generated for your AWS CodeBuild project. This allows anyone to view the status of an AWS CodeBuild project. Build badges do not contain any security information, so they do not require authentication.

Create a Build Project with Build Badges Enabled (Console)

1. Open the AWS CodeBuild console at https://console.aws.amazon.com/codebuild/.

2. If a welcome page is displayed, choose **Get started**. If a welcome page is not displayed, on the navigation pane, choose **Build projects**, and then choose **Create project**.

3. On the **Configure your project** page, for **Project name**, type a name for this build project. Build project names must be unique across each AWS account.

4. In **Source: What to build**, for **Source provider**, choose the source code provider type, and then do one of the following:

   - If you chose **Amazon S3**, then for **Bucket**, choose the name of the input bucket that contains the source code. For **S3 object key**, type the name of the ZIP file that contains the source code.
   - If you chose **AWS CodeCommit**, then for **Repository**, choose the name of the repository. Select the **Build Badge** check box to make your project's build status visible and embeddable.
   - If you chose **GitHub**, follow the instructions to connect (or reconnect) with GitHub. On the GitHub **Authorize application** page, for **Organization access**, choose **Request access** next to each repository you want AWS CodeBuild to be able to access. After you choose **Authorize application**, back in the AWS CodeBuild console, for **Repository**, choose the name of the repository that contains the source code. Select the **Build Badge** check box to make your project's build status visible and embeddable.
   - If you chose **Bitbucket**, follow the instructions to connect (or reconnect) with Bitbucket. On the Bitbucket **Confirm access to your account** page, for **Organization access**, choose **Grant access**. After you choose **Grant access**, back in the AWS CodeBuild console, for **Repository**, choose the name of the repository that contains the source code. Select the **Build Badge** check box to make your project's build status visible and embeddable. **Important**
     If you update your project source, then this could affect the accuracy of the project's build badges.

5. In **Environment: How to build**:

   For **Environment image**, do one of the following:

   - To use a Docker image managed by AWS CodeBuild, choose **Use an image managed by AWS CodeBuild**, and then make selections from **Operating system**, **Runtime**, and **Version**.
   - To use another Docker image, choose **Specify a Docker image**. For **Custom image type**, choose **Other** or **Amazon ECR**. If you choose **Other**, then for **Custom image ID**, type the name and tag of the Docker image in Docker Hub, using the format `repository-name/image-name:image-tag`. If you choose **Amazon ECR**, then use **Amazon ECR repository** and **Amazon ECR image** to choose the Docker image in your AWS account.

   For **Build specification**, do one of the following:

   - Use the buildspec.yml file in the source code root directory.
   - Override the build specification by inserting the build commands.

   For more information, see the Build Spec Reference.

6. In **Artifacts: Where to put the artifacts from this build project**, for **Artifacts type**, do one of the following:

- If you do not want to create any build output artifacts, choose **No artifacts**.
- To store the build output in an Amazon S3 bucket, choose **Amazon S3**, and then do the following:
  - If you want to use your project name for the build output ZIP file or folder, leave **Artifacts name** blank. Otherwise, type the name in the **Artifacts name** box. (By default, the artifact name is the project name. If you want to specify a different name, type it in the artifacts name box. If you want to output a ZIP file, then include the zip extension.
  - For **Bucket name**, choose the name of the output bucket.
  - If you chose **Insert build commands** earlier in this procedure, then for **Output files**, type the locations of the files from the build that you want to put into the build output ZIP file or folder. For multiple locations, separate each location with a comma (for example, `appspec.yml, target/my-app.jar`). For more information, see the description of `files` in Build Spec Syntax.

7. In **Service role**, do one of the following:

   - If you do not have an AWS CodeBuild service role, choose **Create a service role in your account**. In **Role name**, accept the default name or type your own.
   - If you have an AWS CodeBuild service role, choose **Choose an service existing role from your account**. In **Role name**, choose the service role. **Note**
     When you use the console to create or update a build project, you can create an AWS CodeBuild service role at the same time. By default, the role works with that build project only. If you use the console to associate this service role with another build project, the role is updated to work with the other build project. A service role can work with up to 10 build projects.

8. Expand **Show advanced settings** and set the other advanced settings as appropriate.

9. Choose **Continue**. On the **Review** page, choose **Save and build** or, to run the build later, choose **Save**.

Create a Build Project with Build Badges Enabled (CLI)

For information on creating a build project, see Create a Build Project (AWS CLI). To include build badges with your AWS CodeBuild project, you must specify *badgeEnabled* with a value of `true` .

Access Your AWS CodeBuild Build Badges

You can use the AWS CodeBuild console or AWS CLI to access build badges.

- In the AWS CodeBuild console, in the list of build projects, in the **Project** column, choose the link that corresponds to the build project. On the **Build project:** *project-name* page, expand **Project details**. The build badge URL appears under **Advanced**. For more information, see View a Build Project's Details (Console).
- In the AWS CLI, run the `batch-get-projects` command. The build badge URL is included in the project environment details section of the output. For more information, see View a Build Project's Details (AWS CLI).

Important
The given build badge request URL is for the master branch, but you can specify any branch in your source repository with which you have run a build.

Publish Your AWS CodeBuild Build Badges

You can include your build badge request URL in a markdown file in your preferred repository (for example, GitHub or AWS CodeCommit) to display the status of the latest build.

Sample markdown code:

```
1  ![Build Status](https://codebuild.us-east-1.amazon.com/badges?uuid=...&branch=master)
```

AWS CodeBuild Badge Statuses

- **PASSING** The most recent build on the given branch passed.
- **FAILING** The most recent build on the given branch timed out, failed, faulted, or was stopped.
- **IN_PROGRESS** The most recent build on the given branch is in progress.
- **UNKNOWN** The project has not yet run a build for the given branch or at all. Also, the build badges feature might have been disabled.

Build Notifications Sample for AWS CodeBuild

Amazon CloudWatch Events has built-in support for AWS CodeBuild. CloudWatch Events is a stream of system events describing changes in your AWS resources. With CloudWatch Events, you write declarative rules to associate events of interest with automated actions to be taken. This sample uses Amazon CloudWatch Events and Amazon Simple Notification Service (Amazon SNS) to send build notifications to subscribers whenever builds succeed, fail, go from one build phase to another, or any combination of these events.

Important
Running this sample may result in charges to your AWS account. These include possible charges for AWS CodeBuild and for AWS resources and actions related to Amazon CloudWatch and Amazon SNS. For more information, see AWS CodeBuild Pricing, Amazon CloudWatch Pricing, and Amazon SNS Pricing.

Running the Sample

To run this sample:

1. If you already have a topic set up and subscribed to in Amazon SNS that you want to use for this sample, skip ahead to step 4. Otherwise, if you are using an IAM user instead of an AWS root account or an administrator IAM user to work with Amazon SNS, add the following statement (between *### BEGIN ADDING STATEMENT HERE ###* and *### END ADDING STATEMENT HERE ###*) to the user (or IAM group the user is associated with). (Using an AWS root account is not recommended.) This statement enables viewing, creating, subscribing, and testing the sending of notifications to topics in Amazon SNS. Ellipses (. . .) are used for brevity and to help you locate where to add the statement. Do not remove any statements, and do not type these ellipses into the existing policy.

```
1  {
2    "Statement": [
3      ### BEGIN ADDING STATEMENT HERE ###
4      {
5        "Action": [
6          "sns:CreateTopic",
7          "sns:GetTopicAttributes",
8          "sns:List*",
9          "sns:Publish",
10         "sns:SetTopicAttributes",
11         "sns:Subscribe"
12       ],
13       "Resource": "*",
14       "Effect": "Allow"
15     },
16     ### END ADDING STATEMENT HERE ###
17     ...
18   ],
19   "Version": "2012-10-17"
20 }
```

Note
The IAM entity that modifies this policy must have permission in IAM to modify policies.
For more information, see Editing Customer Managed Policies or the "To edit or delete an inline policy for a group, user, or role" section in Working with Inline Policies (Console) in the *IAM User Guide.*

1. Create or identify a topic in Amazon SNS. AWS CodeBuild will use CloudWatch Events to send build notifications to this topic through Amazon SNS. To create a topic:

   1. Open the Amazon SNS console, at https://console.aws.amazon.com/sns.

2. Choose **Create topic**.

3. In the **Create new topic** dialog box, for **Topic name**, type a name for the topic, for example **CodeBuildDemoTopic**. (If you choose a different name, substitute it throughout this sample.)

4. Choose **Create topic**.

5. On the **Topic details: CodeBuildDemoTopic** page, copy the **Topic ARN** value, as shown in the following screen shot. You will need this value for the next step.

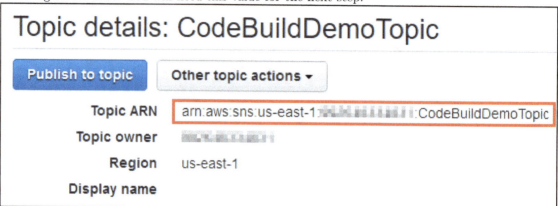

For more information, see Create a Topic in the *Amazon SNS Developer Guide.*

2. Subscribe one or more recipients to the topic to receive email notifications. To subscribe a recipient to a topic:

    1. With the Amazon SNS console open from the previous step, in the navigation pane, choose **Subscriptions**, and then choose **Create subscription**.

    2. In the **Create subscription** dialog box, for **Topic ARN**, paste the topic ARN you copied from the previous step.

    3. For **Protocol**, choose **Email**.

    4. For **Endpoint**, type the recipient's full email address. Compare your results to the following screen shot.

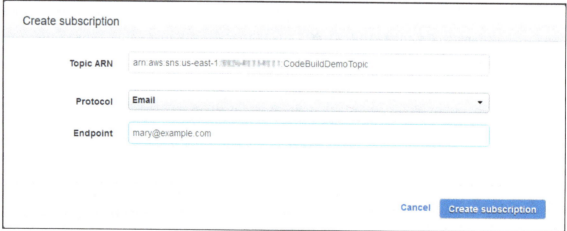

    5. Choose **Create Subscription**.

    6. Amazon SNS sends a subscription confirmation email to the recipient. To begin receiving email notifications, the recipient must choose the **Confirm subscription** link in the subscription confirmation email. After the recipient clicks the link, if successfully subscribed, Amazon SNS displays a confirmation message in the recipient's web browser.

74

For more information, see Subscribe to a Topic in the *Amazon SNS Developer Guide.*

3. If you are using an IAM user instead of an AWS root account or an administrator IAM user to work with CloudWatch Events, add the following statement (between *### BEGIN ADDING STATEMENT HERE ###* and *### END ADDING STATEMENT HERE ###*) to the user (or IAM group the user is associated with). (Using an AWS root account is not recommended.) This statement enables working with CloudWatch Events. Ellipses (. . .) are used for brevity and to help you locate where to add the statement. Do not remove any statements, and do not type these ellipses into the existing policy.

```
1  {
2    "Statement": [
3      ### BEGIN ADDING STATEMENT HERE ###
4      {
5        "Action": [
6          "events:*",
7          "iam:PassRole"
8        ],
9        "Resource": "*",
10       "Effect": "Allow"
11     },
12     ### END ADDING STATEMENT HERE ###
13     ...
14   ],
15   "Version": "2012-10-17"
16 }
```

Note

The IAM entity that modifies this policy must have permission in IAM to modify policies.

For more information, see Editing Customer Managed Policies or the "To edit or delete an inline policy for a group, user, or role" section in Working with Inline Policies (Console) in the *IAM User Guide.*

1. Create a rule in CloudWatch Events. To do this, open the CloudWatch console, at https://console.aws.amazon.com/cloudwatch.

2. In the navigation pane, under **Events**, choose **Rules**, and then choose **Create rule**.

3. On the **Step 1: Create rule page**, the following should already be chosen: **Event Pattern** and **Build event pattern to match events by service**.

4. For **Service Name**, choose **CodeBuild**. For **Event Type**, **All Events** should already be chosen.

5. **Event Pattern Preview** should show the following code.

```
1  {
2    "source": [
3      "aws.codebuild"
4    ]
5  }
```

Compare your results so far to the following screen shot:

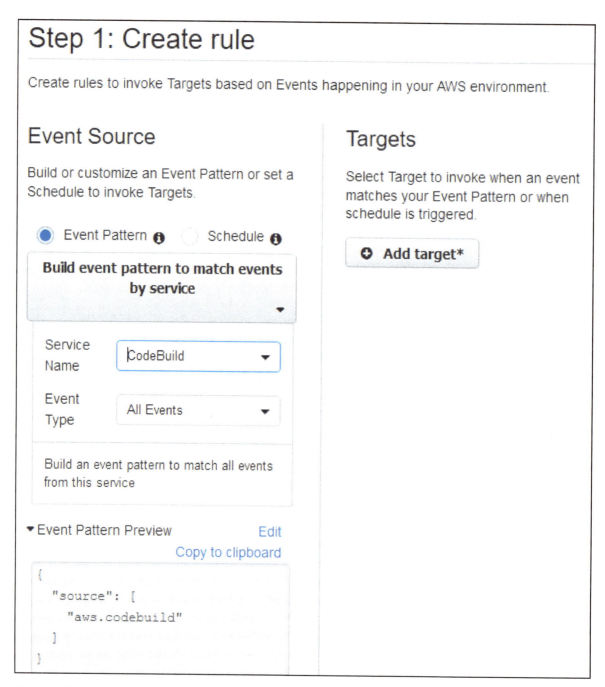

Step 1: Create rule

Create rules to invoke Targets based on Events happening in your AWS environment.

Event Source

Build or customize an Event Pattern or set a Schedule to invoke Targets.

◉ Event Pattern ❶   ○ Schedule ❶

Build event pattern to match events by service ▼

Service Name: `CodeBuild` ▼

Event Type: All Events ▼

Build an event pattern to match all events from this service

▼ Event Pattern Preview   Edit

Copy to clipboard

```
{
  "source": [
    "aws.codebuild"
  ]
}
```

Targets

Select Target to invoke when an event matches your Event Pattern or when schedule is triggered.

⊕ **Add target***

6. Replace the code in **Event Pattern Preview** with one of the following two rule patterns by choosing **Edit**.

This first rule pattern triggers an event whenever a build starts or completes, for the specified build projects in AWS CodeBuild.

```
1  {
2    "source": [
3      "aws.codebuild"
4    ],
5    "detail-type": [
6      "CodeBuild Build State Change"
7    ],
8    "detail": {
```

76

```
9    "build-status": [
10     "IN_PROGRESS",
11     "SUCCEEDED",
12     "FAILED",
13     "STOPPED"
14    ],
15    "project-name": [
16     "my-demo-project-1",
17     "my-demo-project-2"
18    ]
19   }
20 }
```

In the preceding rule, make the following code changes as needed.

- To trigger an event whenever a build starts or completes, either leave all of the values as shown in the `build-status` array, or remove the `build-status` array altogether.
- To trigger an event only when a build completes, remove `IN_PROGRESS` from the `build-status` array.
- To trigger an event only when a build starts, remove all of the values except `IN_PROGRESS` from the `build-status` array.
- To trigger events for all build projects, remove the `project-name` array altogether.
- To trigger events only for individual build projects, specify the name of each build project in the `project-name` array.

This second rule pattern triggers an event whenever a build moves from one build phase to another, for the specified build projects in AWS CodeBuild.

```
1 {
2   "source": [
3     "aws.codebuild"
4   ],
5   "detail-type": [
6     "CodeBuild Build Phase Change"
7   ],
8   "detail": {
9     "completed-phase": [
10      "SUBMITTED",
11      "PROVISIONING",
12      "DOWNLOAD_SOURCE",
13      "INSTALL",
14      "PRE_BUILD",
15      "BUILD",
16      "POST_BUILD",
17      "UPLOAD_ARTIFACTS",
18      "FINALIZING"
19     ],
20     "completed-phase-status": [
21      "TIMED_OUT",
22      "STOPPED",
23      "FAILED",
24      "SUCCEEDED",
25      "FAULT",
26      "CLIENT_ERROR"
27     ],
28     "project-name": [
29      "my-demo-project-1",
```

```
30        "my-demo-project-2"
31    ]
32  }
33 }
```

In the preceding rule, make the following code changes as needed.

- To trigger an event for every build phase change (which may send up to 9 notifications for each build), either leave all of the values as shown in the `completed-phase` array, or remove the `completed-phase` array altogether.
- To trigger events only for individual build phase changes, remove the name of each build phase in the `completed-phase` array that you do not want to trigger an event for.
- To trigger an event for every build phase status change, either leave all of the values as shown in the `completed-phase-status` array, or remove the `completed-phase-status` array altogether.
- To trigger events only for individual build phase status changes, remove the name of each build phase status in the `completed-phase-status` array that you do not want to trigger an event for.
- To trigger events for all build projects, remove the `project-name` array.
- To trigger events for individual build projects, specify the name of each build project in the `project-name` array. **Note**
  If you want to trigger events for both build state changes and build phase changes, you must create two separate rules, one for build state changes and another for build phase changes. If you try to combine both rules into a single rule, the combined rule may produce unexpected results or stop working altogether.

When you have finished replacing the code, choose **Save**.

7. For **Targets**, choose **Add target**.

8. In the list of targets, choose **SNS topic**.

9. For **Topic**, choose the topic you identified or created earlier.

10. Expand **Configure input**, and then choose **Input Transformer**.

11. In the **Input Path** box, type one of the following input paths.

   For a rule with a `detail-type` value of `CodeBuild Build State Change`, type the following.

```
1 {"build-id":"$.detail.build-id","project-name":"$.detail.project-name","build-status":"$.
   detail.build-status"}
```

   For a rule with a `detail-type` value of `CodeBuild Build Phase Change`, type the following.

```
1 {"build-id":"$.detail.build-id","project-name":"$.detail.project-name","completed-phase":"$
   .detail.completed-phase","completed-phase-status":"$.detail.completed-phase-status"}
```

Note
To get other types of information, see the Build Notifications Input Format Reference.

1. In the **Input Template** box, type one of the following input templates.

   For a rule with a `detail-type` value of `CodeBuild Build State Change`, type the following.

```
1 "Build '<build-id>' for build project '<project-name>' has reached the build status of '<
   build-status>'."
```

   For a rule with a `detail-type` value of `CodeBuild Build Phase Change`, type the following.

```
1 "Build '<build-id>' for build project '<project-name>' has completed the build phase of '<
   completed-phase>' with a status of '<completed-phase-status>'."
```

Compare your results so far to the following screen shot, which shows a rule with a `detail-type` value of `CodeBuild Build State Change`:

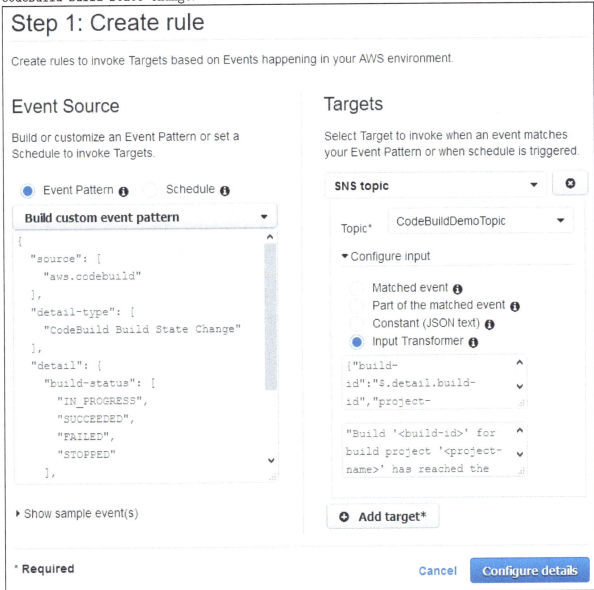

2. Choose **Configure details**.

3. On the **Step 2: Configure rule details** page, type a **Name** and an optional **Description**. Leave the **Enabled** box checked for **State**.

Compare your results so far to the following screen shot:

Step 2: Configure rule details

Rule definition

Name* CodeBuildStateChangeDemo

Description

State ☑ Enabled

CloudWatch Events will add necessary permissions for target(s) so they can be invoked when this rule is triggered.

* Required   Cancel   **Back**   **Create rule**

4. Choose **Create rule**.

5. Create build projects, run the builds, and view build information, for example by following the steps in Run AWS CodeBuild Directly.

6. Confirm that AWS CodeBuild is now successfully sending build notifications. For example, check to see if the build notification emails are now in your inbox.

To change a rule's behavior, in the CloudWatch console, choose the rule you want to change, and then choose **Actions**, **Edit**. Make changes to the rule, and then choose **Configure details**, followed by choosing **Update rule**.

To stop using a rule to send build notifications, in the CloudWatch console, choose the rule you want to stop using, and then choose **Actions**, **Disable**.

To delete a rule altogether, in the CloudWatch console, choose the rule you want to delete, and then choose **Actions**, **Delete**.

Related Resources

- For more information about getting started with AWS CodeBuild, see Getting Started with AWS CodeBuild.
- For more information about troubleshooting problems with AWS CodeBuild, see Troubleshooting AWS CodeBuild.
- For more information about limits in AWS CodeBuild, see Limits for AWS CodeBuild.

Build Notifications Input Format Reference

CloudWatch delivers notifications in JSON format.

Build state change notifications use the following format:

```
1 {
```

```
2     "version": "0",
3     "id": "c030038d-8c4d-6141-9545-00ff7b7153EX",
4     "detail-type": "CodeBuild Build State Change",
5     "source": "aws.codebuild",
6     "account": "123456789012",
7     "time": "2017-09-01T16:14:28Z",
8     "region": "us-west-2",
9     "resources":[
10        "arn:aws:codebuild:us-west-2:123456789012:build/my-sample-project:8745a7a9-c340-456a-9166-
             edf953571bEX"
11    ],
12    "detail":{
13      "build-status": "SUCCEEDED",
14      "project-name": "my-sample-project",
15      "build-id": "arn:aws:codebuild:us-west-2:123456789012:build/my-sample-project:8745a7a9-c340
             -456a-9166-edf953571bEX",
16      "additional-information": {
17        "artifact": {
18          "md5sum": "da9c44c8a9a3cd4b443126e823168fEX",
19          "sha256sum": "6ccc2ae1df9d155ba83c597051611c42d60e09c6329dcb14a312cecc0a8e39EX",
20          "location": "arn:aws:s3:::codebuild-123456789012-output-bucket/my-output-artifact.zip"
21        },
22        "environment": {
23          "image": "aws/codebuild/dot-net:1.1",
24          "privileged-mode": false,
25          "compute-type": "BUILD_GENERAL1_SMALL",
26          "type": "LINUX_CONTAINER",
27          "environment-variables": []
28        },
29        "timeout-in-minutes": 60,
30        "build-complete": true,
31        "initiator": "MyCodeBuildDemoUser",
32        "build-start-time": "Sep 1, 2017 4:12:29 PM",
33        "source": {
34          "location": "codebuild-123456789012-input-bucket/my-input-artifact.zip",
35          "type": "S3"
36        },
37        "logs": {
38          "group-name": "/aws/codebuild/my-sample-project",
39          "stream-name": "8745a7a9-c340-456a-9166-edf953571bEX",
40          "deep-link": "https://console.aws.amazon.com/cloudwatch/home?region=us-west-2#logEvent:
               group=/aws/codebuild/my-sample-project;stream=8745a7a9-c340-456a-9166-edf953571bEX"
41        },
42        "phases": [
43          {
44            "phase-context": [],
45            "start-time": "Sep 1, 2017 4:12:29 PM",
46            "end-time": "Sep 1, 2017 4:12:29 PM",
47            "duration-in-seconds": 0,
48            "phase-type": "SUBMITTED",
49            "phase-status": "SUCCEEDED"
50          },
51          {
52            "phase-context": [],
```

```
53        "start-time": "Sep 1, 2017 4:12:29 PM",
54        "end-time": "Sep 1, 2017 4:13:05 PM",
55        "duration-in-seconds": 36,
56        "phase-type": "PROVISIONING",
57        "phase-status": "SUCCEEDED"
58      },
59      {
60        "phase-context": [],
61        "start-time": "Sep 1, 2017 4:13:05 PM",
62        "end-time": "Sep 1, 2017 4:13:10 PM",
63        "duration-in-seconds": 4,
64        "phase-type": "DOWNLOAD_SOURCE",
65        "phase-status": "SUCCEEDED"
66      },
67      {
68        "phase-context": [],
69        "start-time": "Sep 1, 2017 4:13:10 PM",
70        "end-time": "Sep 1, 2017 4:13:10 PM",
71        "duration-in-seconds": 0,
72        "phase-type": "INSTALL",
73        "phase-status": "SUCCEEDED"
74      },
75      {
76        "phase-context": [],
77        "start-time": "Sep 1, 2017 4:13:10 PM",
78        "end-time": "Sep 1, 2017 4:13:10 PM",
79        "duration-in-seconds": 0,
80        "phase-type": "PRE_BUILD",
81        "phase-status": "SUCCEEDED"
82      },
83      {
84        "phase-context": [],
85        "start-time": "Sep 1, 2017 4:13:10 PM",
86        "end-time": "Sep 1, 2017 4:14:21 PM",
87        "duration-in-seconds": 70,
88        "phase-type": "BUILD",
89        "phase-status": "SUCCEEDED"
90      },
91      {
92        "phase-context": [],
93        "start-time": "Sep 1, 2017 4:14:21 PM",
94        "end-time": "Sep 1, 2017 4:14:21 PM",
95        "duration-in-seconds": 0,
96        "phase-type": "POST_BUILD",
97        "phase-status": "SUCCEEDED"
98      },
99      {
100       "phase-context": [],
101       "start-time": "Sep 1, 2017 4:14:21 PM",
102       "end-time": "Sep 1, 2017 4:14:21 PM",
103       "duration-in-seconds": 0,
104       "phase-type": "UPLOAD_ARTIFACTS",
105       "phase-status": "SUCCEEDED"
106     },
```

```
107        {
108          "phase-context": [],
109          "start-time": "Sep 1, 2017 4:14:21 PM",
110          "end-time": "Sep 1, 2017 4:14:26 PM",
111          "duration-in-seconds": 4,
112          "phase-type": "FINALIZING",
113          "phase-status": "SUCCEEDED"
114        },
115        {
116          "start-time": "Sep 1, 2017 4:14:26 PM",
117          "phase-type": "COMPLETED"
118        }
119      ]
120    },
121    "current-phase": "COMPLETED",
122    "current-phase-context": "[]",
123    "version": "1"
124  }
125 }
```

Build phase change notifications use the following format:

```
1  {
2    "version": "0",
3    "id": "43ddc2bd-af76-9ca5-2dc7-b695e15adeEX",
4    "detail-type": "CodeBuild Build Phase Change",
5    "source": "aws.codebuild",
6    "account": "123456789012",
7    "time": "2017-09-01T16:14:21Z",
8    "region": "us-west-2",
9    "resources":[
10     "arn:aws:codebuild:us-west-2:123456789012:build/my-sample-project:8745a7a9-c340-456a-9166-
           edf953571bEX"
11   ],
12   "detail":{
13     "completed-phase": "COMPLETED",
14     "project-name": "my-sample-project",
15     "build-id": "arn:aws:codebuild:us-west-2:123456789012:build/my-sample-project:8745a7a9-c340
           -456a-9166-edf953571bEX",
16     "completed-phase-context": "[]",
17     "additional-information": {
18       "artifact": {
19         "md5sum": "da9c44c8a9a3cd4b443126e823168fEX",
20         "sha256sum": "6ccc2ae1df9d155ba83c597051611c42d60e09c6329dcb14a312cecc0a8e39EX",
21         "location": "arn:aws:s3:::codebuild-123456789012-output-bucket/my-output-artifact.zip"
22       },
23       "environment": {
24         "image": "aws/codebuild/dot-net:1.1",
25         "privileged-mode": false,
26         "compute-type": "BUILD_GENERAL1_SMALL",
27         "type": "LINUX_CONTAINER",
28         "environment-variables": []
29       },
30       "timeout-in-minutes": 60,
31       "build-complete": true,
```

```
32      "initiator": "MyCodeBuildDemoUser",
33      "build-start-time": "Sep 1, 2017 4:12:29 PM",
34      "source": {
35        "location": "codebuild-123456789012-input-bucket/my-input-artifact.zip",
36        "type": "S3"
37      },
38      "logs": {
39        "group-name": "/aws/codebuild/my-sample-project",
40        "stream-name": "8745a7a9-c340-456a-9166-edf953571bEX",
41        "deep-link": "https://console.aws.amazon.com/cloudwatch/home?region=us-west-2#logEvent:
            group=/aws/codebuild/my-sample-project;stream=8745a7a9-c340-456a-9166-edf953571bEX"
42      },
43      "phases": [
44        {
45          "phase-context": [],
46          "start-time": "Sep 1, 2017 4:12:29 PM",
47          "end-time": "Sep 1, 2017 4:12:29 PM",
48          "duration-in-seconds": 0,
49          "phase-type": "SUBMITTED",
50          "phase-status": "SUCCEEDED"
51        },
52        {
53          "phase-context": [],
54          "start-time": "Sep 1, 2017 4:12:29 PM",
55          "end-time": "Sep 1, 2017 4:13:05 PM",
56          "duration-in-seconds": 36,
57          "phase-type": "PROVISIONING",
58          "phase-status": "SUCCEEDED"
59        },
60        {
61          "phase-context": [],
62          "start-time": "Sep 1, 2017 4:13:05 PM",
63          "end-time": "Sep 1, 2017 4:13:10 PM",
64          "duration-in-seconds": 4,
65          "phase-type": "DOWNLOAD_SOURCE",
66          "phase-status": "SUCCEEDED"
67        },
68        {
69          "phase-context": [],
70          "start-time": "Sep 1, 2017 4:13:10 PM",
71          "end-time": "Sep 1, 2017 4:13:10 PM",
72          "duration-in-seconds": 0,
73          "phase-type": "INSTALL",
74          "phase-status": "SUCCEEDED"
75        },
76        {
77          "phase-context": [],
78          "start-time": "Sep 1, 2017 4:13:10 PM",
79          "end-time": "Sep 1, 2017 4:13:10 PM",
80          "duration-in-seconds": 0,
81          "phase-type": "PRE_BUILD",
82          "phase-status": "SUCCEEDED"
83        },
84        {
```

```
 85          "phase-context": [],
 86          "start-time": "Sep 1, 2017 4:13:10 PM",
 87          "end-time": "Sep 1, 2017 4:14:21 PM",
 88          "duration-in-seconds": 70,
 89          "phase-type": "BUILD",
 90          "phase-status": "SUCCEEDED"
 91        },
 92        {
 93          "phase-context": [],
 94          "start-time": "Sep 1, 2017 4:14:21 PM",
 95          "end-time": "Sep 1, 2017 4:14:21 PM",
 96          "duration-in-seconds": 0,
 97          "phase-type": "POST_BUILD",
 98          "phase-status": "SUCCEEDED"
 99        },
100        {
101          "phase-context": [],
102          "start-time": "Sep 1, 2017 4:14:21 PM",
103          "end-time": "Sep 1, 2017 4:14:21 PM",
104          "duration-in-seconds": 0,
105          "phase-type": "UPLOAD_ARTIFACTS",
106          "phase-status": "SUCCEEDED"
107        },
108        {
109          "phase-context": [],
110          "start-time": "Sep 1, 2017 4:14:21 PM",
111          "end-time": "Sep 1, 2017 4:14:26 PM",
112          "duration-in-seconds": 4,
113          "phase-type": "FINALIZING",
114          "phase-status": "SUCCEEDED"
115        },
116        {
117          "start-time": "Sep 1, 2017 4:14:26 PM",
118          "phase-type": "COMPLETED"
119        }
120      ]
121    },
122    "completed-phase-status": "SUCCEEDED",
123    "completed-phase-duration-seconds": 4,
124    "version": "1",
125    "completed-phase-start": "Sep 1, 2017 4:14:21 PM",
126    "completed-phase-end": "Sep 1, 2017 4:14:26 PM"
127  }
128 }
```

Docker in Custom Image Sample for AWS CodeBuild

This sample builds and runs a Docker image by using AWS CodeBuild and a custom Docker build image (`docker:dind` in Docker Hub).

To learn how to build a Docker image by using a build image provided by AWS CodeBuild with Docker support instead, see our Docker Sample.

Important
Running this sample may result in charges to your AWS account. These include possible charges for AWS CodeBuild and for AWS resources and actions related to Amazon S3, AWS KMS, and CloudWatch Logs. For more information, see AWS CodeBuild Pricing, Amazon S3 Pricing, AWS Key Management Service Pricing, and Amazon CloudWatch Pricing.

Topics

- Running the Sample
- Directory Structure
- Files
- Related Resources

Running the Sample

To run this sample:

1. Create the files as described in the Directory Structure and Files sections of this topic, and then upload them to an Amazon S3 input bucket or an AWS CodeCommit, GitHub, or Bitbucket repository. **Important** Do not upload (`root directory name`), just the files inside of (`root directory name`). If you are using an Amazon S3 input bucket, be sure to create a ZIP file that contains the files, and then upload it to the input bucket. Do not add (`root directory name`) to the ZIP file, just the files inside of (`root directory name`).

2. Create a build project, run the build, and view related build information by following the steps in Run AWS CodeBuild Directly.

    If you use the AWS CLI to create the build project, the JSON-formatted input to the`create-project` command might look similar to this. (Replace the placeholders with your own values.)

```
1  {
2    "name": "sample-docker-custom-image-project",
3    "source": {
4      "type": "S3",
5      "location": "codebuild-region-ID-account-ID-input-bucket/DockerCustomImageSample.zip"
6    },
7    "artifacts": {
8      "type": "NO_ARTIFACTS"
9    },
10   "environment": {
11     "type": "LINUX_CONTAINER",
12     "image": "docker:dind",
13     "computeType": "BUILD_GENERAL1_SMALL",
14     "privilegedMode": true
15   },
16   "serviceRole": "arn:aws:iam::account-ID:role/role-name",
17   "encryptionKey": "arn:aws:kms:region-ID:account-ID:key/key-ID"
18 }
```

3. To see the build results, look in the build's log for the string `Hello, World!`. For more information, see View Build Details.

Directory Structure

This sample assumes this directory structure.

```
1  (root directory name)
2      |-- buildspec.yml
3      `-- Dockerfile
```

Files

The base image of the operating system used in this sample is Ubuntu. The sample uses these files.

`buildspec.yml` (in (root directory name))

```
1  version: 0.2
2
3  phases:
4    install:
5      commands:
6        - nohup /usr/local/bin/dockerd --host=unix:///var/run/docker.sock --host=tcp
             ://127.0.0.1:2375 --storage-driver=overlay&
7        - timeout 15 sh -c "until docker info; do echo .; sleep 1; done"
8    pre_build:
9      commands:
10       - docker build -t helloworld .
11   build:
12     commands:
13       - docker images
14       - docker run helloworld echo "Hello, World!"
```

Note
If the base operating system is Alpine Linux, in the `buildspec.yml` add the `-t` argument to `timeout`:

```
1  - timeout -t 15 sh -c "until docker info; do echo .; sleep 1; done"
```

`Dockerfile` (in (root directory name))

```
1  FROM maven:3.3.9-jdk-8
2
3  RUN echo "Hello World"
```

Related Resources

- For more information about getting started with AWS CodeBuild, see Getting Started with AWS CodeBuild.
- For more information about troubleshooting problems with AWS CodeBuild, see Troubleshooting AWS CodeBuild.
- For more information about limits in AWS CodeBuild, see Limits for AWS CodeBuild.

AWS CodeDeploy Sample for AWS CodeBuild

This sample instructs AWS CodeBuild to use Maven to produce as build output a single JAR file named `my-app-1.0-SNAPSHOT.jar`. This sample then uses AWS CodeDeploy to deploy the JAR file to an Amazon Linux instance. (Alternatively, you can use AWS CodePipeline to automate the use of AWS CodeDeploy to deploy the JAR file to an Amazon Linux instance.) This sample is based on the Maven in 5 Minutes topic on the Apache Maven website.

Important
Running this sample may result in charges to your AWS account. These include possible charges for AWS CodeBuild and for AWS resources and actions related to Amazon S3, AWS KMS, CloudWatch Logs, and Amazon EC2. For more information, see AWS CodeBuild Pricing, Amazon S3 Pricing, AWS Key Management Service Pricing, Amazon CloudWatch Pricing, and Amazon EC2 Pricing.

Running the Sample

To run this sample:

1. Download and install Maven. For more information, see Downloading Apache Maven and Installing Apache Maven on the Apache Maven website.

2. Switch to an empty directory on your local computer or instance, and then run this Maven command.

```
mvn archetype:generate -DgroupId=com.mycompany.app -DartifactId=my-app -
    DarchetypeArtifactId=maven-archetype-quickstart -DinteractiveMode=false
```

If successful, this directory structure and files will be created.

```
(root directory name)
    `-- my-app
        |-- pom.xml
        `-- src
            |-- main
            |   `-- java
            |       `-- com
            |           `-- mycompany
            |               `-- app
            |                   `-- App.java
            `-- test
                `-- java
                    `-- com
                        `-- mycompany
                            `-- app
                                `-- AppTest.java
```

3. Create a file with this content. Name the file `buildspec.yml`, and then add it to the (root directory name)/my-app directory.

```
version: 0.2

phases:
  build:
    commands:
      - echo Build started on `date`
      - mvn test
  post_build:
```

```
 9      commands:
10        - echo Build completed on `date`
11        - mvn package
12  artifacts:
13    files:
14      - target/my-app-1.0-SNAPSHOT.jar
15      - appspec.yml
16    discard-paths: yes
```

4. Create a file with this content. Name the file `appspec.yml`, and then add it to the `(root directory name)/my-app` directory.

```
1  version: 0.0
2  os: linux
3  files:
4    - source: ./my-app-1.0-SNAPSHOT.jar
5      destination: /tmp
```

When finished, your directory structure and file should look like this.

```
 1  (root directory name)
 2       `-- my-app
 3              |-- buildspec.yml
 4              |-- appspec.yml
 5              |-- pom.xml
 6              `-- src
 7                    |-- main
 8                    |      `-- java
 9                    |            `-- com
10                    |                  `-- mycompany
11                    |                        `-- app
12                    |                              `-- App.java
13                    `-- test
14                          `-- java
15                                `-- com
16                                      `-- mycompany
17                                            `-- app
18                                                  ` -- AppTest.java
```

5. Create a ZIP file that contains the directory structure and files inside of `(root directory name)/my-app`, and then upload the ZIP file to a source code repository type supported by AWS CodeBuild and AWS CodeDeploy, such as an Amazon S3 input bucket or a GitHub or Bitbucket repository. **Important**
If you want to use AWS CodePipeline to deploy the resulting build output artifact, you cannot upload the source code to a Bitbucket repository.
Do not add `(root directory name)` or `(root directory name)/my-app` to the ZIP file, just the directories and files inside of `(root directory name)/my-app`. The ZIP file should contain these directories and files:

```
1  CodeDeploySample.zip
2        |--buildspec.yml
3        |-- appspec.yml
4        |-- pom.xml
5        `-- src
6              |-- main
7              |      `-- java
8              |            `-- com
```

```
 9     |                        `-- mycompany
10     |                            `-- app
11     |                                `-- App.java
12     `-- test
13          `-- java
14              `-- com
15                  `-- mycompany
16                      `-- app
17                          ` -- AppTest.java
```

6. Create a build project by following the steps in Create a Build Project.

   If you use the AWS CLI to create the build project, the JSON-formatted input to the `create-project` command might look similar to this. (Replace the placeholders with your own values.)

```
 1  {
 2    "name": "sample-codedeploy-project",
 3    "source": {
 4      "type": "S3",
 5      "location": "codebuild-region-ID-account-ID-input-bucket/CodeDeploySample.zip"
 6    },
 7    "artifacts": {
 8      "type": "S3",
 9      "location": "codebuild-region-ID-account-ID-output-bucket",
10      "packaging": "ZIP",
11      "name": "CodeDeployOutputArtifact.zip"
12    },
13    "environment": {
14      "type": "LINUX_CONTAINER",
15      "image": "aws/codebuild/java:openjdk-8",
16      "computeType": "BUILD_GENERAL1_SMALL"
17    },
18    "serviceRole": "arn:aws:iam::account-ID:role/role-name",
19    "encryptionKey": "arn:aws:kms:region-ID:account-ID:key/key-ID"
20  }
```

7. If you plan to deploy the build output artifact with AWS CodeDeploy, then follow the steps in Run a Build. Otherwise, skip this step. (This is because if you plan to deploy the build output artifact with AWS CodePipeline, then AWS CodePipeline will use AWS CodeBuild to run the build automatically.)

8. Complete the setup steps for using AWS CodeDeploy, including:

   - Grant the IAM user access to AWS CodeDeploy and the AWS services and actions AWS CodeDeploy depends on. For more information, see Provision an IAM User in the *AWS CodeDeploy User Guide*.
   - Create or identify a service role to enable AWS CodeDeploy to identify the instances where it will deploy the build output artifact. For more information, see Creating a Service Role for AWS CodeDeploy in the *AWS CodeDeploy User Guide*.
   - Create or identify an IAM instance profile to enable your instances to access the Amazon S3 input bucket or GitHub repository that contains the build output artifact. For more information, see Creating an IAM Instance Profile for Your Amazon EC2 Instances in the *AWS CodeDeploy User Guide*.

9. Create or identify an Amazon Linux instance compatible with AWS CodeDeploy where the build output artifact will be deployed. For more information, see Working with Instances for AWS CodeDeploy in the *AWS CodeDeploy User Guide*.

10. Create or identify an AWS CodeDeploy application and deployment group. For more information, see Creating an Application with AWS CodeDeploy in the *AWS CodeDeploy User Guide*.

11. Deploy the build output artifact to the instance.

    To deploy with AWS CodeDeploy, see Deploying a Revision with AWS CodeDeploy in the *AWS CodeDeploy User Guide*.

    To deploy with AWS CodePipeline, see Use AWS CodePipeline with AWS CodeBuild.

12. To find the build output artifact after the deployment is complete, sign in to the instance and look in the `/tmp` directory for the file named `my-app-1.0-SNAPSHOT.jar`.

Related Resources

- For more information about getting started with AWS CodeBuild, see Getting Started with AWS CodeBuild.
- For more information about troubleshooting problems with AWS CodeBuild, see Troubleshooting AWS CodeBuild.
- For more information about limits in AWS CodeBuild, see Limits for AWS CodeBuild.

AWS Lambda Sample for AWS CodeBuild

To define a standard model for serverless applications that use resources such as Lambda, AWS created the AWS Serverless Application Model (AWS SAM). For more information, see the AWS Serverless Application Model repository on GitHub.

You can use AWS CodeBuild to package and deploy serverless applications that follow the AWS SAM standard. For the deployment step, AWS CodeBuild can use AWS CloudFormation. To automate the building and deployment of serverless applications with AWS CodeBuild and AWS CloudFormation, you can use AWS CodePipeline.

For more information, see Deploying Lambda-based Applications in the *AWS Lambda Developer Guide*. To experiment with a serverless application sample that uses AWS CodeBuild along with Lambda, AWS Cloud-Formation, and AWS CodePipeline, see Automating Deployment of Lambda-based Applications in the *AWS Lambda Developer Guide*.

Related Resources

- For more information about getting started with AWS CodeBuild, see Getting Started with AWS CodeBuild.
- For more information about troubleshooting problems with AWS CodeBuild, see Troubleshooting AWS CodeBuild.
- For more information about limits in AWS CodeBuild, see Limits for AWS CodeBuild.

AWS Elastic Beanstalk Sample for AWS CodeBuild

This sample instructs AWS CodeBuild to use Maven to produce as build output a single WAR file named `my-web-app.war`. This sample then deploys the WAR file to the instances in an Elastic Beanstalk environment. This sample is based on the Java Sample.

Important
Running this sample may result in charges to your AWS account. These include possible charges for AWS CodeBuild and for AWS resources and actions related to Amazon S3, AWS KMS, CloudWatch Logs, and Amazon EC2. For more information, see AWS CodeBuild Pricing, Amazon S3 Pricing, AWS Key Management Service Pricing, Amazon CloudWatch Pricing, and Amazon EC2 Pricing.

Create the Source Code

In this section, you will use Maven to produce the source code to be built. Later on, you will use AWS CodeBuild to build a WAR file based on this source code.

1. Download and install Maven. For information, see Downloading Apache Maven and Installing Apache Maven on the Apache Maven website.

2. Switch to an empty directory on your local computer or instance, and then run this Maven command.

```
mvn archetype:generate -DgroupId=com.mycompany.app -DartifactId=my-web-app -
    DarchetypeArtifactId=maven-archetype-webapp -DinteractiveMode=false
```

If successful, this directory structure and files will be created.

```
(root directory name)
    `-- my-web-app
        |-- pom.xml
        `-- src
            `-- main
                |-- resources
                `-- webapp
                    |-- WEB-INF
                    |   `-- web.xml
                    `-- index.jsp
```

After you run Maven, continue with one of the following scenarios:

- Scenario A: Run AWS CodeBuild Manually and Deploy to Elastic Beanstalk Manually
- Scenario B: Use AWS CodePipeline to Run AWS CodeBuild and Deploy to Elastic Beanstalk
- Scenario C: Use the Elastic Beanstalk Command Line Interface (EB CLI) to Run AWS CodeBuild and Deploy to an Elastic Beanstalk Environment

Scenario A: Run AWS CodeBuild Manually and Deploy to Elastic Beanstalk Manually

In this scenario, you will manually create and upload the source code to be built. You will then use the AWS CodeBuild and Elastic Beanstalk consoles to build the source code, create an Elastic Beanstalk application and environment, and deploy the build output to the environment.

Step A1: Add Files to the Source Code

In this step, you will add an Elastic Beanstalk configuration file and a build spec file to the code in Create the Source Code. You will then upload the source code to an Amazon S3 input bucket or an AWS CodeCommit or GitHub repository.

1. Create a subdirectory named `.ebextensions` inside of the `(root directory name)/my-web-app` directory. In the `.ebextensions` subdirectory, create a file named `fix-path.config` with this content.

```
1 container_commands:
2   fix_path:
3     command: "unzip my-web-app.war 2>&1 > /var/log/my_last_deploy.log"
```

2. Create a file named `buildspec.yml` with the following contents. Store the file in the `(root directory name)/my-web-app` directory.

```
1 version: 0.2
2
3 phases:
4   post_build:
5     commands:
6       - mvn package
7       - mv target/my-web-app.war my-web-app.war
8 artifacts:
9   files:
10     - my-web-app.war
11     - .ebextensions/**/*
```

3. Your file structure should now look like this.

```
1 (root directory name)
2    `-- my-web-app
3        |-- .ebextensions
4        |    `-- fix-path.config
5        |-- src
6        |    `-- main
7        |        |-- resources
8        |        `-- webapp
9        |            |-- WEB-INF
10       |            |   `-- web.xml
11       |            `-- index.jsp
12       |-- buildpsec.yml
13       `-- pom.xml
```

4. Upload this contents of the `my-web-app` directory to an Amazon S3 input bucket or an AWS CodeCommit, GitHub, or Bitbucket repository. **Important**
Do not upload `(root directory name)` or `(root directory name)/my-web-app`, just the directories and files inside of `(root directory name)/my-web-app`.
If you are using an Amazon S3 input bucket, be sure to create a ZIP file that contains the directory structure and files, and then upload it to the input bucket. Do not add `(root directory name)` or `(root directory name)/my-web-app` to the ZIP file, just the directories and files inside of `(root directory name)/my-web-app`.

Step A2: Create the Build Project and Run the Build

In this step, you will use the AWS CodeBuild console to create a build project and then run a build.

1. Create or identify an Amazon S3 output bucket to store the build output. If you're storing the source code in an Amazon S3 input bucket, the output bucket must be in the same AWS region as the input bucket.

2. Open the AWS CodeBuild console at https://console.aws.amazon.com/codebuild/.

   Use the AWS region selector to choose a region that supports AWS CodeBuild and matches the region where your Amazon S3 output bucket is stored.

3. Create a build project and then run a build. For more information, see Create a Build Project (Console) and Run a Build (Console). Leave all settings at their default values, except for these settings.

   - For **Environment: How to build**:
     - For **Environment image**, choose **Use an image managed by AWS CodeBuild**.
     - For **Operating system**, choose **Ubuntu**.
     - For **Runtime**, choose **Java**.
     - For **Version**, choose **aws/codebuild/java:openjdk-8**.
   - For **Artifacts: Where to put the artifacts from this build project**:
     - For **Artifacts name**, type a build output file name that's easy for you to remember. Include the `.zip` extension.
   - For **Show advanced settings**:
     - For **Artifacts packaging**, choose **Zip**.

Step A3: Create the Application and Environment and Deploy

In this step, you will use the Elastic Beanstalk console to create an application and environment. As part of creating the environment, you will deploy the build output from the previous step to the environment.

1. Open the Elastic Beanstalk console at https://console.aws.amazon.com/elasticbeanstalk.

   Use the AWS region selector to choose the region that matches the one where your Amazon S3 output bucket is stored.

2. Create an Elastic Beanstalk application. For more information, see Managing and Configuring AWS Elastic Beanstalk Applications.

3. Create an Elastic Beanstalk environment for this application. For more information, see The Create New Environment Wizard. Leave all settings at their default values, except for these settings.

   - For **Platform**, choose **Tomcat**.
   - For **Application code**, choose **Upload your code**, and then choose **Upload**. For **Source code origin**, choose **Public S3 URL**, and then type the full URL to the build output ZIP file in the output bucket. Then choose **Upload**.

4. After Elastic Beanstalk deploys the build output to the environment, you can see the results in a web browser. Go to the environment URL for the instance (for example, `http://my-environment-name.random-string .region-ID.elasticbeanstalk.com`). The web browser should display the text `Hello World!`.

Scenario B: Use AWS CodePipeline to Run AWS CodeBuild and Deploy to Elastic Beanstalk

In this scenario, you will finish manually preparing and uploading the source code to be built. You will then use the AWS CodePipeline console to create a pipeline and an Elastic Beanstalk application and environment. After you create the pipeline, AWS CodePipeline automatically builds the source code and deploys the build output to the environment.

Step B1: Add a Build Spec File to the Source Code

In this step, you will create an add a build spec file to the code you created in Create the Source Code. You will then upload the source code to an Amazon S3 input bucket or an AWS CodeCommit or GitHub repository.

1. Create a file named `buildspec.yml` with the following contents. Store the file inside of the `(root directory name)/my-web-app` directory.

```
1  version: 0.2
2
3  phases:
4    post_build:
5      commands:
6        - mvn package
7  artifacts:
8    files:
9      - '**/*'
10   base-directory: 'target/my-web-app'
```

2. Your file structure should now look like this.

```
1  (root directory name)
2      `-- my-web-app
3          |-- src
4          |    `-- main
5          |          |-- resources
6          |          `-- webapp
7          |                |-- WEB-INF
8          |                |    `-- web.xml
9          |                `-- index.jsp
10         |-- buildpsec.yml
11         `-- pom.xml
```

3. Upload this contents of the `my-web-app` directory to an Amazon S3 input bucket or an AWS CodeCommit, GitHub, or Bitbucket repository. **Important**
Do not upload `(root directory name)` or `(root directory name)/my-web-app`, just the directories and files inside of `(root directory name)/my-web-app`.
If you are using an Amazon S3 input bucket, be sure to create a ZIP file that contains the directory structure and files, and then upload it to the input bucket. Do not add `(root directory name)` or `(root directory name)/my-web-app` to the ZIP file, just the directories and files inside of `(root directory name)/my-web-app`.

Step B2: Create the Pipeline and Deploy

In this step, you will use the AWS CodePipeline and Elastic Beanstalk consoles to create a pipeline, an application, and an environment. After you create the pipeline and it runs, AWS CodePipeline uses AWS CodeBuild to build the source code, and then it uses Elastic Beanstalk to deploy the build output to the environment.

1. Create or identify a service role that AWS CodePipeline, AWS CodeBuild, and Elastic Beanstalk can use to do their work on your behalf. For more information, see Prerequisites.

2. Open the AWS CodePipeline console at https://console.aws.amazon.com/codepipeline/.

   Use the AWS region selector to choose a region that supports AWS CodeBuild and, if you're storing the source code in an Amazon S3 input bucket, choose the region that matches the one where your input bucket is stored.

3. Create a pipeline. For information, see Create a Pipeline that Uses AWS CodeBuild (AWS CodePipeline Console). Leave all settings at their default values, except for these settings.

- For **Step 3: Build**, for **Configure your project**, choose **Create a new build project**. For **Environment: How to build**:
  - For **Environment image**, choose **Use an image managed by AWS CodeBuild**.
  - For **Operating system**, choose **Ubuntu**.
  - For **Runtime**, choose **Java**.
  - For **Version**, choose **aws/codebuild/java:openjdk-8**.
- For **Step 4: Beta**, for **Deployment provider**, choose **AWS Elastic Beanstalk**.
  - For the application, choose the **create a new one in Elastic Beanstalk** link. This opens the Elastic Beanstalk console. For more information, see Managing and Configuring AWS Elastic Beanstalk Applications. After you create the application, return to the AWS CodePipeline console, and then select the application you just created.
  - For the environment, choose the **create a new one in Elastic Beanstalk** link. This opens the Elastic Beanstalk console. For more information, see The Create New Environment Wizard. Leave all but one setting at their default values: for **Platform**, choose **Tomcat**. After you create the environment, return to the AWS CodePipeline console, and then select the environment you just created.

4. After the pipeline has run successfully, you can see the results in a web browser. Go to the environment URL for the instance (for example, `http://my-environment-name.random-string.region-ID.elasticbeanstalk.com`). The web browser should display the text `Hello World!`.

Now, whenever you make changes to the source code and upload those changes to the original Amazon S3 input bucket or AWS CodeCommit, GitHub, or Bitbucket repository, AWS CodePipeline detects the change and runs the pipeline again. This causes AWS CodeBuild to automatically rebuild the code and then causes Elastic Beanstalk to automatically deploy the rebuilt output to the environment.

Scenario C: Use the Elastic Beanstalk Command Line Interface (EB CLI) to Run AWS CodeBuild and Deploy to an Elastic Beanstalk Environment

In this scenario, you will finish manually preparing and uploading the source code to be built. You will then run the EB CLI to create an Elastic Beanstalk application and environment, use AWS CodeBuild to build the source code, and then deploy the build output to the environment. For more information, see Using the EB CLI with AWS CodeBuild in the *AWS Elastic Beanstalk Developer Guide*.

Step C1: Add Files to the Source Code

In this step, you will add an Elastic Beanstalk configuration file and a build spec file to the code you created in Create the Source Code. You will also create or identify a service role for the build spec file.

1. Create or identify a service role that Elastic Beanstalk and the EB CLI can use on your behalf. For information, see Create an AWS CodeBuild Service Role.

2. Create a subdirectory named `.ebextensions` inside of the `(root directory name)/my-web-app` directory. In the `.ebextensions` subdirectory, create a file named `fix-path.config` with this content.

```
1  container_commands:
2    fix_path:
3      command: "unzip my-web-app.war 2>&1 > /var/log/my_last_deploy.log"
```

3. Create a file named `buildspec.yml` with the following contents. Store the file inside of the `(root directory name)/my-web-app` directory.

```
1 version: 0.2
2
3 phases:
4   post_build:
5     commands:
6       - mvn package
7       - mv target/my-web-app.war my-web-app.war
8 artifacts:
9   files:
10     - my-web-app.war
11     - .ebextensions/**/*
12 eb_codebuild_settings:
13   CodeBuildServiceRole: my-service-role-name
14   ComputeType: BUILD_GENERAL1_SMALL
15   Image: aws/codebuild/java:openjdk-8
16   Timeout: 60
```

In the preceding code, replace *my-service-role-name* with the name of the service role you created or identified earlier.

4. Your file structure should now look like this.

```
1 (root directory name)
2     `-- my-web-app
3         |-- .ebextensions
4         |     `-- fix-path.config
5         |-- src
6         |    `-- main
7         |         |-- resources
8         |         `-- webapp
9         |              |-- WEB-INF
10        |              |    `-- web.xml
11        |              `-- index.jsp
12        |-- buildpsec.yml
13        `-- pom.xml
```

Step C2: Install and Run the EB CLI

1. If you have not already done so, install and configure the EB CLI on the same computer or instance where you created the source code. For information, see Install the Elastic Beanstalk Command Line Interface (EB CLI) and Configure the EB CLI.

2. From your computer's or instance's command line or terminal, run the cd command or similar to switch to your (root directory name)/my-web-app directory. Run the eb init command to configure the EB CLI.

```
1 eb init
```

When prompted:

- Choose an AWS region where AWS CodeBuild is supported and matches where you want to create your Elastic Beanstalk application and environment.
- Create an Elastic Beanstalk application, and type a name for the application.
- Choose the Tomcat platform.
- Choose the Tomcat 8 Java 8 version.
- Choose whether you want to use SSH to set up access to your environment's instances.

3. From the same directory, run the eb create command to create an Elastic Beanstalk environment.

When prompted:

- Type the name for the new environment, or accept the suggested name.
- Type the DNS CNAME prefix for the environment, or accept the suggested value.
- For this sample, accept the Classic load balancer type.

1. After you run the eb create command, the EB CLI does the following:

   1. Creates a ZIP file from the source code and then uploads the ZIP file to an Amazon S3 bucket in your account.

   2. Creates an Elastic Beanstalk application and application version.

   3. Creates an AWS CodeBuild project.

   4. Runs a build based on the new project.

   5. Deletes the project after the build is complete.

   6. Creates an Elastic Beanstalk environment.

   7. Deploys the build output to the environment.

2. After the EB CLI deploys the build output to the environment, you can see the results in a web browser. Go to the environment URL for the instance (for example, `http://my-environment-name.random-string.region-ID.elasticbeanstalk.com`). The web browser should display the text `Hello World!`.

If you want, you can make changes to the source code and then run the eb deploy command from the same directory. The EB CLI performs the same steps as the eb create command, but it deploys the build output to the existing environment instead of creating a new environment.

Related Resources

- For more information about getting started with AWS CodeBuild, see Getting Started with AWS CodeBuild.
- For more information about troubleshooting problems with AWS CodeBuild, see Troubleshooting AWS CodeBuild.
- For more information about limits in AWS CodeBuild, see Limits for AWS CodeBuild.

AWS CodeBuild Code-Based Samples

Refer to these code-based samples to experiment with AWS CodeBuild:

Name	Description
C++ Sample	Uses C++ to output a single .out file.
Go Sample	Uses Go to output a single binary file.
Maven Sample	Uses Apache Maven to produce a single JAR file.
Node.js Sample	Uses Mocha to test whether an internal variable in code contains a specific string value. Produces a single .js file.
Python Sample	Uses Python to test whether an internal variable in code is set to a specific string value. Produces a single .py file.
Ruby Sample	Uses RSpec to test whether an internal variable in code is set to a specific string value. Produces a single .rb file.
Scala Sample	Uses sbt to produce a single JAR file.
Java Sample	Uses Apache Maven to produce a single WAR file.
.NET Core in Linux Sample	Uses .NET Core to build an executable file out of code written in C#.

C++ Hello World Sample for AWS CodeBuild

This C++ sample produces as build output a single binary file named `hello.out`.

Important
Running this sample may result in charges to your AWS account. These include possible charges for AWS CodeBuild and for AWS resources and actions related to Amazon S3, AWS KMS, and CloudWatch Logs. For more information, see AWS CodeBuild Pricing, Amazon S3 Pricing, AWS Key Management Service Pricing, and Amazon CloudWatch Pricing.

Topics

- Running the Sample
- Directory Structure
- Files
- Related Resources

Running the Sample

To run this sample:

1. Create the files as described in the Directory Structure and Files sections of this topic, and then upload them to an Amazon S3 input bucket or an AWS CodeCommit, GitHub, or Bitbucket repository. **Important**
   Do not upload (`root directory name`), just the files inside of (`root directory name`).
   If you are using an Amazon S3 input bucket, be sure to create a ZIP file that contains the files, and then upload it to the input bucket. Do not add (`root directory name`) to the ZIP file, just the files inside of (`root directory name`).

2. Create a build project, run the build, and view related build information by following the steps in Run AWS CodeBuild Directly.

   If you use the AWS CLI to create the build project, the JSON-formatted input to the `create-project` command might look similar to this. (Replace the placeholders with your own values.)

```
1  {
2    "name": "sample-c-plus-plus-project",
3    "source": {
4      "type": "S3",
5      "location": "codebuild-region-ID-account-ID-input-bucket/CPlusPlusSample.zip"
6    },
7    "artifacts": {
8      "type": "S3",
9      "location": "codebuild-region-ID-account-ID-output-bucket",
10     "packaging": "ZIP",
11     "name": "CPlusPlusOutputArtifact.zip"
12   },
13   "environment": {
14     "type": "LINUX_CONTAINER",
15     "image": "aws/codebuild/ubuntu-base:14.04",
16     "computeType": "BUILD_GENERAL1_SMALL"
17   },
18   "serviceRole": "arn:aws:iam::account-ID:role/role-name",
19   "encryptionKey": "arn:aws:kms:region-ID:account-ID:key/key-ID"
20 }
```

3. To get the build output artifact, open your Amazon S3 output bucket.

4. Download the `CPlusPlusOutputArtifact.zip` file to your local computer or instance, and then extract the contents of the file. In the extracted contents, get the `hello.out` file.

Directory Structure

This sample assumes this directory structure.

```
1 (root directory name)
2     |-- buildspec.yml
3     `-- hello.cpp
```

Files

This sample uses these files.

`buildspec.yml` (in (root directory name))

```
1 version: 0.2
2
3 phases:
4   install:
5     commands:
6       - apt-get update -y
7       - apt-get install -y build-essential
8   build:
9     commands:
10      - echo Build started on `date`
11      - echo Compiling the C++ code...
12      - g++ hello.cpp -o hello.out
13  post_build:
14    commands:
15      - echo Build completed on `date`
16 artifacts:
17   files:
18     - hello.out
```

`hello.cpp` (in (root directory name))

```cpp
1 #include <iostream>
2
3 int main()
4 {
5   std::cout << "Hello, World!\n";
6 }
```

Related Resources

- For more information about getting started with AWS CodeBuild, see Getting Started with AWS CodeBuild.
- For more information about troubleshooting problems with AWS CodeBuild, see Troubleshooting AWS CodeBuild.
- For more information about limits in AWS CodeBuild, see Limits for AWS CodeBuild.

Go Hello World Sample for AWS CodeBuild

This Go sample produces as build output a single binary file named `hello`.

Important
Running this sample may result in charges to your AWS account. These include possible charges for AWS CodeBuild and for AWS resources and actions related to Amazon S3, AWS KMS, and CloudWatch Logs. For more information, see AWS CodeBuild Pricing, Amazon S3 Pricing, AWS Key Management Service Pricing, and Amazon CloudWatch Pricing.

Note
Did you know you can use AWS Cloud9 to work with the code in this topic? AWS Cloud9 is an online, cloud-based integrated development environment (IDE) you can use to write, run, debug, and deploy code—using just a browser from an internet-connected machine. AWS Cloud9 includes a code editor, debugger, terminal, and essential tools, such as the AWS CLI and Git. In many cases, you don't need to install files or configure your development machine to start working with code. Learn more in the AWS Cloud9 User Guide.

Topics

- Running the Sample
- Directory Structure
- Files
- Related Resources

Running the Sample

To run this sample:

1. Create the files as described in the Directory Structure and Files sections of this topic, and then upload them to an Amazon S3 input bucket or an AWS CodeCommit, GitHub, or Bitbucket repository. **Important**
   Do not upload (`root directory name`), just the files inside of (`root directory name`).
   If you are using an Amazon S3 input bucket, be sure to create a ZIP file that contains the files, and then upload it to the input bucket. Do not add (`root directory name`) to the ZIP file, just the files inside of (`root directory name`).

2. Create a build project, run the build, and view related build information by following the steps in Run AWS CodeBuild Directly.

   If you use the AWS CLI to create the build project, the JSON-formatted input to the `create-project` command might look similar to this. (Replace the placeholders with your own values.)

```
1  {
2    "name": "sample-go-project",
3    "source": {
4      "type": "S3",
5      "location": "codebuild-region-ID-account-ID-input-bucket/GoSample.zip"
6    },
7    "artifacts": {
8      "type": "S3",
9      "location": "codebuild-region-ID-account-ID-output-bucket",
10     "packaging": "ZIP",
11     "name": "GoOutputArtifact.zip"
12   },
13   "environment": {
14     "type": "LINUX_CONTAINER",
15     "image": "aws/codebuild/golang:1.7.3",
16     "computeType": "BUILD_GENERAL1_SMALL"
```

```
17    },
18    "serviceRole": "arn:aws:iam::account-ID:role/role-name",
19    "encryptionKey": "arn:aws:kms:region-ID:account-ID:key/key-ID"
20 }
```

3. To get the build output artifact, open your Amazon S3 output bucket.

4. Download the GoOutputArtifact.zip file to your local computer or instance, and then extract the contents of the file. In the extracted contents, get the hello file.

Directory Structure

This sample assumes this directory structure.

```
1 (root directory name)
2    |-- buildspec.yml
3    `-- hello.go
```

Files

This sample uses these files.

buildspec.yml (in (root directory name))

```
1 version: 0.2
2
3 phases:
4   build:
5     commands:
6       - echo Build started on `date`
7       - echo Compiling the Go code...
8       - go build hello.go
9   post_build:
10     commands:
11       - echo Build completed on `date`
12 artifacts:
13   files:
14     - hello
```

hello.go (in (root directory name))

```
1 package main
2 import "fmt"
3
4 func main() {
5   fmt.Println("hello world")
6   fmt.Println("1+1 =", 1+1)
7   fmt.Println("7.0/3.0 =", 7.0/3.0)
8   fmt.Println(true && false)
9   fmt.Println(true || false)
10  fmt.Println(!true)
11 }
```

Related Resources

- For more information about getting started with AWS CodeBuild, see Getting Started with AWS CodeBuild.
- For more information about troubleshooting problems with AWS CodeBuild, see Troubleshooting AWS CodeBuild.
- For more information about limits in AWS CodeBuild, see Limits for AWS CodeBuild.

Maven in 5 Minutes Sample for AWS CodeBuild

This Maven sample produces as build output a single JAR file named `my-app-1.0-SNAPSHOT.jar`. This sample is based on the Maven in 5 Minutes topic on the Apache Maven website.

Important

Running this sample may result in charges to your AWS account. These include possible charges for AWS CodeBuild and for AWS resources and actions related to Amazon S3, AWS KMS, and CloudWatch Logs. For more information, see AWS CodeBuild Pricing, Amazon S3 Pricing, AWS Key Management Service Pricing, and Amazon CloudWatch Pricing.

Running the Sample

To run this sample:

1. Download and install Maven. For more information, see Downloading Apache Maven and Installing Apache Maven on the Apache Maven website.

2. Switch to an empty directory on your local computer or instance, and then run this Maven command.

```
1 mvn archetype:generate -DgroupId=com.mycompany.app -DartifactId=my-app -
    DarchetypeArtifactId=maven-archetype-quickstart -DinteractiveMode=false
```

If successful, this directory structure and files will be created.

```
1 (root directory name)
2     `-- my-app
3         |-- pom.xml
4         `-- src
5             |-- main
6             |   `-- java
7             |       `-- com
8             |           `-- mycompany
9             |               `-- app
10            |                   `-- App.java
11            `-- test
12                `-- java
13                    `-- com
14                        `-- mycompany
15                            `-- app
16                                `-- AppTest.java
```

3. Create a file with this content. Name the file `buildspec.yml`, and then add it to the `(root directory name)/my-app` directory.

```
1 version: 0.2
2
3 phases:
4   build:
5     commands:
6       - echo Build started on `date`
7       - mvn test
8   post_build:
9     commands:
10      - echo Build completed on `date`
11      - mvn package
```

```
12 artifacts:
13   files:
14     - target/my-app-1.0-SNAPSHOT.jar
```

When finished, your directory structure and file should look like this.

```
1 (root directory name)
2       `-- my-app
3              |-- buildspec.yml
4              |-- pom.xml
5              `-- src
6                   |-- main
7                   |      `-- java
8                   |           `-- com
9                   |                `-- mycompany
10                  |                     `-- app
11                  |                          `-- App.java
12                  `-- test
13                         `-- java
14                              `-- com
15                                   `-- mycompany
16                                        `-- app
17                                             ` -- AppTest.java
```

4. Upload this contents of the `my-app` directory to an Amazon S3 input bucket or an AWS CodeCommit, GitHub, or Bitbucket repository. **Important**
Do not upload (`root directory name`) or (`root directory name`)/`my-app`, just the directories and files inside of (`root directory name`)/`my-app`.
If you are using an Amazon S3 input bucket, be sure to create a ZIP file that contains the directory structure and files, and then upload it to the input bucket. Do not add (`root directory name`) or (`root directory name`)/`my-app` to the ZIP file, just the directories and files inside of (`root directory name`)/`my-app`.

5. Create a build project, run the build, and view related build information by following the steps in Run AWS CodeBuild Directly.

If you use the AWS CLI to create the build project, the JSON-formatted input to the `create-project` command might look similar to this. (Replace the placeholders with your own values.)

```
1 {
2   "name": "sample-maven-in-5-minutes-project",
3   "source": {
4     "type": "S3",
5     "location": "codebuild-region-ID-account-ID-input-bucket/MavenIn5MinutesSample.zip"
6   },
7   "artifacts": {
8     "type": "S3",
9     "location": "codebuild-region-ID-account-ID-output-bucket",
10    "packaging": "ZIP",
11    "name": "MavenIn5MinutesOutputArtifact.zip"
12  },
13  "environment": {
14    "type": "LINUX_CONTAINER",
15    "image": "aws/codebuild/java:openjdk-8",
16    "computeType": "BUILD_GENERAL1_SMALL"
17  },
18  "serviceRole": "arn:aws:iam::account-ID:role/role-name",
```

```
19    "encryptionKey": "arn:aws:kms:region-ID:account-ID:key/key-ID"
20  }
```

6. To get the build output artifact, open your Amazon S3 output bucket.

7. Download the `MavenIn5MinutesOutputArtifact.zip` file to your local computer or instance, and then extract the contents of the `MavenIn5MinutesOutputArtifact.zip` file. In the extracted contents, open the `target` folder to get the `my-app-1.0-SNAPSHOT.jar` file.

Related Resources

- For more information about getting started with AWS CodeBuild, see Getting Started with AWS CodeBuild.
- For more information about troubleshooting problems with AWS CodeBuild, see Troubleshooting AWS CodeBuild.
- For more information about limits in AWS CodeBuild, see Limits for AWS CodeBuild.

Node.js Hello World Sample for AWS CodeBuild

This Node.js sample tests whether an internal variable in code starts with the string `Hello`. It produces as build output a single file named `HelloWorld.js`.

Important
Running this sample may result in charges to your AWS account. These include possible charges for AWS CodeBuild and for AWS resources and actions related to Amazon S3, AWS KMS, and CloudWatch Logs. For more information, see AWS CodeBuild Pricing, Amazon S3 Pricing, AWS Key Management Service Pricing, and Amazon CloudWatch Pricing.

Note
Did you know you can use AWS Cloud9 to work with the code in this topic? AWS Cloud9 is an online, cloud-based integrated development environment (IDE) you can use to write, run, debug, and deploy code—using just a browser from an internet-connected machine. AWS Cloud9 includes a code editor, debugger, terminal, and essential tools, such as the AWS CLI and Git. In many cases, you don't need to install files or configure your development machine to start working with code. Learn more in the AWS Cloud9 User Guide.

Topics

- Running the Sample
- Directory Structure
- Files
- Related Resources

Running the Sample

To run this sample:

1. On your local computer or instance, create the files as described in the Directory Structure and Files sections of this topic, and then upload them to an Amazon S3 input bucket or an AWS CodeCommit, GitHub, or Bitbucket repository. **Important**
   Do not upload (root directory name), just the files inside of (root directory name).
   If you are using an Amazon S3 input bucket, be sure to create a ZIP file that contains the files, and then upload it to the input bucket. Do not add (root directory name) to the ZIP file, just the files inside of (root directory name).

2. Create a build project, run the build, and view related build information by following the steps in Run AWS CodeBuild Directly.

   If you use the AWS CLI to create the build project, the JSON-formatted input to the `start-build` command might look similar to this. (Replace the placeholders with your own values.)

```
1  {
2    "name": "sample-nodejs-project",
3    "source": {
4      "type": "S3",
5      "location": "codebuild-region-ID-account-ID-input-bucket/NodeJSSample.zip"
6    },
7    "artifacts": {
8      "type": "S3",
9      "location": "codebuild-region-ID-account-ID-output-bucket",
10     "packaging": "ZIP",
11     "name": "NodeJSOutputArtifact.zip"
12   },
13   "environment": {
14     "type": "LINUX_CONTAINER",
```

```
15        "image": "aws/codebuild/nodejs:6.3.1",
16        "computeType": "BUILD_GENERAL1_SMALL"
17      },
18      "serviceRole": "arn:aws:iam::account-ID:role/role-name",
19      "encryptionKey": "arn:aws:kms:region-ID:account-ID:key/key-ID"
20    }
```

3. To get the build output artifact, open your Amazon S3 output bucket.

4. Download the `NodeJSOutputArtifact.zip` file to your local computer or instance, and then extract the contents of the file. In the extracted contents, get the `HelloWorld.js` file.

Directory Structure

This sample assumes this directory structure.

```
1 (root directory name)
2     |-- buildspec.yml
3     `-- HelloWorld.js
```

Files

This sample uses these files.

`buildspec.yml` (in `(root directory name)`)

```
1 version: 0.2
2
3 phases:
4   install:
5     commands:
6       - echo Installing Mocha...
7       - npm install -g mocha
8   pre_build:
9     commands:
10      - echo Installing source NPM dependencies...
11      - npm install unit.js
12  build:
13    commands:
14      - echo Build started on `date`
15      - echo Compiling the Node.js code
16      - mocha HelloWorld.js
17  post_build:
18    commands:
19      - echo Build completed on `date`
20 artifacts:
21   files:
22     - HelloWorld.js
```

`HelloWorld.js` (in `(root directory name)`)

```
1 var test = require('unit.js');
2 var str = 'Hello, world!';
3
4 test.string(str).startsWith('Hello');
```

110

```
5
6 if (test.string(str).startsWith('Hello')) {
7   console.log('Passed');
8 }
```

Related Resources

- For more information about getting started with AWS CodeBuild, see Getting Started with AWS CodeBuild.
- For more information about troubleshooting problems with AWS CodeBuild, see Troubleshooting AWS CodeBuild.
- For more information about limits in AWS CodeBuild, see Limits for AWS CodeBuild.

Python Hello World Sample for AWS CodeBuild

This Python sample tests whether an internal variable in code contains the string `Hello world!`. It produces as build output a single file named `HelloWorld.py`.

Important
Running this sample may result in charges to your AWS account. These include possible charges for AWS CodeBuild and for AWS resources and actions related to Amazon S3, AWS KMS, and CloudWatch Logs. For more information, see AWS CodeBuild Pricing, Amazon S3 Pricing, AWS Key Management Service Pricing, and Amazon CloudWatch Pricing.

Note
Did you know you can use AWS Cloud9 to work with the code in this topic? AWS Cloud9 is an online, cloud-based integrated development environment (IDE) you can use to write, run, debug, and deploy code—using just a browser from an internet-connected machine. AWS Cloud9 includes a code editor, debugger, terminal, and essential tools, such as the AWS CLI and Git. In many cases, you don't need to install files or configure your development machine to start working with code. Learn more in the AWS Cloud9 User Guide.

Topics

- Running the Sample
- Directory Structure
- Files
- Related Resources

Running the Sample

To run this sample:

1. Create the files as described in the Directory Structure and Files sections of this topic, and then upload them to an Amazon S3 input bucket or an AWS CodeCommit, GitHub, or Bitbucket repository. **Important**
   Do not upload (root directory name), just the files inside of (root directory name).
   If you are using an Amazon S3 input bucket, be sure to create a ZIP file that contains the files, and then upload it to the input bucket. Do not add (root directory name) to the ZIP file, just the files inside of (root directory name).

2. Create a build project, run the build, and view related build information by following the steps in Run AWS CodeBuild Directly.

   If you use the AWS CLI to create the build project, the JSON-formatted input to the create-project command might look similar to this. (Replace the placeholders with your own values.)

```
1  {
2    "name": "sample-python-project",
3    "source": {
4      "type": "S3",
5      "location": "codebuild-region-ID-account-ID-input-bucket/PythonSample.zip"
6    },
7    "artifacts": {
8      "type": "S3",
9      "location": "codebuild-region-ID-account-ID-output-bucket",
10     "packaging": "ZIP",
11     "name": "PythonOutputArtifact.zip"
12   },
13   "environment": {
14     "type": "LINUX_CONTAINER",
15     "image": "aws/codebuild/python:3.5.2",
```

```
16       "computeType": "BUILD_GENERAL1_SMALL"
17     },
18     "serviceRole": "arn:aws:iam::account-ID:role/role-name",
19     "encryptionKey": "arn:aws:kms:region-ID:account-ID:key/key-ID"
20 }
```

3. To get the build output artifact, open your Amazon S3 output bucket.

4. Download the `PythonOutputArtifact.zip` file to your local computer or instance, and then extract the contents of the file. In the extracted contents, get the `HelloWorld.py` file.

Directory Structure

This sample assumes this directory structure.

```
1 (root directory name)
2     |-- buildspec.yml
3     |-- HelloWorld.py
4     `-- HelloWorld_tst.py
```

Files

This sample uses these files.

`buildspec.yml` (in (root directory name))

```
1 version: 0.2
2
3 phases:
4   build:
5     commands:
6       - echo Build started on `date`
7       - echo Compiling the Python code...
8       - python HelloWorld_tst.py
9   post_build:
10     commands:
11       - echo Build completed on `date`
12 artifacts:
13   files:
14       - HelloWorld.py
```

`HelloWorld.py` (in (root directory name))

```
1 class HelloWorld:
2   def __init__(self):
3     self.message = 'Hello world!'
```

`HelloWorld_tst.py` (in (root directory name))

```
1 import unittest
2 from HelloWorld import HelloWorld
3
4 class MyTestCase(unittest.TestCase):
5   def test_default_greeting_set(self):
6     hw = HelloWorld()
7     self.assertEqual(hw.message, 'Hello world!')
```

```
 8
 9 if __name__ == '__main__':
10   unittest.main()
```

Related Resources

- For more information about getting started with AWS CodeBuild, see Getting Started with AWS CodeBuild.
- For more information about troubleshooting problems with AWS CodeBuild, see Troubleshooting AWS CodeBuild.
- For more information about limits in AWS CodeBuild, see Limits for AWS CodeBuild.

Ruby Hello World Sample for AWS CodeBuild

This Ruby sample tests whether an internal variable in code contains the string `Hello, world!`. It produces as build output a single file named `HelloWorld.rb`.

Important
Running this sample may result in charges to your AWS account. These include possible charges for AWS CodeBuild and for AWS resources and actions related to Amazon S3, AWS KMS, and CloudWatch Logs. For more information, see AWS CodeBuild Pricing, Amazon S3 Pricing, AWS Key Management Service Pricing, and Amazon CloudWatch Pricing.

Note
Did you know you can use AWS Cloud9 to work with the code in this topic? AWS Cloud9 is an online, cloud-based integrated development environment (IDE) you can use to write, run, debug, and deploy code—using just a browser from an internet-connected machine. AWS Cloud9 includes a code editor, debugger, terminal, and essential tools, such as the AWS CLI and Git. In many cases, you don't need to install files or configure your development machine to start working with code. Learn more in the AWS Cloud9 User Guide.

Topics

- Running the Sample
- Directory Structure
- Files
- Related Resources

Running the Sample

To run this sample:

1. Create the files as described in the Directory Structure and Files sections of this topic, and then upload them to an Amazon S3 input bucket or an AWS CodeCommit, GitHub, or Bitbucket repository. **Important**
Do not upload (`root directory name`), just the files inside of (`root directory name`).
If you are using an Amazon S3 input bucket, be sure to create a ZIP file that contains the files, and then upload it to the input bucket. Do not add (`root directory name`) to the ZIP file, just the files inside of (`root directory name`).

2. Create a build project, run the build, and view related build information by following the steps in Run AWS CodeBuild Directly.

   If you use the AWS CLI to create the build project, the JSON-formatted input to the `create-project` command might look similar to this. (Replace the placeholders with your own values.)

```
1  {
2    "name": "sample-ruby-project",
3    "source": {
4      "type": "S3",
5      "location": "codebuild-region-ID-account-ID-input-bucket/RubySample.zip"
6    },
7    "artifacts": {
8      "type": "S3",
9      "location": "codebuild-region-ID-account-ID-output-bucket",
10     "packaging": "ZIP",
11     "name": "RubyOutputArtifact.zip"
12   },
13   "environment": {
14     "type": "LINUX_CONTAINER",
15     "image": "aws/codebuild/ruby:2.3.1",
```

```
16      "computeType": "BUILD_GENERAL1_SMALL"
17    },
18    "serviceRole": "arn:aws:iam::account-ID:role/role-name",
19    "encryptionKey": "arn:aws:kms:region-ID:account-ID:key/key-ID"
20  }
```

3. To get the build output artifact, open your Amazon S3 output bucket.

4. Download the `RubyOutputArtifact.zip` file to your local computer or instance, and then extract the contents of the file. In the extracted contents, get the `HelloWorld.rb` file.

Directory Structure

This sample assumes this directory structure.

```
1 (root directory name)
2     |-- buildspec.yml
3     |-- HelloWorld.rb
4     `-- HelloWorld_spec.rb
```

Files

This sample uses these files.

`buildspec.yml` (in `(root directory name)`)

```
1 version: 0.2
2
3 phases:
4   install:
5     commands:
6       - echo Installing RSpec...
7       - gem install rspec
8   build:
9     commands:
10      - echo Build started on `date`
11      - echo Compiling the Ruby code...
12      - rspec HelloWorld_spec.rb
13  post_build:
14    commands:
15      - echo Build completed on `date`
16 artifacts:
17   files:
18     - HelloWorld.rb
```

`HelloWorld.rb` (in `(root directory name)`)

```
1 class HelloWorld
2   def say_hello()
3     return 'Hello, world!'
4   end
5 end
```

`HelloWorld_spec.rb` (in `(root directory name)`)

```
1 require './HelloWorld'
2
3 describe HelloWorld do
4   context "When testing the HelloWorld class" do
5     it "The say_hello method should return 'Hello World'" do
6       hw = HelloWorld.new
7       message = hw.say_hello
8       puts 'Succeed' if expect(message).to eq "Hello, world!"
9     end
10  end
11 end
```

Related Resources

- For more information about getting started with AWS CodeBuild, see Getting Started with AWS CodeBuild.
- For more information about troubleshooting problems with AWS CodeBuild, see Troubleshooting AWS CodeBuild.
- For more information about limits in AWS CodeBuild, see Limits for AWS CodeBuild.

Scala Hello World Sample for AWS CodeBuild

This Scala sample produces as build output a single JAR file named `core_2.11-1.0.0.jar`.

Important
Running this sample may result in charges to your AWS account. These include possible charges for AWS CodeBuild and for AWS resources and actions related to Amazon S3, AWS KMS, and CloudWatch Logs. For more information, see AWS CodeBuild Pricing, Amazon S3 Pricing, AWS Key Management Service Pricing, and Amazon CloudWatch Pricing.

Topics

- Running the Sample
- Directory Structure
- Files
- Related Resources

Running the Sample

To run this sample:

1. Identify a Docker image that contains sbt, a build tool for Scala projects. To find a compatible Docker image, search Docker Hub for **sbt**.

2. Create the directory structure and files as described in the Directory Structure and Files sections of this topic, and then upload them to an Amazon S3 input bucket or an AWS CodeCommit, GitHub, or Bitbucket repository. **Important**
Do not upload (`root directory name`), just the directories and files inside of (`root directory name`). If you are using an Amazon S3 input bucket, be sure to create a ZIP file that contains the directory structure and files, and then upload it to the input bucket. Do not add (`root directory name`) to the ZIP file, just the directories and files inside of (`root directory name`).

3. Create a build project, run the build, and view related build information by following the steps in Run AWS CodeBuild Directly.

   If you use the AWS CLI to create the build project, the JSON-formatted input to the `create-project` command might look similar to this. (Replace the placeholders with your own values.)

```
 1 {
 2    "name": "sample-scala-project",
 3    "source": {
 4      "type": "S3",
 5      "location": "codebuild-region-ID-account-ID-input-bucket/ScalaSample.zip"
 6    },
 7    "artifacts": {
 8      "type": "S3",
 9      "location": "codebuild-region-ID-account-ID-output-bucket",
10      "packaging": "ZIP",
11      "name": "ScalaOutputArtifact.zip"
12    },
13    "environment": {
14      "type": "LINUX_CONTAINER",
15      "image": "scala-image-ID",
16      "computeType": "BUILD_GENERAL1_SMALL"
17    },
18    "serviceRole": "arn:aws:iam::account-ID:role/role-name",
19    "encryptionKey": "arn:aws:kms:region-ID:account-ID:key/key-ID"
```

```
20 }
```

4. To get the build output artifact, open your Amazon S3 output bucket.

5. Download the `ScalaOutputArtifact.zip` file to your local computer or instance, and then extract the contents of the file. In the extracted contents, open the `core/target/scala-2.11` folder to get the `core_2.11-1.0.0.jar` file.

Directory Structure

This sample assumes this directory structure.

```
1 (root directory name)
2     |-- buildspec.yml
3     |-- core
4     |      `-- src
5     |            `-- main
6     |                   `-- scala
7     |                          `-- Test.scala
8     |-- macros
9     |      `-- src
10    |            `-- main
11    |                   `-- scala
12    |                          `-- Macros.scala
13    `-- project
14           |-- Build.scala
15           `-- build.properties
```

Files

This sample uses these files.

`buildspec.yml` (in (root directory name))

```
1 version: 0.2
2
3 phases:
4   build:
5     commands:
6       - echo Build started on `date`
7       - echo Run the test and package the code...
8       - sbt run
9   post_build:
10    commands:
11      - echo Build completed on `date`
12      - sbt package
13 artifacts:
14   files:
15     - core/target/scala-2.11/core_2.11-1.0.0.jar
```

`Test.scala` (in (root directory name)/core/src/main/scala)

```
1 object Test extends App {
2   Macros.hello
3 }
```

Macros.scala (in (root directory name)/macros/src/main/scala)

```scala
1 import scala.language.experimental.macros
2 import scala.reflect.macros.Context
3
4 object Macros {
5   def impl(c: Context) = {
6     import c.universe._
7     c.Expr[Unit](q"""println("Hello World")""")
8   }
9
10   def hello: Unit = macro impl
11 }
```

Build.scala (in (root directory name)/project)

```scala
1 import sbt._
2 import Keys._
3
4 object BuildSettings {
5   val buildSettings = Defaults.defaultSettings ++ Seq(
6     organization := "org.scalamacros",
7     version := "1.0.0",
8     scalaVersion := "2.11.8",
9     crossScalaVersions := Seq("2.10.2", "2.10.3", "2.10.4", "2.10.5", "2.10.6", "2.11.0",
10         "2.11.1", "2.11.2", "2.11.3", "2.11.4", "2.11.5", "2.11.6", "2.11.7", "2.11.8"),
10    resolvers += Resolver.sonatypeRepo("snapshots"),
11    resolvers += Resolver.sonatypeRepo("releases"),
12    scalacOptions ++= Seq()
13  )
14 }
15
16 object MyBuild extends Build {
17   import BuildSettings._
18
19   lazy val root: Project = Project(
20     "root",
21     file("."),
22     settings = buildSettings ++ Seq(
23       run <<= run in Compile in core)
24   ) aggregate(macros, core)
25
26   lazy val macros: Project = Project(
27     "macros",
28     file("macros"),
29     settings = buildSettings ++ Seq(
30       libraryDependencies <+= (scalaVersion)("org.scala-lang" % "scala-reflect" % _),
31       libraryDependencies := {
32         CrossVersion.partialVersion(scalaVersion.value) match {
33           // if Scala 2.11+ is used, quasiquotes are available in the standard distribution
34           case Some((2, scalaMajor)) if scalaMajor >= 11 =>
35             libraryDependencies.value
36           // in Scala 2.10, quasiquotes are provided by macro paradise
37           case Some((2, 10)) =>
38             libraryDependencies.value ++ Seq(
```

```
39        compilerPlugin("org.scalamacros" % "paradise" % "2.1.0-M5" cross CrossVersion.full
               ),
40        "org.scalamacros" %% "quasiquotes" % "2.1.0-M5" cross CrossVersion.binary)
41      }
42    }
43  )
44  )
45
46  lazy val core: Project = Project(
47    "core",
48    file("core"),
49    settings = buildSettings
50  ) dependsOn(macros)
51 }
```

build.properties (in (root directory name)/project)

```
1 sbt.version=0.13.7
```

Related Resources

- For more information about getting started with AWS CodeBuild, see Getting Started with AWS CodeBuild.
- For more information about troubleshooting problems with AWS CodeBuild, see Troubleshooting AWS CodeBuild.
- For more information about limits in AWS CodeBuild, see Limits for AWS CodeBuild.

WAR Hello World Sample for AWS CodeBuild

This Maven sample produces as build output a single Web application ARchive (WAR) file named `my-web-app.war`.

Important

Running this sample may result in charges to your AWS account. These include possible charges for AWS CodeBuild and for AWS resources and actions related to Amazon S3, AWS KMS, and CloudWatch Logs. For more information, see AWS CodeBuild Pricing, Amazon S3 Pricing, AWS Key Management Service Pricing, and Amazon CloudWatch Pricing.

Running the Sample

To run this sample:

1. Download and install Maven. For more information, see Downloading Apache Maven and Installing Apache Maven on the Apache Maven website.

2. Switch to an empty directory on your local computer or instance, and then run this Maven command.

```
1 mvn archetype:generate -DgroupId=com.mycompany.app -DartifactId=my-web-app -
      DarchetypeArtifactId=maven-archetype-webapp -DinteractiveMode=false
```

   If successful, this directory structure and files will be created.

```
1  (root directory name)
2      `-- my-web-app
3          |-- pom.xml
4          `-- src
5              `-- main
6                  |-- resources
7                  `-- webapp
8                      |-- WEB-INF
9                      |   `-- web.xml
10                     `-- index.jsp
```

3. Create a file with this content. Name the file `buildspec.yml`, and then add it to the `(root directory name)/my-web-app` directory.

```
1  version: 0.2
2
3  phases:
4    post_build:
5      commands:
6        - echo Build completed on `date`
7        - mvn package
8  artifacts:
9    files:
10       - target/my-web-app.war
11   discard-paths: yes
```

   When finished, your directory structure and file should look like this.

```
1  (root directory name)
2      `-- my-web-app
3          |-- buildspec.yml
4          |-- pom.xml
```

```
5              `-- src
6                   `-- main
7                        |-- resources
8                        `-- webapp
9                             |-- WEB-INF
10                            |    `-- web.xml
11                            `-- index.jsp
```

4. Upload the contents of the `my-web-app` directory to an Amazon S3 input bucket or an AWS CodeCommit, GitHub, or Bitbucket repository. **Important**

   Do not upload (`root directory name`) or (`root directory name`)/`my-web-app`, just the directories and files inside of (`root directory name`)/`my-web-app`.

   If you are using an Amazon S3 input bucket, be sure to create a ZIP file that contains the directory structure and files, and then upload it to the input bucket. Do not add (`root directory name`) or (`root directory name`)/`my-web-app` to the ZIP file, just the directories and files inside of (`root directory name`)/`my-web-app`. For example, the ZIP file should contain these directories and files:

```
1  WebArchiveHelloWorldSample.zip
2       |-- buildpsec.yml
3       |-- pom.xml
4       `-- src
5            `-- main
6                 |-- resources
7                 `-- webapp
8                      |-- WEB-INF
9                      |    `-- web.xml
10                     `-- index.jsp
```

5. Create a build project, run the build, and view related build information by following the steps in Run AWS CodeBuild Directly.

   If you use the AWS CLI to create the build project, the JSON-formatted input to the `create-project` command might look similar to this. (Replace the placeholders with your own values.)

```
1  {
2    "name": "sample-web-archive-project",
3    "source": {
4      "type": "S3",
5      "location": "codebuild-region-ID-account-ID-input-bucket/WebArchiveHelloWorldSample.zip
          "
6    },
7    "artifacts": {
8      "type": "S3",
9      "location": "codebuild-region-ID-account-ID-output-bucket",
10     "packaging": "ZIP",
11     "name": "WebArchiveHelloWorldOutputArtifact.zip"
12   },
13   "environment": {
14     "type": "LINUX_CONTAINER",
15     "image": "aws/codebuild/java:openjdk-8",
16     "computeType": "BUILD_GENERAL1_SMALL"
17   },
18   "serviceRole": "arn:aws:iam::account-ID:role/role-name",
19   "encryptionKey": "arn:aws:kms:region-ID:account-ID:key/key-ID"
20 }
```

6. To get the build output artifact, open your Amazon S3 output bucket.

7. Download the `WebArchiveHelloWorldOutputArtifact.zip` file to your local computer or instance, and then extract the contents of the file. In the extracted contents, open the `target` folder to get the `my-web-app.war` file.

Related Resources

- For more information about getting started with AWS CodeBuild, see Getting Started with AWS CodeBuild.
- For more information about troubleshooting problems with AWS CodeBuild, see Troubleshooting AWS CodeBuild.
- For more information about limits in AWS CodeBuild, see Limits for AWS CodeBuild.

.NET Core in Linux Sample for AWS CodeBuild

This sample uses a AWS CodeBuild build environment running .NET Core to build an executable file out of code written in C#.

Important
Running this sample may result in charges to your AWS account. These include possible charges for AWS CodeBuild and for AWS resources and actions related to Amazon S3, AWS KMS, and CloudWatch Logs. For more information, see AWS CodeBuild Pricing, Amazon S3 Pricing, AWS Key Management Service Pricing, and Amazon CloudWatch Pricing.

Running the Sample

To run this sample:

1. Create the files as described in the Directory Structure and Files sections of this topic, and then upload them to an Amazon S3 input bucket or an AWS CodeCommit, GitHub, or Bitbucket repository. **Important**
   Do not upload (`root directory name`), just the files inside of (`root directory name`).
   If you are using an Amazon S3 input bucket, be sure to create a ZIP file that contains the files, and then upload it to the input bucket. Do not add (`root directory name`) to the ZIP file, just the files inside of (`root directory name`).

2. Create a build project, run the build, and view related build information by following the steps in Run AWS CodeBuild Directly.

   If you use the AWS CLI to create the build project, the JSON-formatted input to the `create-project` command might look similar to this. (Replace the placeholders with your own values.)

```
1  {
2    "name": "sample-dot-net-core-project",
3    "source": {
4      "type": "S3",
5      "location": "codebuild-region-ID-account-ID-input-bucket/windows-dotnetcore.zip"
6    },
7    "artifacts": {
8      "type": "S3",
9      "location": "codebuild-region-ID-account-ID-output-bucket",
10     "packaging": "ZIP",
11     "name": "dot-net-core-output-artifact.zip"
12   },
13   "environment": {
14     "type": "LINUX_CONTAINER",
15     "image": "aws/codebuild/dot-net:core-2.0",
16     "computeType": "BUILD_GENERAL1_SMALL"
17   },
18   "serviceRole": "arn:aws:iam::account-ID:role/role-name",
19   "encryptionKey": "arn:aws:kms:region-ID:account-ID:key/key-ID"
20 }
```

3. To get the build output artifact, in your Amazon S3 output bucket, download the `dot-net-core-output-artifact.zip` file to your local computer or instance. Extract the contents to get to the executable file `HelloWorldSample.dll`, which be found in the `bin\Debug\netcoreapp2.0` directory.

Directory Structure

This sample assumes this directory structure.

```
1 (root directory name)
2     |-- buildspec.yml
3     |-- HelloWorldSample.csproj
4     `-- Program.cs
```

Files

This sample uses these files.

buildspec.yml (in (root directory name))

```
1 version: 0.2
2
3 phases:
4   build:
5     commands:
6       - dotnet restore
7       - dotnet build
8 artifacts:
9   files:
10      - bin/Debug/netcoreapp2.0/*
```

HelloWorldSample.csproj (in (root directory name))

```
1 <Project Sdk="Microsoft.NET.Sdk">
2   <PropertyGroup>
3     <OutputType>Exe</OutputType>
4     <TargetFramework>netcoreapp2.0</TargetFramework>
5   </PropertyGroup>
6 </Project>
```

Program.cs (in (root directory name))

```
1 using System;
2
3 namespace HelloWorldSample {
4   public static class Program {
5     public static void Main() {
6       Console.WriteLine("Hello, World!");
7     }
8   }
9 }
```

Related Resources

- For more information about getting started with AWS CodeBuild, see Getting Started with AWS CodeBuild.
- For more information about troubleshooting problems with AWS CodeBuild, see Troubleshooting AWS CodeBuild.
- For more information about limits in AWS CodeBuild, see Limits for AWS CodeBuild.

Plan a Build for AWS CodeBuild

Before you run your build with AWS CodeBuild, you must answer these questions:

1. **Where is the source code located?** AWS CodeBuild currently supports building from the following source code repository providers. The source code must contain a build specification (build spec) file, or the build spec must be declared as part of a build project definition. A *build spec* is a collection of build commands and related settings, in YAML format, that AWS CodeBuild uses to run a build.

[See the AWS documentation website for more details]

1. **Which build commands do you need to run and in what order?** By default, AWS CodeBuild downloads the build input from the provider you specify and uploads the build output to the bucket you specify. You use the build spec to instruct how to turn the downloaded build input into the expected build output. For more information, see the Build Spec Reference.

2. **Which runtimes and tools do you need to run the build?** For example, are you building for Java, Ruby, Python, or Node.js? Does the build need Maven or Ant or a compiler for Java, Ruby, or Python? Does the build need Git, the AWS CLI, or other tools?

   AWS CodeBuild runs builds in build environments that use Docker images. These Docker images must be stored in a repository type supported by AWS CodeBuild. These include the AWS CodeBuild Docker image repository, Docker Hub, and Amazon Elastic Container Registry (Amazon ECR). For more information about the AWS CodeBuild Docker image repository, see Docker Images Provided by AWS CodeBuild.

3. **Do you need AWS resources that aren't provided automatically by AWS CodeBuild? If so, which security policies will those resources need?** For example, you might need to modify the AWS CodeBuild service role to allow AWS CodeBuild to work with those resources.

4. **Do you want AWS CodeBuild to work with your VPC?** If so, you need the VPC ID, the subnet IDs, and security group IDs for your VPC configuration. For more information, see Use AWS CodeBuild with Amazon Virtual Private Cloud.

After you have answered these questions, you should have the settings and resources you need to run a build successfully. To run your build, you can:

- Use the AWS CodeBuild console, AWS CLI, or AWS SDKs. For more information, see Run AWS CodeBuild Directly.
- Create or identify a pipeline in AWS CodePipeline, and then add a build or test action that instructs AWS CodeBuild to automatically test your code, run your build, or both. For more information, see Use AWS CodePipeline with AWS CodeBuild.

Build Specification Reference for AWS CodeBuild

This topic provides important reference information about build specifications (build specs). A *build spec* is a collection of build commands and related settings, in YAML format, that AWS CodeBuild uses to run a build. You can include a build spec as part of the source code or you can define a build spec when you create a build project. For information about how a build spec works, see How AWS CodeBuild Works.

Topics

- Build Spec File Name and Storage Location
- Build Spec Syntax
- Build Spec Example
- Build Spec Versions

Build Spec File Name and Storage Location

If you include a build spec as part of the source code, by default, the build spec file must be named `buildspec.yml` and be placed in the root of your source directory.

You can also override the default build spec file name and location. For example, you can:

- Use a different build spec file for different builds in the same repository, such as `buildspec_debug.yml` and `buildspec_release.yml`.
- Store a build spec file somewhere other than the root of your source directory, such as `config/buildspec.yml`.

You can specify only one build spec for a build project, regardless of the build spec file's name.

To override the default build spec file name, location, or both, do one of the following:

- Run the AWS CLI `create-project` or `update-project` command, setting the `buildspec` value to the path to the alternate build spec file relative to the value of the built-in environment variable `CODEBUILD_SRC_DIR`. You can also do the equivalent with the create project operation in the AWS SDKs. For more information, see Create a Build Project or Change a Build Project's Settings.
- Run the AWS CLI `start-build` command, setting the `buildspecOverride` value to the path to the alternate build spec file relative to the value of the built-in environment variable `CODEBUILD_SRC_DIR`. You can also do the equivalent with the start build operation in the AWS SDKs. For more information, see Run a Build.
- In an AWS CloudFormation template, set the `BuildSpec` property of `Source` in a resource of type `AWS::CodeBuild::Project` to the path to the alternate build spec file relative to the value of the built-in environment variable `CODEBUILD_SRC_DIR`. For more information, see the "BuildSpec" property in AWS CodeBuild Project Source in the *AWS CloudFormation User Guide*.

Build Spec Syntax

Build specs must be expressed in YAML format.

The build spec has the following syntax:

```
1 version: 0.2
2
3 env:
4   variables:
5     key: "value"
6     key: "value"
7   parameter-store:
8     key: "value"
```

```
 9      key: "value"
10
11 phases:
12   install:
13     commands:
14       - command
15       - command
16   pre_build:
17     commands:
18       - command
19       - command
20   build:
21     commands:
22       - command
23       - command
24   post_build:
25     commands:
26       - command
27       - command
28 artifacts:
29   files:
30     - location
31     - location
32   discard-paths: yes
33   base-directory: location
34 cache:
35   paths:
36     - path
37     - path
```

The build spec contains the following:

- **version**: Required mapping. Represents the build spec version. We recommend you use 0.2. **Note** Version 0.1 is still supported. However, we recommend that you use version 0.2 whenever possible. For more information, see Build Spec Versions.

- **env**: Optional sequence. Represents information for one or more custom environment variables.

  - **variables**: Required if **env** is specified, and you want to define custom environment variables in plain text. Contains a mapping of *key/value* scalars, where each mapping represents a single custom environment variable in plain text. *key* is the name of the custom environment variable, and *value* is that variable's value. **Important**
    We strongly discourage using environment variables to store sensitive values, especially AWS access key IDs and secret access keys. Environment variables can be displayed in plain text using tools such as the AWS CodeBuild console and the AWS CLI. For sensitive values, we recommend you use the **parameter-store** mapping instead, as described later in this section.
    Any environment variables you set will replace existing environment variables. For example, if the Docker image already contains an environment variable named **MY_VAR** with a value of **my_value**, and you set an environment variable named **MY_VAR** with a value of **other_value**, then **my_value** will be replaced by **other_value**. Similarly, if the Docker image already contains an environment variable named **PATH** with a value of **/usr/local/sbin:/usr/local/bin**, and you set an environment variable named **PATH** with a value of **$PATH:/usr/share/ant/bin**, then **/usr/local/sbin:/usr/local/bin** will be replaced by the literal value **$PATH:/usr/share/ant/bin**.
    Do not set any environment variable with a name that begins with **CODEBUILD_**. This prefix is reserved for internal use.
    If an environment variable with the same name is defined in multiple places, the value is determined

as follows:

The value in the start build operation call takes highest precedence. The value in the build project definition takes next precedence. The value in the build spec declaration takes lowest precedence.

- `parameter-store`: Required if `env` is specified, and you want to retrieve custom environment variables stored in Amazon EC2 Systems Manager Parameter Store. Contains a mapping of *key/value* scalars, where each mapping represents a single custom environment variable stored in Amazon EC2 Systems Manager Parameter Store. *key* is the name you will use later in your build commands to refer to this custom environment variable, and *value* is the name of the custom environment variable stored in Amazon EC2 Systems Manager Parameter Store. To store sensitive values, see Systems Manager Parameter Store and Systems Manager Parameter Store Console Walkthrough in the *Amazon EC2 Systems Manager User Guide*. **Important**

  To allow AWS CodeBuild to retrieve custom environment variables stored in Amazon EC2 Systems Manager Parameter Store, you must add the `ssm:GetParameters` action to your AWS CodeBuild service role. For more information, see Create an AWS CodeBuild Service Role.

  Any environment variables you retrieve from Amazon EC2 Systems Manager Parameter Store will replace existing environment variables. For example, if the Docker image already contains an environment variable named `MY_VAR` with a value of `my_value`, and you retrieve an environment variable named `MY_VAR` with a value of `other_value`, then `my_value` will be replaced by `other_value`. Similarly, if the Docker image already contains an environment variable named `PATH` with a value of `/usr/local/sbin:/usr/local/bin`, and you retrieve an environment variable named `PATH` with a value of `$PATH:/usr/share/ant/bin`, then `/usr/local/sbin:/usr/local/bin` will be replaced by the literal value `$PATH:/usr/share/ant/bin`.

  Do not store any environment variable with a name that begins with `CODEBUILD_`. This prefix is reserved for internal use.

  If an environment variable with the same name is defined in multiple places, the value is determined as follows:

  The value in the start build operation call takes highest precedence. The value in the build project definition takes next precedence. The value in the build spec declaration takes lowest precedence.

- `phases`: Required sequence. Represents the commands AWS CodeBuild will run during each phase of the build. **Note**

  In build spec version 0.1, AWS CodeBuild runs each command in a separate instance of the default shell in the build environment. This means that each command runs in isolation from all other commands. Therefore, by default, you cannot run a single command that relies on the state of any previous commands (for example, changing directories or setting environment variables). To get around this limitation, we recommend you use version 0.2, which solves this issue. If you must use build spec version 0.1 for some reason, we recommend the approaches in Shells and Commands in Build Environments.

The allowed build phase names are:

- `install`: Optional sequence. Represents the commands, if any, that AWS CodeBuild will run during installation. We recommend you use the `install` phase only for installing packages in the build environment. For example, you might use this phase to install a code testing framework such as Mocha or RSpec.
  - `commands`: Required sequence if `install` is specified. Contains a sequence of scalars, where each scalar represents a single command that AWS CodeBuild will run during installation. AWS CodeBuild runs each command, one at a time, in the order listed, from beginning to end.
- `pre_build`: Optional sequence. Represents the commands, if any, that AWS CodeBuild will run before the build. For example, you might use this phase to log in to Amazon ECR, or you might install npm dependencies.
  - `commands`: Required sequence if `pre_build` is specified. Contains a sequence of scalars, where each scalar represents a single command that AWS CodeBuild will run before the build. AWS CodeBuild runs each command, one at a time, in the order listed, from beginning to end.
- `build`: Optional sequence. Represents the commands, if any, that AWS CodeBuild will run during the build. For example, you might use this phase to run Mocha, RSpec, or sbt.
  - `commands`: Required if `build` is specified. Contains a sequence of scalars, where each scalar

represents a single command that AWS CodeBuild will run during the build. AWS CodeBuild runs each command, one at a time, in the order listed, from beginning to end.

- `post_build`: Optional sequence. Represents the commands, if any, that AWS CodeBuild will run after the build. For example, you might use Maven to package the build artifacts into a JAR or WAR file, or you might push a Docker image into Amazon ECR. Then you might send a build notification through Amazon SNS.
  - `commands`: Required if `post_build` is specified. Contains a sequence of scalars, where each scalar represents a single command that AWS CodeBuild will run after the build. AWS CodeBuild runs each command, one at a time, in the order listed, from beginning to end. **Important** Commands in some build phases might not be run if commands in earlier build phases fail. For example, if a command fails during the `install` phase, none of the commands in the `pre_build`, `build`, and `post_build` phases will be run for that build's lifecycle. For more information, see Build Phase Transitions.

- `artifacts`: Optional sequence. Represents information about where AWS CodeBuild can find the build output and how AWS CodeBuild will prepare it for uploading to the Amazon S3 output bucket. This sequence is not required if, for example, you are building and pushing a Docker image to Amazon ECR, or you are running unit tests on your source code but not building it.
  - `files`: Required sequence. Represents the locations containing the build output artifacts in the build environment. Contains a sequence of scalars, with each scalar representing a separate location where AWS CodeBuild can find build output artifacts, relative to the original build location or, if set, the base directory. Locations can include the following:
    - A single file (for example, `my-file.jar`).
    - A single file in a subdirectory (for example, `my-subdirectory/my-file.jar` or `my-parent-subdirectory/my-subdirectory/my-file.jar`).
    - `'**/*'` represents all files recursively.
    - `my-subdirectory/*` represents all files in a subdirectory named *my-subdirectory*.
    - `my-subdirectory/**/*` represents all files recursively starting from a subdirectory named *my-subdirectory*.

  When you specify build output artifact locations, AWS CodeBuild can locate the original build location in the build environment. You do not have to prepend your build artifact output locations with the path to the original build location or specify `./` or similar. If you want to know the path to this location, you can run a command such as `echo $CODEBUILD_SRC_DIR` during a build. The location for each build environment might be slightly different.

  - `discard-paths`: Optional mapping. Represents whether paths to files in the build output artifact are discarded. `yes` if paths are discarded; otherwise, `no` or not specified (the default). For example, if a path to a file in the build output artifact would be `com/mycompany/app/HelloWorld.java`, then specifying `yes` would shorten this path to simply `HelloWorld.java`.

  - `base-directory`: Optional mapping. Represents one or more top-level directories, relative to the original build location, that AWS CodeBuild uses to determine which files and subdirectories to include in the build output artifact. Valid values include:
    - A single top-level directory (for example, `my-directory`).
    - `'my-directory*'` represents all top-level directories with names starting with `my-directory`.

  Matching top-level directories are not included in the build output artifact, only their files and subdirectories.

  You can use `files` and `discard-paths` to further restrict which files and subdirectories are included. For example, for the following directory structure:

```
1 |-- my-build1
2 |      `-- my-file1.txt
3 `-- my-build2
4        |-- my-file2.txt
```

```
5         `-- my-subdirectory
6              `-- my-file3.txt
```

And for the following `artifacts` sequence:

```
1 artifacts:
2   files:
3     - '*/my-file3.txt'
4   base-directory: my-build2
```

The following subdirectory and file would be included in the build output artifact:

```
1 my-subdirectory
2   `-- my-file3.txt
```

While for the following `artifacts` sequence:

```
1 artifacts:
2   files:
3     - '**/*'
4   base-directory: 'my-build*'
5   discard-paths: yes
```

The following files would be included in the build output artifact:

```
1 |-- my-file1.txt
2 |-- my-file2.txt
3 `-- my-file3.txt
```

- **cache**: Optional sequence. Represents information about where AWS CodeBuild can prepare the files for uploading cache to an Amazon S3 cache bucket. This sequence is not required if the cache type of the project is `No Cache`.

  - **paths**: Required sequence. Represents the locations of the cache. Contains a sequence of scalars, with each scalar representing a separate location where AWS CodeBuild can find build output artifacts, relative to the original build location or, if set, the base directory. Locations can include the following:
    - A single file (for example, `my-file.jar`).
    - A single file in a subdirectory (for example, `my-subdirectory/my-file.jar` or `my-parent-subdirectory/my-subdirectory/my-file.jar`).
    - `'**/*'` represents all files recursively.
    - `my-subdirectory/*` represents all files in a subdirectory named *my-subdirectory*.
    - `my-subdirectory/**/*` represents all files recursively starting from a subdirectory named *my-subdirectory*.

Important

Because a build spec declaration must be valid YAML, the spacing in a build spec declaration is important. If the number of spaces in your build spec declaration is invalid, builds might fail immediately. You can use a YAML validator to test whether your build spec declarations are valid YAML.

If you use the AWS CLI, or the AWS SDKs to declare a build spec when you create or update a build project, the build spec must be a single string expressed in YAML format, along with required whitespace and newline escape characters. There is an example in the next section.

If you use the AWS CodeBuild or AWS CodePipeline consoles instead of a buildspec.yml file, you can insert commands for the `build` phase only. Instead of using the preceding syntax, you list, in a single line, all of the commands you want to run during the build phase. For multiple commands, separate each command by `&&` (for example, `mvn test && mvn package`).

You can use the AWS CodeBuild or AWS CodePipeline consoles instead of a buildspec.yml file to specify the locations of the build output artifacts in the build environment. Instead of using the preceding syntax, you list, in a single line, all of the locations. For multiple locations, separate each location with a comma (for example, `appspec.yml, target/my-app.jar`).

Build Spec Example

Here is an example of a buildspec.yml file.

```
1  version: 0.2
2
3  env:
4    variables:
5      JAVA_HOME: "/usr/lib/jvm/java-8-openjdk-amd64"
6    parameter-store:
7      LOGIN_PASSWORD: "dockerLoginPassword"
8
9  phases:
10   install:
11     commands:
12       - echo Entered the install phase...
13       - apt-get update -y
14       - apt-get install -y maven
15   pre_build:
16     commands:
17       - echo Entered the pre_build phase...
18       - docker login -u User -p $LOGIN_PASSWORD
19   build:
20     commands:
21       - echo Entered the build phase...
22       - echo Build started on `date`
23       - mvn install
24   post_build:
25     commands:
26       - echo Entered the post_build phase...
27       - echo Build completed on `date`
28 artifacts:
29   files:
30     - target/messageUtil-1.0.jar
31   discard-paths: yes
32 cache:
33   paths:
34     - '/root/.m2/**/*'
```

Here is an example of the preceding build spec, expressed as a single string, for use with the AWS CLI, or the AWS SDKs.

```
1  "version: 0.2\n\nenv:\n  variables:\n    JAVA_HOME: "/usr/lib/jvm/java-8-openjdk-amd64"\n
   parameter-store:\n    LOGIN_PASSWORD: "dockerLoginPassword"\n\nphases:\n  install:\n
   commands:\n      - apt-get update -y\n      - apt-get install -y maven\n  pre_build:\n
   commands:\n      - echo Entered the pre_build phase...\n  build:\n    commands:\n      -
   echo Build started on `date`\n      - mvn install\n  post_build:\n    commands:\n      -
   echo Build completed on `date`\nartifacts:\n  files:\n    - target/messageUtil-1.0.jar\n
   discard-paths: yes"
```

Here is an example of the commands in the build phase, for use with the AWS CodeBuild or AWS CodePipeline consoles.

```
1  echo Build started on `date` && mvn install
```

In these examples:

- A custom environment variable in plain text with the key of `JAVA_HOME` and the value of `/usr/lib/jvm/java-8-openjdk-amd64` will be set.
- A custom environment variable named `dockerLoginPassword` you stored in Amazon EC2 Systems Manager Parameter Store will be referenced later in build commands by using the key `LOGIN_PASSWORD`.
- You cannot change these build phase names. The commands that will be run in this example are `apt-get update -y` and `apt-get install -y maven` (to install Apache Maven), `mvn install` (to compile, test, and package the source code into a build output artifact and to perform other actions, such as install the build output artifact in its internal repository), `docker login` (to log in to Docker with the password that corresponds to the value of the custom environment variable `dockerLoginPassword` you set in Amazon EC2 Systems Manager Parameter Store), and several `echo` commands. The `echo` commands are included here to show how AWS CodeBuild runs commands and the order in which it runs them.
- `files` represents the files to upload to the build output location. In this example, AWS CodeBuild will upload the single file `messageUtil-1.0.jar`. The `messageUtil-1.0.jar` file can be found in the relative directory named `target` in the build environment. Because `discard-paths: yes` is specified, `messageUtil-1.0.jar` will be uploaded directly (and not to an intermediate `target` directory). The file name `messageUtil-1.0.jar` and the relative directory name of `target` is based on the way Apache Maven creates and stores build output artifacts for this example only. In your own scenarios, these file names and directories will be different.

Build Spec Versions

The following table lists the build spec versions and the changes between versions.

Version	Changes
0.2	`environment_variables` has been renamed to `env`. `plaintext` has been renamed to `variables`. In version 0.1, AWS CodeBuild runs each build command in a separate instance of the default shell in the build environment. In verson 0.2, this issue is addressed; AWS CodeBuild runs all build commands in the same instance of the default shell in the build environment.
0.1	This is the initial definition of the build specification format.

Build Environment Reference for AWS CodeBuild

When you call AWS CodeBuild to run a build, you must provide information about the build environment AWS CodeBuild will use. A *build environment* represents a combination of operating system, programming language runtime, and tools that AWS CodeBuild uses to run a build. For information about how a build environment works, see How AWS CodeBuild Works.

A build environment contains a Docker image. For information, see Docker Glossary: Image on the Docker Docs website.

When you provide information to AWS CodeBuild about the build environment, you specify the identifier of a Docker image in a supported repository type. These include the AWS CodeBuild Docker image repository, publicly available images in Docker Hub, and Amazon Elastic Container Registry (Amazon ECR) repositories in your AWS account:

- We recommend that you use Docker images stored in the AWS CodeBuild Docker image repository, because they are optimized for use with the service. For more information, see Docker Images Provided by AWS CodeBuild.
- To get the identifier of a publicly available Docker image stored in Docker Hub, see Searching for images on the Docker Docs website.
- To learn how to work with Docker images stored in Amazon ECR repositories in your AWS account, see our Amazon ECR Sample.

In addition to a Docker image identifier, you also specify a set of computing resources that the build environment will use. For more information, see Build Environment Compute Types.

Topics

- Docker Images Provided by AWS CodeBuild
- Build Environment Compute Types
- Shells and Commands in Build Environments
- Environment Variables in Build Environments
- Background Tasks in Build Environments

Docker Images Provided by AWS CodeBuild

AWS CodeBuild manages the following Docker images that are available in the AWS CodeBuild and AWS CodePipeline consoles.

Note

If you do not find your image on this page, it most likely contains components that are no longer supported by a vendor. Images with one or more unsupported components are not available from the AWS CodeBuild console or the AWS CodeBuild SDK. The images might still be available in the CLI, but they are not supported and will not be updated.

Platform	Programming language or framework	Runtime version	Image identifier	Definition
Ubuntu 14.04	(Base image)		aws/codebuild/ubu base:14.04	ubuntu/ubuntu-base/14.04
Ubuntu 14.04	Android	26.1.1	aws/codebuild/andi java-8:26.1.1	ubuntu/android-java-8/26.1.1
Ubuntu 14.04	Android	24.4.1	aws/codebuild/andi java-8:24.4.1	ubuntu/android-java-8/24.4.1
Ubuntu 14.04	Docker	17.09.0	aws/codebuild/-docker:17.09.0	ubuntu/dock-er/17.09.0
Ubuntu 14.04	Golang	1.10	aws/codebuild/-golang:1.10	ubuntu/-golang/1.10
Ubuntu 14.04	Java	8	aws/codebuild/-java:openjdk-8	ubuntu/java/openjdk-8
Ubuntu 14.04	Java	9	aws/codebuild/-java:openjdk-9	ubuntu/java/openjdk-9
Ubuntu 14.04	Node.js	10.1.0	aws/codebuild/n-odejs:10.1.0	ubuntu/node-js/10.1.0
Ubuntu 14.04	Node.js	8.11.0	aws/codebuild/n-odejs:8.11.0	ubuntu/node-js/8.11.0
Ubuntu 14.04	Node.js	6.3.1	aws/codebuild/n-odejs:6.3.1	ubuntu/node-js/6.3.1
Ubuntu 14.04	PHP	5.6	aws/code-build/php:5.6	ubuntu/php/5.6
Ubuntu 14.04	PHP	7.0	aws/code-build/php:7.0	ubuntu/php/7.0
Ubuntu 14.04	Python	3.6.5	aws/code-build/python:3.6.5	ubun-tu/python/3.6.5
Ubuntu 14.04	Python	3.5.2	aws/code-build/python:3.5.2	ubun-tu/python/3.5.2
Ubuntu 14.04	Python	3.4.5	aws/code-build/python:3.4.5	ubun-tu/python/3.4.5
Ubuntu 14.04	Python	3.3.6	aws/code-build/python:3.3.6	ubun-tu/python/3.3.6
Ubuntu 14.04	Python	2.7.12	aws/code-build/python:2.7.12	ubun-tu/python/2.7.12
Ubuntu 14.04	Ruby	2.5.1	aws/code-build/ruby:2.5.1	ubun-tu/ruby/2.5.1
Ubuntu 14.04	Ruby	2.3.1	aws/code-build/ruby:2.3.1	ubun-tu/ruby/2.3.1

Platform	Programming language or framework	Runtime version	Image identifier	Definition
Ubuntu 14.04	Ruby	2.2.5	aws/codebuild/ruby:2.2.5	ubuntu/ruby/2.2.5
Ubuntu 14.04	.NET Core	1.1	aws/codebuild/dotnet:core-1	ubuntu/dotnet/core-1
Ubuntu 14.04	.NET Core	2.0	aws/codebuild/dotnet:core-2.0	ubuntu/dotnet/core-2
Windows Server Core 2016	(Base Image)		aws/codebuild/win base:1.0	

AWS CodeBuild also manages the following Docker images that are not in the AWS CodeBuild and AWS CodePipeline consoles.

Platform	Programming language or framework	Runtime version	Additional components	Image identifier
Amazon Linux 2016.03, 64-bit v2.3.2	Golang	1.6	Apache Maven 3.3.3, Apache Ant 1.9.6, Gradle 2.7	aws/codebuild/eb-go-1.6-amazonlinux-64:2.3.2
Amazon Linux 2016.03, 64-bit v2.1.6	Golang	1.5.3	Apache Maven 3.3.3, Apache Ant 1.9.6, Gradle 2.7	aws/codebuild/eb-go-1.5-amazonlinux-64:2.1.6
Amazon Linux 2016.03, 64-bit v2.1.3	Golang	1.5.3	Apache Maven 3.3.3, Apache Ant 1.9.6, Gradle 2.7	aws/codebuild/eb-go-1.5-amazonlinux-64:2.1.3
Amazon Linux 2016.03, 64-bit v2.4.3	Java	1.8.0	Apache Maven 3.3.3, Apache Ant 1.9.6, Gradle 2.7	aws/codebuild/eb-java-8-amazonlinux-64:2.4.3
Amazon Linux 2016.03, 64-bit v2.1.6	Java	1.8.0	Apache Maven 3.3.3, Apache Ant 1.9.6, Gradle 2.7	aws/codebuild/eb-java-8-amazonlinux-64:2.1.6
Amazon Linux 2016.03, 64-bit v2.1.3	Java	1.8.0	Apache Maven 3.3.3, Apache Ant 1.9.6, Gradle 2.7	aws/codebuild/eb-java-8-amazonlinux-64:2.1.3
Amazon Linux 2016.03, 64-bit v2.4.3	Java	1.7.0	Apache Maven 3.3.3, Apache Ant 1.9.6, Gradle 2.7	aws/codebuild/eb-java-7-amazonlinux-64:2.4.3
Amazon Linux 2016.03, 64-bit v2.1.6	Java	1.7.0	Apache Maven 3.3.3, Apache Ant 1.9.6, Gradle 2.7	aws/codebuild/eb-java-7-amazonlinux-64:2.1.6

Platform		Programming language or framework	Runtime version	Additional components	Image identifier
Amazon 2016.03, v2.1.3	Linux 64-bit	Java	1.7.0	Apache Maven 3.3.3, Apache Ant 1.9.6, Gradle 2.7	aws/codebuild/eb-java-7-amazonlinux-64:2.1.3
Amazon 2016.03, v4.0.0	Linux 64-bit	Node.js	6.10.0	Git 2.7.4, npm 2.15.5	aws/codebuild/eb-nodejs-6.10.0-amazonlinux-64:4.0.0
Amazon 2016.03, v2.1.3	Linux 64-bit	Node.js	4.4.6	Git 2.7.4, npm 2.15.5	aws/codebuild/eb-nodejs-4.4.6-amazonlinux-64:2.1.3
Amazon 2016.03, v2.1.6	Linux 64-bit	Python	3.4.3	meld3 1.0.2, pip 7.1.2, setuptools 18.4	aws/codebuild/eb-python-3.4-amazonlinux-64:2.1.6
Amazon 2016.03, v2.1.3	Linux 64-bit	Python	3.4.3	meld3 1.0.2, pip 7.1.2, setuptools 18.4	aws/codebuild/eb-python-3.4-amazonlinux-64:2.1.3
Amazon 2016.03, v2.3.2	Linux 64-bit	Python	3.4	meld3 1.0.2, pip 7.1.2, setuptools 18.4	aws/codebuild/eb-python-3.4-amazonlinux-64:2.3.2
Amazon 2016.03, v2.1.6	Linux 64-bit	Python	2.7.10	meld3 1.0.2, pip 7.1.2, setuptools 18.4	aws/codebuild/eb-python-2.7-amazonlinux-64:2.1.6
Amazon 2016.03, v2.1.3	Linux 64-bit	Python	2.7.10	meld3 1.0.2, pip 7.1.2, setuptools 18.4	aws/codebuild/eb-python-2.7-amazonlinux-64:2.1.3
Amazon 2016.03, v2.3.2	Linux 64-bit	Python	2.7	meld3 1.0.2, pip 7.1.2, setuptools 18.4	aws/codebuild/eb-python-2.7-amazonlinux-64:2.3.2
Amazon 2016.03, v2.1.6	Linux 64-bit	Python	2.6.9	meld3 1.0.2, pip 7.1.2, setuptools 18.4	aws/codebuild/eb-python-2.6-amazonlinux-64:2.1.6
Amazon 2016.03, v2.1.3	Linux 64-bit	Python	2.6.9	meld3 1.0.2, pip 7.1.2, setuptools 18.4	aws/codebuild/eb-python-2.6-amazonlinux-64:2.1.3
Amazon 2016.03, v2.3.2	Linux 64-bit	Python	2.6	meld3 1.0.2, pip 7.1.2, setuptools 18.4	aws/codebuild/eb-python-2.6-amazonlinux-64:2.3.2

Platform		Programming language or framework	Runtime version	Additional components	Image identifier
Amazon 2016.03, v2.1.6	Linux 64-bit	Ruby	2.3.1	Bundler, RubyGems	aws/codebuild/eb-ruby-2.3-amazonlinux-64:2.1.6
Amazon 2016.03, v2.1.3	Linux 64-bit	Ruby	2.3.1	Bundler, RubyGems	aws/codebuild/eb-ruby-2.3-amazonlinux-64:2.1.3
Amazon 2016.03, v2.3.2	Linux 64-bit	Ruby	2.3	Bundler, RubyGems	aws/codebuild/eb-ruby-2.3-amazonlinux-64:2.3.2
Amazon 2016.03, v2.1.6	Linux 64-bit	Ruby	2.2.5	Bundler, RubyGems	aws/codebuild/eb-ruby-2.2-amazonlinux-64:2.1.6
Amazon 2016.03, v2.1.3	Linux 64-bit	Ruby	2.2.5	Bundler, RubyGems	aws/codebuild/eb-ruby-2.2-amazonlinux-64:2.1.3
Amazon 2016.03, v2.3.2	Linux 64-bit	Ruby	2.2	Bundler, RubyGems	aws/codebuild/eb-ruby-2.2-amazonlinux-64:2.3.2
Amazon 2016.03, v2.1.6	Linux 64-bit	Ruby	2.1.9	Bundler, RubyGems	aws/codebuild/eb-ruby-2.1-amazonlinux-64:2.1.6
Amazon 2016.03, v2.1.3	Linux 64-bit	Ruby	2.1.9	Bundler, RubyGems	aws/codebuild/eb-ruby-2.1-amazonlinux-64:2.1.3
Amazon 2016.03, v2.3.2	Linux 64-bit	Ruby	2.1	Bundler, RubyGems	aws/codebuild/eb-ruby-2.1-amazonlinux-64:2.3.2
Amazon 2016.03, v2.3.2	Linux 64-bit	Ruby	2.0	Bundler, RubyGems	aws/codebuild/eb-ruby-2.0-amazonlinux-64:2.3.2
Amazon 2016.03, v2.1.6	Linux 64-bit	Ruby	2.0.0	Bundler, RubyGems	aws/codebuild/eb-ruby-2.0-amazonlinux-64:2.1.6
Amazon 2016.03, v2.1.3	Linux 64-bit	Ruby	2.0.0	Bundler, RubyGems	aws/codebuild/eb-ruby-2.0-amazonlinux-64:2.1.3

Platform		Programming language or framework	Runtime version	Additional components	Image identifier
Amazon 2016.03, v2.1.6	Linux 64-bit	Ruby	1.9.3	Bundler, RubyGems	aws/codebuild/eb-ruby-1.9-amazonlinux-64:2.1.6
Amazon 2016.03, v2.1.3	Linux 64-bit	Ruby	1.9.3	Bundler, RubyGems	aws/codebuild/eb-ruby-1.9-amazonlinux-64:2.1.3
Amazon 2016.03, v2.3.2	Linux 64-bit	Ruby	1.9	Bundler, RubyGems	aws/codebuild/eb-ruby-1.9-amazonlinux-64:2.3.2

For more information about the Docker images that contain `eb-` in their identifier, see Supported Platforms and Platform History in the *AWS Elastic Beanstalk Developer Guide*. Docker images that contain `eb-` in their identifier are available for use in Elastic Beanstalk; but are not available in the AWS CodeBuild and AWS CodePipeline consoles.

You can use a build specification to install other components (for example, the AWS CLI, Apache Maven, Apache Ant, Mocha, RSpec, or similar) during the `install` build phase. For more information, see Build Spec Example.

AWS CodeBuild frequently updates the list of Docker images. To get the most current list, do one of the following:

- In the AWS CodeBuild console, in the **Create project** wizard or **Update project** page, for **Environment image**, choose **Use an image managed by AWS CodeBuild**. Choose from the **Operating system**, **Runtime**, and **Version** drop-down lists. For more information, see Create a Build Project (Console) or Change a Build Project's Settings (Console).

- In the AWS CodePipeline console, in the **Create pipeline** wizard on the **Step 3: Build** page, or in the **AWS CodeBuild** section of the **Add action** or **Edit action** pane, choose **Create a new build project**. In **Environment: How to build**, for **Environment image**, choose **Use an image managed by AWS CodeBuild**. Choose from the **Operating system**, **Runtime**, and **Version** drop-down lists. For more information, see Create a Pipeline that Uses AWS CodeBuild (AWS CodePipeline Console) or Add an AWS CodeBuild Build Action to a Pipeline (AWS CodePipeline Console).

- For the AWS CLI, run the `list-curated-environment-images` command:

```
1 aws codebuild list-curated-environment-images
```

- For the AWS SDKs, call the `ListCuratedEnvironmentImages` operation for your target programming language. For more information, see the AWS SDKs and Tools Reference.

To confirm the version of a component installed on a Docker image, you can run a command during a build. The version number for the component will appear in the output. For example, include one or more of the following commands in your build specification:

- For the Microsoft .NET Framework, run `reg query "HKEY_LOCAL_MACHINE\SOFTWARE\Microsoft\NET Framework Setup\NDP"`.
- For .NET Core, run `dotnet --version`.
- For Apache Ant, run `ant -version`.
- For Apache Maven, run `mvn -version`.
- For the AWS CLI, run `aws --version`.
- For Bundler, run `bundle version`.
- For Git, run `git --version`.
- For Gradle, run `gradle --version`.
- For Java, run `java -version`.
- For NPM, run `npm --version`.
- For PHP, run `php --version`.
- For pip, run `pip --version`.
- For Python, run `python --version`.
- For RubyGems, run `gem --version`.
- For setuptools, run `easy_install --version`.

The following build command (entered through the AWS CodeBuild or AWS CodePipeline console as part of a build project's settings) returns the versions of the AWS CLI, Git, pip, and Python on a Docker image that has these components installed: `aws --version && git --version && pip --version && python --version`.

Build Environment Compute Types

AWS CodeBuild provides build environments with the following available memory, vCPUs, and available disk space:

Compute type	computeType value	Memory	vCPUs	Disk space
build.general1.small	BUILD_GENERAL1_SMALL	3 GB	2	64 GB
build.general1.medium	BUILD_GENERAL1_MEDIUM	7 GB	4	128 GB
build.general1.large	BUILD_GENERAL1_LARGE	15 GB	8	128 GB

Note

For custom build environment images, AWS CodeBuild supports Docker images up to 10 GB uncompressed, regardless of the compute type. To check your build image's size, use Docker to run the `docker images REPOSITORY:TAG` command.

To choose one of these compute types:

- In the AWS CodeBuild console, in the **Create Project** wizard or **Update project** page, expand **Show advanced settings**, and then choose one of the options from **Compute type**. For more information, see Create a Build Project (Console) or Change a Build Project's Settings (Console).
- In the AWS CodePipeline console, in the **Create Pipeline** wizard on the **Step 3: Build** page, or in the **Add action** or **Edit action** pane, choose **Create a new build project**, expand **Advanced**, and then choose one of the options in **Compute type**. For more information, see Create a Pipeline that Uses AWS CodeBuild (AWS CodePipeline Console) or Add an AWS CodeBuild Build Action to a Pipeline (AWS CodePipeline Console).
- For the AWS CLI, run the `create-project` or `update-project` command, specifying the `computeType` value of the `environment` object. For more information, see Create a Build Project (AWS CLI) or Change a Build Project's Settings (AWS CLI).
- For the AWS SDKs, call the equivalent of the `CreateProject` or `UpdateProject` operation for your target programming language, specifying the equivalent of `computeType` value of the `environment` object. For more information, see the AWS SDKs and Tools Reference.

Shells and Commands in Build Environments

You provide a set of commands for AWS CodeBuild to run in a build environment during the lifecycle of a build (for example, installing build dependencies and testing and compiling your source code). There are several ways to specify these commands:

- Create a build spec file and include it with your source code. In this file, specify the commands you want to run in each phase of the build lifecycle. For more information, see the Build Specification Reference for AWS CodeBuild.
- Use the AWS CodeBuild or AWS CodePipeline console to create a build project. In **Insert build commands**, for **Build command**, specify the commands you want to run in the `build` phase. For more information, see the description of **Insert build commands** in Create a Build Project (Console) or Use AWS CodePipeline with AWS CodeBuild.
- Use the AWS CodeBuild console to change the settings of a build project. In **Insert build commands**, for **Build command**, specify the commands you want to run in the `build` phase. For more information, see the description of **Insert build commands** in Change a Build Project's Settings (Console).
- Use the AWS CLI, or AWS SDKs to create a build project or change the settings of a build project. Reference the source code that contains a build spec file with your commands, or specify a single string that includes the contents of an equivalent build spec file. For more information, see the description for the `buildspec` value in Create a Build Project or Change a Build Project's Settings.
- Use the AWS CLI, or AWS SDKs to start a build, specifying a build spec file or a single string that includes the contents of an equivalent build spec file. For more information, see the description for the `buildspecOverride` value in Run a Build.

You can specify any command that is supported by the build environment's default shell (`- sh` is the default shell in curated image). In build spec version 0.1, AWS CodeBuild runs each command in a separate instance of the default shell in the build environment. This means that each command runs in isolation from all other commands. Therefore, by default, you cannot run a single command that relies on the state of any previous commands (for example, changing directories or setting environment variables). To get around this limitation, we recommend you use version 0.2, which solves this issue. If you must use version 0.1 for some reason, we recommend the following approaches:

- Include a shell script in your source code that contains the commands you want to run in a single instance of the default shell. For example, you could include a file named `my-script.sh` in your source code that contains commands such as `cd MyDir; mkdir -p mySubDir; cd mySubDir; pwd;`. Then, in your build spec file, specify the command `./my-script.sh`.
- In your build spec file, or for the console's **Build command** setting for the `build` phase only, specify a single command that includes all of the commands you want to run in a single instance of the default shell (for example, `cd MyDir && mkdir -p mySubDir && cd mySubDir && pwd`).

If AWS CodeBuild encounters an error, the error might be more difficult to troubleshoot compared to running a single command in its own instance of the default shell.

Environment Variables in Build Environments

AWS CodeBuild provides several environment variables that you can use in your build commands:

- `AWS_DEFAULT_REGION`: The AWS region where the build is running (for example, `us-east-1`). This environment variable is used primarily by the AWS CLI.
- `AWS_REGION`: The AWS region where the build is running (for example, `us-east-1`). This environment variable is used primarily by the AWS SDKs.
- `CODEBUILD_BUILD_ARN`: The Amazon Resource Name (ARN) of the build (for example, `arn:aws:codebuild:region-ID:account-ID:build/codebuild-demo-project:b1e6661e-e4f2-4156-9ab9-82a19EXAMPLE`).
- `CODEBUILD_BUILD_IMAGE`: The AWS CodeBuild build image identifier (for example, `aws/codebuild/java:openjdk-8`).
- `CODEBUILD_BUILD_SUCCEEDING`: Whether the current build is succeeding. Set to `0` if the build is failing, or `1` if the build is succeeding.
- `CODEBUILD_INITIATOR`: The entity that started the build. If AWS CodePipeline started the build, this is the pipeline's name, for example `codepipeline/my-demo-pipeline`. If an IAM user started the build, this is the user's name, for example `MyUserName`. If the Jenkins plugin for AWS CodeBuild started the build, this is the string `CodeBuild-Jenkins-Plugin`.
- `CODEBUILD_KMS_KEY_ID`: The identifier of the AWS KMS key that AWS CodeBuild is using to encrypt the build output artifact (for example, `arn:aws:kms:region-ID:account-ID:key/key-ID` or `alias/key-alias`).
- `CODEBUILD_RESOLVED_SOURCE_VERSION`: For builds run by AWS CodePipeline, the commit ID or Amazon S3 version ID of the source code to be built. Note that this value is available only if the pipeline's related Source action is based on an Amazon S3, AWS CodeCommit, or GitHub repository.
- `CODEBUILD_SOURCE_REPO_URL`: The URL to the input artifact or source code repository. For Amazon S3, this is `s3://` followed by the bucket name and path to the input artifact. For AWS CodeCommit and GitHub, this is the repository's clone URL.
- `CODEBUILD_SOURCE_VERSION`: For Amazon S3, the version ID associated with the input artifact. For AWS CodeCommit, the commit ID or branch name associated with the version of the source code to be built. For GitHub, the commit ID, branch name, or tag name associated with the version of the source code to be built.
- `CODEBUILD_SRC_DIR`: The directory path that AWS CodeBuild uses for the build (for example, `/tmp/src123456789/src`).
- `HOME`: This environment variable is always set to `/root`.

You can also provide build environments with your own environment variables. For more information, see the following topics:

- Use AWS CodePipeline with AWS CodeBuild
- Create a Build Project
- Change a Build Project's Settings
- Run a Build
- Build Spec Reference

To list all of the available environment variables in a build environment, you can run the `printenv` command (for Linux-based build environment) or `"Get-ChildItem Env:"` (for Windows-based build environments) during a build. With the exception of those previously listed, environment variables that start with `CODEBUILD_` are for AWS CodeBuild internal use. They should not be used in your build commands.

Important

We strongly discourage using environment variables to store sensitive values, especially AWS access key IDs and secret access keys. Environment variables can be displayed in plain text using tools such as the AWS CodeBuild console and the AWS CLI.

For sensitive values, we recommend you store them in the Amazon EC2 Systems Manager Parameter Store and then retrieve them from your build spec. To store sensitive values, see Systems Manager Parameter Store and

Systems Manager Parameter Store Console Walkthrough in the *Amazon EC2 Systems Manager User Guide*. To retrieve them, see the `parameter-store` mapping in Build Spec Syntax.

Background Tasks in Build Environments

You can run background tasks in build environments. To do this, in your build spec, use the `nohup` command to run a command as a task in the background, even if the build process exits the shell. Use the `disown` command to forcibly stop a running background task.

Examples:

- Start a background process and wait for it to complete later:

```
1 nohup sleep 30 & ; echo $! > pidfile…
2
3 wait $(cat pidfile)
```

- Start a background process and do not wait for it to ever complete:

```
1 nohup sleep 30 & ; disown $!
```

- Start a background process and kill it later:

```
1 nohup sleep 30 & ; echo $! > pidfile…
2
3 kill $(cat pidfile)
```

Test and Debug Locally with the AWS CodeBuild Agent

This topic provides information about how to run the AWS CodeBuild agent and subscribe to notifications about new versions of the agent.

Test and Debug on a Local Machine with the AWS CodeBuild Agent

You can use the AWS CodeBuild agent to test and debug builds on a local machine. To use the agent, run the following command:

```
1  docker run -it -v /var/run/docker.sock:/var/run/docker.sock -e \
2          "IMAGE_NAME=amazon/aws-codebuild-local" -e \
3          "ARTIFACTS=absolute-path-to-your-artifact-output-directory" -e \
4          "SOURCE=absolute-path-to-your-source-directory" name-of-the-agent -e \
5          "BUILDSPEC=absolute-or-relative-path-to-your-buildspec-file"
```

The AWS CodeBuild agent is available from https://hub.docker.com/r/amazon/aws-codebuild-local/. Its Secure Hash Algorithm (SHA) signature is ceb83dccf6febea461317457279bc66b9fa88a707da15bcd720bcb7d339e55ba. You can use this to identify the version of the agent. To see the agent's SHA signature, run the following command:

```
1  docker inspect amazon/aws-codebuild-local
```

Receive Notifications for New AWS CodeBuild Agent Versions

Amazon SNS can notify you when new versions of the AWS CodeBuild Agent are released. Use the following procedure to subscribe to these notifications.

** To subscribe to the AWS CodeBuild Agent notifications:**

1. Open the Amazon SNS console at https://console.aws.amazon.com/sns/v2/home.

2. In the navigation bar, if it's not already selected, change the region to **US East (N. Virginia)**, if it not already selected. You must select this region because the SNS notifications that you are subscribing to are created in this region.

3. In the navigation pane, choose **Subscriptions**.

4. Choose **Create subscription**.

5. In the **Create subscription** dialog box:

6. For **Topic ARN**, use the following Amazon Resource Name (ARN):

```
1  ```
2  arn:aws:sns:us-east-1:850632864840:AWS-CodeBuild-Local-Agent-Updates
3  ```
```

1. For **Protocol** choose **Email** or **SMS**.

2. For **Endpoint** choose where to receive the notifications:

- If you choose **Email**, type an email address.
- If you choose **SMS**, type a phone number, including area code.

1. Choose **Create subscription**.

2. If you choose **Email**, you'll receive an email asking you to confirm your subscription. Follow the directions in the email to complete your subscription.

When a new version of the AWS CodeBuild agent is released, subscribers receive notifications. If you no longer want to receive these notifications, use the following procedure to unsubscribe.

** To unsubscribe from AWS CodeBuild agent notifications:**

1. Open the Amazon SNS console at https://console.aws.amazon.com/sns/v2/home.

2. In the navigation pane, choose **Subscriptions**.

3. Select the subscription and then from **Actions**, choose **Delete subscriptions**. When you are prompted to confirm, choose **Delete**.

Run AWS CodeBuild Directly

To set up, run, and monitor builds directly with AWS CodeBuild, you can use the AWS CodeBuild console, AWS CLI, or AWS SDK.

Not what you're looking for? To use AWS CodePipeline to run AWS CodeBuild, see Use AWS CodePipeline with AWS CodeBuild.

Topics

- Prerequisites
- Run AWS CodeBuild Directly (Console)
- Run AWS CodeBuild Directly (AWS CLI)

Prerequisites

Answer the questions in Plan a Build.

Run AWS CodeBuild Directly (Console)

1. Create the build project. For information, see Create a Build Project (Console).

2. Run the build. For information, see Run a Build (Console).

3. Get information about the build. For information, see View Build Details (Console).

Run AWS CodeBuild Directly (AWS CLI)

For more information about using the AWS CLI with AWS CodeBuild, see the Command Line Reference.

1. Create the build project. For information, see Create a Build Project (AWS CLI).

2. Run the build. For information, see Run a Build (AWS CLI).

3. Get information about the build. For information, see View Build Details (AWS CLI).

Use AWS CodeBuild with Amazon Virtual Private Cloud

Typically, resources in an VPC are not accessible by AWS CodeBuild. To enable access, you must provide additional VPC-specific configuration information as part of your AWS CodeBuild project configuration. This includes the VPC ID, the VPC subnet IDs, and the VPC security group IDs. VPC-enabled builds are then able to access resources inside your VPC. For more information about setting up a VPC in Amazon VPC, see the VPC User Guide.

Topics

- Use Cases
- Enabling Amazon VPC Access in Your AWS CodeBuild Projects
- Best Practices for VPCs
- Troubleshooting Your VPC Setup
- Use VPC Endpoints
- AWS CloudFormation VPC Template

Use Cases

VPC connectivity from AWS CodeBuild builds makes it possible to:

- Run integration tests from your build against data in an Amazon RDS database that's isolated on a private subnet.
- Query data in an Amazon ElastiCache cluster directly from tests.
- Interact with internal web services hosted on Amazon EC2, Amazon ECS, or services that use internal Elastic Load Balancing.
- Retrieve dependencies from self-hosted, internal artifact repositories, such as PyPI for Python, Maven for Java, and npm for Node.js.
- Access objects in an Amazon S3 bucket configured to allow access through an Amazon VPC endpoint only.
- Query external web services that require fixed IP addresses through the Elastic IP address of the NAT gateway or NAT instance associated with your subnet(s).

Your builds can access any resource that's hosted in your VPC.

Enabling Amazon VPC Access in Your AWS CodeBuild Projects

Include these settings in your VPC configuration:

- For **VPC ID**, choose the VPC ID that AWS CodeBuild uses.
- For **Subnets**, choose the subnets that include resources that AWS CodeBuild uses.
- For **Security Groups**, choose the security groups that AWS CodeBuild uses to allow access to resources in the VPCs.

Create a build project (console)

For information about creating a build project, see Create a Build Project (Console). When you create or change your AWS CodeBuild project, in **VPC**, choose your VPC ID, subnets, and security groups.

Create a build project (AWS CLI)

For information about creating a build project, see Create a Build Project (AWS CLI). If you are using the AWS CLI with AWS CodeBuild, the service role used by AWS CodeBuild to interact with services on behalf of the IAM user must have the following policy attached: Allow AWS CodeBuild Access to AWS Services Required to Create a VPC Network Interface.

The *vpcConfig* object should include your *vpcId*, *securityGroupIds*, and *subnets*.

- *vpcId*: Required value. The VPC ID that AWS CodeBuild uses. To get a list of all Amazon VPC IDs in your region, run this command:

```
1 aws ec2 describe-vpcs
```

- *subnets*: Required value. The subnet IDs that include resources used by AWS CodeBuild. To obtain these IDs, run this command:

```
1 aws ec2 describe-subnets --filters "Name=vpc-id,Values=<vpc-id>" --region us-east-1
```

Note
Replace us-east-1 with your region.

- *securityGroupIds*: Required value. The security group IDs used by AWS CodeBuild to allow access to resources in the VPCs. To obtain these IDs, run this command:

```
1 aws ec2 describe-security-groups --filters "Name=vpc-id,Values=<vpc-id>" --region us-east-1
```

Note
Replace us-east-1 with your region.

Best Practices for VPCs

Use this checklist when setting up a VPC to work with AWS CodeBuild.

- Set up your VPC with public and private subnets and a NAT gateway. For more information, see VPC with Public and Private Subnets (NAT). **Important**
  You need a NAT gateway or NAT instance in order to use AWS CodeBuild with your Amazon VPC so that AWS CodeBuild can reach public endpoints (for example, to execute CLI commands when running builds). You cannot use the internet gateway instead of a NAT gateway or a NAT instance because AWS CodeBuild does not support assigning elastic IP addresses to the network interfaces that it creates, and auto-assigning a public IP address is not supported by Amazon EC2 for any network interfaces created outside of Amazon EC2 instance launches.
- Include multiple Availability Zones with your VPC.
- Make sure that your security groups have no inbound (ingress) traffic allowed to your builds. For more information, see Security Groups Rules.
- Set up separate subnets for your builds.
- When you set up your AWS CodeBuild projects to access your VPC, choose private subnets only.

For more information about setting up a VPC in Amazon VPC, see the Amazon VPC User Guide.

For more information about using AWS CloudFormation to configure an Amazon VPC to use the AWS CodeBuild VPC feature, see the AWS CloudFormation VPC Template.

Troubleshooting Your VPC Setup

When troubleshooting VPC issues, use the information that appears in the error message to help you identify, diagnose, and address issues.

The following are some guidelines to assist you when troubleshooting a common AWS CodeBuild VPC error: "Build does not have internet connectivity. Please check subnet network configuration".

1. Make sure that your internet gateway is attached to VPC.

2. Make sure that the route table for your public subnet points to the internet gateway.

3. Make sure that your network ACLs allow traffic to flow.

4. Make sure that your security groups allow traffic to flow.

5. Troubleshoot your NAT gateway.

6. Make sure that the route table for private subnets points to the NAT gateway.

7. Make sure that the service role used by AWS CodeBuild to interact with services on behalf of the IAM user has the permissions in this policy. For more information, see Create an AWS CodeBuild Service Role.

   If AWS CodeBuild is missing permissions, you might receive an error that says, "Unexpected EC2 error: UnauthorizedOperation." This error can occur if AWS CodeBuild does not have the Amazon EC2 permissions required to work with an Amazon VPC.

Use VPC Endpoints

You can improve the security of your builds by configuring AWS CodeBuild to use an interface VPC endpoint. Interface endpoints are powered by PrivateLink, a technology that enables you to privately access Amazon EC2 and AWS CodeBuild by using private IP addresses. PrivateLink restricts all network traffic between your managed instances, AWS CodeBuild, and Amazon EC2 to the Amazon network (managed instances don't have access to the internet). Also, you don't need an Internet gateway, a NAT device, or a virtual private gateway. You are not required to configure PrivateLink, but it's recommended. For more information about Private Link and VPC endpoints, see Accessing AWS Services Through PrivateLink .

Before You Create VPC Endpoints

Before you configure VPC endpoints for AWS CodeBuild, be aware of the following restrictions and limitations.

Note
The following services must communicate with the internet. You can use VPC endpoints with AWS CodeBuild and these services with an Amazon VPC NAT Gateway.
AWS CodeCommit, which might be a source repository. Amazon ECR, which might be used with a custom Docker image. Active Directory. Amazon CloudWatch Events and Amazon CloudWatch Logs.

- VPC endpoints only support Amazon-provided DNS through Amazon Route 53. If you want to use your own DNS, you can use conditional DNS forwarding. For more information, see DHCP Option Sets in the Amazon VPC User Guide.
- VPC endpoints currently do not support cross-region requests. Ensure that you create your endpoint in the same region as any Amazon S3 buckets that store your build input and output. You can find the location of your bucket by using the by using the Amazon S3 console, or by using the get-bucket-location command. Use a region-specific Amazon S3 endpoint to access your bucket; for example, `mybucket.s3 -us-west-2.amazonaws.com`. For more information about region-specific endpoints for Amazon S3, see Amazon Simple Storage Service (Amazon S3) in Amazon Web Services General Reference*Amazon Web Services General Reference*. If you use the AWS CLI to make requests to Amazon S3, set your default region to the same region as your bucket, or use the `--region` parameter in your requests.

Creating VPC Endpoints for AWS CodeBuild

Use Creating an Interface Endpoint to create the endpoint ** com.amazonaws.*region*.codebuild**. This is a VPC endpoint for the AWS CodeBuild service.

Service Name com.amazonaws.us-west-2.codebuild ⓘ

Service Name	Owner	Type
○ com.amazonaws.us-west-2.cloudformation	amazon	Interface
● com.amazonaws.us-west-2.codebuild	amazon	Interface
○ com.amazonaws.us-west-2.codebuild-fips	amazon	Interface
○ com.amazonaws.us-west-2.dynamodb	amazon	Gateway
○ com.amazonaws.us-west-2.ec2	amazon	Interface

region represents the region identifier for an AWS region supported by AWS CodeBuild, such as `us-east-2` for the US East (Ohio) Region. For a list of supported **region** values, see the Region column in the AWS CodeBuild table of regions and endpoints in the * AWS General Reference*. The endpoint is prepopulated with the region you specified when you logged into AWS. If you change your region, then the VPC endpoint will update with the new region.

AWS CloudFormation VPC Template

AWS CloudFormation enables you to create and provision AWS infrastructure deployments predictably and repeatedly, by using template files to create and delete a collection of resources together as a single unit (a stack). For more information, see the AWS CloudFormation User Guide.

The following is an AWS CloudFormation YAML template for configuring an Amazon VPC to use the AWS CodeBuild VPC feature. It is available for download from https://s3.amazonaws.com/codebuild-cloudformation-templates-public/vpc_cloudformation_template.yml.

```
1  Description:
2
3      This template deploys a VPC, with a pair of public and private subnets spread
4
5      across two Availability Zones. It deploys an Internet Gateway, with a default
6
7      route on the public subnets. It deploys a pair of NAT Gateways (one in each AZ),
8
9      and default routes for them in the private subnets.
10
11
12
13  Parameters:
14
15
16
17      EnvironmentName:
18
19          Description: An environment name that will be prefixed to resource names
20
21          Type: String
22
23
24
25      VpcCIDR:
26
27          Description: Please enter the IP range (CIDR notation) for this VPC
28
29          Type: String
30
31          Default: 10.192.0.0/16
32
33
34
35      PublicSubnet1CIDR:
36
37          Description: Please enter the IP range (CIDR notation) for the public subnet in the
                  first Availability Zone
38
39          Type: String
40
41          Default: 10.192.10.0/24
42
43
44
```

155

```
45    PublicSubnet2CIDR:
46
47        Description: Please enter the IP range (CIDR notation) for the public subnet in the
              second Availability Zone
48
49        Type: String
50
51        Default: 10.192.11.0/24
52
53
54
55    PrivateSubnet1CIDR:
56
57        Description: Please enter the IP range (CIDR notation) for the private subnet in the
              first Availability Zone
58
59        Type: String
60
61        Default: 10.192.20.0/24
62
63
64
65    PrivateSubnet2CIDR:
66
67        Description: Please enter the IP range (CIDR notation) for the private subnet in the
              second Availability Zone
68
69        Type: String
70
71        Default: 10.192.21.0/24
72
73
74
75  Resources:
76
77
78
79    VPC:
80
81        Type: AWS::EC2::VPC
82
83        Properties:
84
85            CidrBlock: !Ref VpcCIDR
86
87            Tags:
88
89                - Key: Name
90
91                  Value: !Ref EnvironmentName
92
93
94
95    InternetGateway:
```

```
96
97      Type: AWS::EC2::InternetGateway
98
99      Properties:
100
101          Tags:
102
103              - Key: Name
104
105                Value: !Ref EnvironmentName
106
107
108
109  InternetGatewayAttachment:
110
111      Type: AWS::EC2::VPCGatewayAttachment
112
113      Properties:
114
115          InternetGatewayId: !Ref InternetGateway
116
117          VpcId: !Ref VPC
118
119
120
121  PublicSubnet1:
122
123      Type: AWS::EC2::Subnet
124
125      Properties:
126
127          VpcId: !Ref VPC
128
129          AvailabilityZone: !Select [ 0, !GetAZs '' ]
130
131          CidrBlock: !Ref PublicSubnet1CIDR
132
133          MapPublicIpOnLaunch: true
134
135          Tags:
136
137              - Key: Name
138
139                Value: !Sub ${EnvironmentName} Public Subnet (AZ1)
140
141
142
143  PublicSubnet2:
144
145      Type: AWS::EC2::Subnet
146
147      Properties:
148
149          VpcId: !Ref VPC
```

```
150
151          AvailabilityZone: !Select [ 1, !GetAZs '' ]
152
153          CidrBlock: !Ref PublicSubnet2CIDR
154
155          MapPublicIpOnLaunch: true
156
157          Tags:
158
159              - Key: Name
160
161                Value: !Sub ${EnvironmentName} Public Subnet (AZ2)
162
163
164
165    PrivateSubnet1:
166
167        Type: AWS::EC2::Subnet
168
169        Properties:
170
171          VpcId: !Ref VPC
172
173          AvailabilityZone: !Select [ 0, !GetAZs '' ]
174
175          CidrBlock: !Ref PrivateSubnet1CIDR
176
177          MapPublicIpOnLaunch: false
178
179          Tags:
180
181              - Key: Name
182
183                Value: !Sub ${EnvironmentName} Private Subnet (AZ1)
184
185
186
187    PrivateSubnet2:
188
189        Type: AWS::EC2::Subnet
190
191        Properties:
192
193          VpcId: !Ref VPC
194
195          AvailabilityZone: !Select [ 1, !GetAZs '' ]
196
197          CidrBlock: !Ref PrivateSubnet2CIDR
198
199          MapPublicIpOnLaunch: false
200
201          Tags:
202
203              - Key: Name
```

```yaml
204
205                     Value: !Sub ${EnvironmentName} Private Subnet (AZ2)
206
207
208
209      NatGateway1EIP:
210
211          Type: AWS::EC2::EIP
212
213          DependsOn: InternetGatewayAttachment
214
215          Properties:
216
217              Domain: vpc
218
219
220
221      NatGateway2EIP:
222
223          Type: AWS::EC2::EIP
224
225          DependsOn: InternetGatewayAttachment
226
227          Properties:
228
229              Domain: vpc
230
231
232
233      NatGateway1:
234
235          Type: AWS::EC2::NatGateway
236
237          Properties:
238
239              AllocationId: !GetAtt NatGateway1EIP.AllocationId
240
241              SubnetId: !Ref PublicSubnet1
242
243
244
245      NatGateway2:
246
247          Type: AWS::EC2::NatGateway
248
249          Properties:
250
251              AllocationId: !GetAtt NatGateway2EIP.AllocationId
252
253              SubnetId: !Ref PublicSubnet2
254
255
256
257      PublicRouteTable:
```

```
    Type: AWS::EC2::RouteTable

    Properties:

        VpcId: !Ref VPC

        Tags:

            - Key: Name

              Value: !Sub ${EnvironmentName} Public Routes



DefaultPublicRoute:

    Type: AWS::EC2::Route

    DependsOn: InternetGatewayAttachment

    Properties:

        RouteTableId: !Ref PublicRouteTable

        DestinationCidrBlock: 0.0.0.0/0

        GatewayId: !Ref InternetGateway



PublicSubnet1RouteTableAssociation:

    Type: AWS::EC2::SubnetRouteTableAssociation

    Properties:

        RouteTableId: !Ref PublicRouteTable

        SubnetId: !Ref PublicSubnet1



PublicSubnet2RouteTableAssociation:

    Type: AWS::EC2::SubnetRouteTableAssociation

    Properties:

        RouteTableId: !Ref PublicRouteTable

        SubnetId: !Ref PublicSubnet2
```

```
312
313
314
315    PrivateRouteTable1:
316
317        Type: AWS::EC2::RouteTable
318
319        Properties:
320
321            VpcId: !Ref VPC
322
323            Tags:
324
325                - Key: Name
326
327                  Value: !Sub ${EnvironmentName} Private Routes (AZ1)
328
329
330
331    DefaultPrivateRoute1:
332
333        Type: AWS::EC2::Route
334
335        Properties:
336
337            RouteTableId: !Ref PrivateRouteTable1
338
339            DestinationCidrBlock: 0.0.0.0/0
340
341            NatGatewayId: !Ref NatGateway1
342
343
344
345    PrivateSubnet1RouteTableAssociation:
346
347        Type: AWS::EC2::SubnetRouteTableAssociation
348
349        Properties:
350
351            RouteTableId: !Ref PrivateRouteTable1
352
353            SubnetId: !Ref PrivateSubnet1
354
355
356
357    PrivateRouteTable2:
358
359        Type: AWS::EC2::RouteTable
360
361        Properties:
362
363            VpcId: !Ref VPC
364
365            Tags:
```

```
366
367                    - Key: Name
368
369                        Value: !Sub ${EnvironmentName} Private Routes (AZ2)
370
371
372
373     DefaultPrivateRoute2:
374
375         Type: AWS::EC2::Route
376
377         Properties:
378
379             RouteTableId: !Ref PrivateRouteTable2
380
381             DestinationCidrBlock: 0.0.0.0/0
382
383             NatGatewayId: !Ref NatGateway2
384
385
386
387     PrivateSubnet2RouteTableAssociation:
388
389         Type: AWS::EC2::SubnetRouteTableAssociation
390
391         Properties:
392
393             RouteTableId: !Ref PrivateRouteTable2
394
395             SubnetId: !Ref PrivateSubnet2
396
397
398
399     NoIngressSecurityGroup:
400
401         Type: AWS::EC2::SecurityGroup
402
403         Properties:
404
405             GroupName: "no-ingress-sg"
406
407             GroupDescription: "Security group with no ingress rule"
408
409             VpcId: !Ref VPC
410
411
412
413 Outputs:
414
415
416
417     VPC:
418
419         Description: A reference to the created VPC
```

```
420
421        Value: !Ref VPC
422
423
424
425    PublicSubnets:
426
427        Description: A list of the public subnets
428
429        Value: !Join [ ",", [ !Ref PublicSubnet1, !Ref PublicSubnet2 ]]
430
431
432
433    PrivateSubnets:
434
435        Description: A list of the private subnets
436
437        Value: !Join [ ",", [ !Ref PrivateSubnet1, !Ref PrivateSubnet2 ]]
438
439
440
441    PublicSubnet1:
442
443        Description: A reference to the public subnet in the 1st Availability Zone
444
445        Value: !Ref PublicSubnet1
446
447
448
449    PublicSubnet2:
450
451        Description: A reference to the public subnet in the 2nd Availability Zone
452
453        Value: !Ref PublicSubnet2
454
455
456
457    PrivateSubnet1:
458
459        Description: A reference to the private subnet in the 1st Availability Zone
460
461        Value: !Ref PrivateSubnet1
462
463
464
465    PrivateSubnet2:
466
467        Description: A reference to the private subnet in the 2nd Availability Zone
468
469        Value: !Ref PrivateSubnet2
470
471
472
473    NoIngressSecurityGroup:
```

```
474
475        Description: Security group with no ingress rule
476
477        Value: !Ref NoIngressSecurityGroup
```

Use AWS CodePipeline with AWS CodeBuild to Test Code and Run Builds

You can automate your release process by using AWS CodePipeline to test your code and run your builds with AWS CodeBuild.

The following table lists tasks and the methods available for performing them. Using the AWS SDKs to accomplish these tasks is outside the scope of this topic.

Task	Available approaches	Approaches described in this topic
Create a continuous delivery (CD) pipeline with AWS CodePipeline that automates builds with AWS CodeBuild	[See the AWS documentation website for more details]	[See the AWS documentation website for more details]
Add test and build automation with AWS CodeBuild to an existing pipeline in AWS CodePipeline	[See the AWS documentation website for more details]	[See the AWS documentation website for more details]

Topics

- Prerequisites
- Create a Pipeline that Uses AWS CodeBuild (AWS CodePipeline Console)
- Create a Pipeline that Uses AWS CodeBuild (AWS CLI)
- Add an AWS CodeBuild Build Action to a Pipeline (AWS CodePipeline Console)
- Add an AWS CodeBuild Test Action to a Pipeline (AWS CodePipeline Console)

Prerequisites

1. Answer the questions in Plan a Build.

2. If you are using an IAM user to access AWS CodePipeline instead of an AWS root account or an administrator IAM user, attach the managed policy named `AWSCodePipelineFullAccess` to the user (or to the IAM group to which the user belongs). (Using an AWS root account is not recommended.) This enables the user to create the pipeline in AWS CodePipeline. For more information, see Attaching Managed Policies in the *IAM User Guide*. **Note**
   The IAM entity that attaches the policy to the user (or to the IAM group to which the user belongs) must have permission in IAM to attach policies. For more information, see Delegating Permissions to Administer IAM Users, Groups, and Credentials in the *IAM User Guide*.

3. Create an AWS CodePipeline service role, if you do not already have one available in your AWS account. This service role enables AWS CodePipeline to interact with other AWS services, including AWS CodeBuild, on your behalf. For example, to create an AWS CodePipeline service role by using the AWS CLI, run the IAM `create-role` command:

For Linux, macOS, or Unix:

```
1 aws iam create-role --role-name AWS-CodePipeline-CodeBuild-Service-Role --assume-role-
    policy-document '{"Version":"2012-10-17","Statement":{"Effect":"Allow","Principal":{"
    Service":"codepipeline.amazonaws.com"},"Action":"sts:AssumeRole"}}'
```

For Windows:

```
1 aws iam create-role --role-name AWS-CodePipeline-CodeBuild-Service-Role --assume-role-
    policy-document "{\"Version\":\"2012-10-17\",\"Statement\":{\"Effect\":\"Allow\",\"
    Principal\":{\"Service\":\"codepipeline.amazonaws.com\"},\"Action\":\"sts:AssumeRole
    \"}}"
```

Note
The IAM entity that creates this AWS CodePipeline service role must have permission in IAM to create service roles.

1. After you create an AWS CodePipeline service role or identify an existing one, you must add a policy statement to it. Add the default AWS CodePipeline service role policy to the service role as described in Review the Default AWS CodePipeline Service Role Policy in the *AWS CodePipeline User Guide*. **Note** The IAM entity that adds this AWS CodePipeline service role policy must have permission in IAM to add service role policies to service roles.

2. Create and upload the source code to a repository type supported by AWS CodeBuild and AWS CodePipeline, such as AWS CodeCommit, Amazon S3, or GitHub. (AWS CodePipeline does not currently support Bitbucket.) Make sure the source code contains a build spec file (or you can declare a build spec when you define a build project later in this topic), which provides instructions for building the source code. For more information, see the Build Spec Reference. **Important**
If you plan to use the pipeline to deploy built source code, then the build output artifact must be compatible with the deployment system you will use.
For AWS CodeDeploy, see the AWS CodeDeploy Sample in this guide and see Prepare a Revision for AWS CodeDeploy in the *AWS CodeDeploy User Guide*. For AWS Elastic Beanstalk, see the Elastic Beanstalk Sample in this guide and see Create an Application Source Bundle in the *AWS Elastic Beanstalk Developer Guide*. For AWS OpsWorks, see Application Source and Using AWS CodePipeline with AWS OpsWorks in the *AWS OpsWorks User Guide*.

Create a Pipeline that Uses AWS CodeBuild (AWS CodePipeline Console)

Use the following procedure to create a pipeline that uses AWS CodeBuild to build and deploy your source code.

To create a pipeline that only tests your source code, your options are to:

- Use the following procedure to create the pipeline, and then delete the Build and Beta stages from the pipeline. Then use the Add an AWS CodeBuild Test Action to a Pipeline (AWS CodePipeline Console) procedure in this topic to add to the pipeline a test action that uses AWS CodeBuild.
- Use one of the other procedures in this topic to create the pipeline, and then use the Add an AWS CodeBuild Test Action to a Pipeline (AWS CodePipeline Console) procedure in this topic to add to the pipeline a test action that uses AWS CodeBuild.

To use the create pipeline wizard in AWS CodePipeline to create a pipeline that uses AWS CodeBuild

1. Complete the steps in Prerequisites.

2. Open the AWS CodePipeline console, at https://console.aws.amazon.com/codepipeline.

   You need to have already signed in to the AWS Management Console by using one of the following:

   - Your AWS root account. This is not recommended. For more information, see The Account Root User in the *IAM User Guide*.

   - An administrator IAM user in your AWS account. For more information, see Creating Your First IAM Admin User and Group in the *IAM User Guide*.

   - An IAM user in your AWS account with permission to use the following minimum set of actions:

```
1 codepipeline:*
2 iam:ListRoles
```

```
3 iam:PassRole
4 s3:CreateBucket
5 s3:GetBucketPolicy
6 s3:GetObject
7 s3:ListAllMyBuckets
8 s3:ListBucket
9 s3:PutBucketPolicy
10 codecommit:ListBranches
11 codecommit:ListRepositories
12 codedeploy:GetApplication
13 codedeploy:GetDeploymentGroup
14 codedeploy:ListApplications
15 codedeploy:ListDeploymentGroups
16 elasticbeanstalk:DescribeApplications
17 elasticbeanstalk:DescribeEnvironments
18 lambda:GetFunctionConfiguration
19 lambda:ListFunctions
20 opsworks:DescribeStacks
21 opsworks:DescribeApps
22 opsworks:DescribeLayers
```

3. In the AWS region selector, choose the region where your pipeline and related AWS resources are located. This region must also support AWS CodeBuild. For more information, see AWS CodeBuild in the "Regions and Endpoints" topic in the *Amazon Web Services General Reference*.

4. Create a pipeline as follows:

   If a welcome page is displayed, choose **Get started**.

   If an **All Pipelines** page is displayed, choose **Create pipeline**.

5. On the **Step 1: Name** page, for **Pipeline name**, type a name for the pipeline; for example, **CodeBuildDemoPipeline**. If you choose a different name, substitute it throughout this procedure. Choose **Next step**.

6. On the **Step 2: Source** page, for **Source provider**, do one of the following:

   - If your source code is stored in an Amazon S3 bucket, choose **Amazon S3**. For **Amazon S3 location**, type the path to the source code, using the format s3://bucket-name/path/to/file-name.zip. Choose **Next step**.
   - If your source code is stored in an AWS CodeCommit repository, choose **AWS CodeCommit**. For **Repository name**, choose the name of the repository that contains the source code. For **Branch name**, choose the name of the branch that represents the version of the source code you want to build. Choose **Next step**.
   - If your source code is stored in a GitHub repository, choose **GitHub**. Choose **Connect to GitHub**, and follow the instructions to authenticate with GitHub. For **Repository**, choose the name of the repository that contains the source code. For **Branch**, choose the name of the branch that represents the version of the source code you want to build. Choose **Next step**.

7. On the **Step 3: Build** page, for **Build provider**, choose **AWS CodeBuild**.

8. If you already have a build project you want to use, choose **Select an existing build project**. For **Project name**, choose the name of the build project, and then skip ahead to step 17 in this procedure. **Note**
   If you choose an existing build project, it must have build output artifact settings already defined (even though AWS CodePipeline will override them). For more information, see the description of **Artifacts: Where to put the artifacts from this build project** in Create a Build Project (Console) or Change a Build Project's Settings (Console). **Important**
   If you enable webhooks for an AWS CodeBuild project, and the project is used as a build step in AWS

CodePipeline, then two identical builds will be created for each commit. One build is triggered through webhooks, and one through AWS CodePipeline. Because billing is on a per-build basis, you will be billed for both builds. Therefore, if you are using AWS CodePipeline, we recommend that you disable webhooks in CodeBuild. In the AWS CodeBuild console, clear the Webhook box. For more information, see step 9 in Change a Build Project's Settings (Console)

9. Choose **Create a new build project**.

10. For **Project name**, type a name for this build project. Build project names must be unique across each AWS account.

11. (Optional) Type a description in the **Description** box.

12. For **Environment image**, do one of the following:

    - To use a build environment based on a Docker image that is managed by AWS CodeBuild, choose **Use an image managed by AWS CodeBuild**. Make your selections from the **Operating system**, **Runtime**, and **Version** drop-down lists. For more information, see Docker Images Provided by AWS CodeBuild.
    - To use a build environment based on a Docker image in an Amazon ECR repository in your AWS account, choose **Specify a Docker image**. For **Custom image type**, choose **Amazon ECR**. Use the **Amazon ECR repository** and **Amazon ECR image** drop-down lists to specify the desired Amazon ECR repository and Docker image in that repository.
    - To use a build environment based on a publicly available Docker image in Docker Hub, choose **Specify a Docker image**. For **Custom image type**, choose **Other**. In the **Custom image ID** box, type the Docker image ID, using the format `docker-repo-name/docker-image-name:tag`.

13. For **Build specification**, do one of the following:

    - If your source code includes a build spec file, choose **Use the buildspec.yml in the source code root directory**.
    - If your source code does not include a build spec file, choose **Insert build commands**. For **Build command**, type the commands you want to run during the build phase in the build environment; for multiple commands, separate each command with **&&** for Linux-based build environments or ; for Windows-based build environments. For **Output files**, type the paths to the build output files in the build environment that you want to send to AWS CodePipeline; for multiple files, separate each file path with a comma. For more information, see the tooltips in the console.

14. For **AWS CodeBuild service role**, do one of the following:

    - If you do not have an AWS CodeBuild service role in your AWS account, choose **Create a service role in your account**. In the **Role name** box, type a name for the service role or leave the suggested name. (Service role names must be unique across your AWS account.) **Note**
      If you use the console to create an AWS CodeBuild service role, by default this service role works with this build project only. If you use the console to associate this service role with another build project, this role will be updated to work with the other build project. A single AWS CodeBuild service role can work with up to ten build projects.
    - If you have an AWS CodeBuild service role in your AWS account, choose **Choose an existing service role from your account**. In the **Role name** box, choose the name of the service role.

15. Expand **Advanced**.

    To specify a build timeout other than 60 minutes (the default), use the **hours** and **minutes** boxes to set a timeout between 5 and 480 minutes (8 hours) .

    Select the **Privileged** check box only if you plan to use this build project to build Docker images, and the build environment image you chose is not one provided by AWS CodeBuild with Docker support. Otherwise, all associated builds that attempt to interact with the Docker daemon will fail. Note that you must also start the Docker daemon so that your builds can interact with it as needed. One way to do this is to initialize the Docker daemon in the `install` phase of your build spec by running the following build commands. (Do not run the following build commands if you chose a build environment image provided by AWS CodeBuild with Docker support.)

```
1 - nohup /usr/local/bin/dockerd --host=unix:///var/run/docker.sock --host=tcp
     ://127.0.0.1:2375 --storage-driver=overlay&
2 - timeout -t 15 sh -c "until docker info; do echo .; sleep 1; done"
```

For **Compute**, choose one of the available options.

For **Environment variables**, use **Name** and **Value** to specify any optional environment variables for the build environment to use. To add more environment variables, choose **Add row. Important**
We strongly discourage using environment variables to store sensitive values, especially AWS access key IDs and secret access keys. Environment variables can be displayed in plain text using tools such as the AWS CodeBuild console and the AWS CLI.
To store and retrieve sensitive values, we recommend your build commands use the AWS CLI to interact with the Amazon EC2 Systems Manager Parameter Store. The AWS CLI comes preinstalled and preconfigured on all build environments provided by AWS CodeBuild. For more information, see Systems Manager Parameter Store and Systems Manager Parameter Store CLI Walkthrough in the *Amazon EC2 Systems Manager User Guide*

16. Choose **Save build project**.

17. After the build project is saved, choose **Next step**.

18. On the **Step 4: Deploy** page, do one of the following:

    - If you do not want to deploy the build output artifact, for **Deployment provider**, choose **No Deployment**.
    - If you want to deploy the build output artifact, for **Deployment provider**, choose a deployment provider, and then specify the settings when prompted.

19. Choose **Next step**.

20. On the **Step 5: Service Role** page, for **Role name**, choose the AWS CodePipeline service role you created or identified as part of this topic's prerequisites.

    Do not use this page to create a AWS CodePipeline service role. If you do, the service role will not have the permissions required to work with AWS CodeBuild.

21. Choose **Next step**.

22. On the **Step 6: Review** page, choose **Create pipeline**.

23. After the pipeline runs successfully, you can get the build output artifact. With the pipeline displayed in the AWS CodePipeline console, in the **Build** action, rest your mouse pointer on the tooltip. Make a note of the value for **Output artifact** (for example, **MyAppBuild**). **Note**
You can also get the build output artifact by choosing the **Build artifacts** link on the build details page in the AWS CodeBuild console. To get to this page, skip the rest of the steps in this procedure, and see View Build Details (Console).

24. Open the Amazon S3 console at https://console.aws.amazon.com/s3/.

25. In the list of buckets, open the bucket used by the pipeline. The name of the bucket should follow the format `codepipeline-region-ID-random-number`. You can use the AWS CLI to run the AWS CodePipeline `get-pipeline` command to get the name of the bucket, where *my-pipeline-name* is the display name of your pipeline:

```
1 aws codepipeline get-pipeline --name my-pipeline-name
```

In the output, the `pipeline` object contains an `artifactStore` object, which contains a `location` value with the name of the bucket.

26. Open the folder that matches the name of your pipeline (depending on the length of the pipeline's name, the folder name might be truncated), and then open the folder matching the value for **Output artifact** that you noted in step 23 of this procedure.

27. Extract the contents of the file. If there are multiple files in that folder, extract the contents of the file with the latest **Last Modified** timestamp. (You might need to give the file the `.zip` extension so that you can work with it in your system's ZIP utility.) The build output artifact will be in the extracted contents of the file.

28. If you instructed AWS CodePipeline to deploy the build output artifact, use the deployment provider's instructions to get to the build output artifact on the deployment targets.

Create a Pipeline that Uses AWS CodeBuild (AWS CLI)

Use the following procedure to create a pipeline that uses AWS CodeBuild to build your source code.

To use the AWS CLI to create a pipeline that deploys your built source code or that only tests your source code, you can adapt the instructions in Edit a Pipeline (AWS CLI) and the AWS CodePipeline Pipeline Structure Reference in the *AWS CodePipeline User Guide*.

1. Complete the steps in Prerequisites.

2. Create or identify a build project in AWS CodeBuild. For more information, see Create a Build Project.
   Important
   The build project must define build output artifact settings (even though AWS CodePipeline will override them). For more information, see the description of `artifacts` in Create a Build Project (AWS CLI).

3. Make sure you have configured the AWS CLI with the AWS access key and AWS secret access key that correspond to one of the IAM entities described in this topic. For more information, see Getting Set Up with the AWS Command Line Interface in the *AWS Command Line Interface User Guide*.

4. Create a JSON-formatted file that represents the structure of the pipeline. Name the file `create-pipeline` `.json` or similar. For example, this JSON-formatted structure creates a pipeline with a source action that references an Amazon S3 input bucket and a build action that uses AWS CodeBuild:

```
1  {
2    "pipeline": {
3      "roleArn": "arn:aws:iam::account-id:role/my-AWS-CodePipeline-service-role-name",
4      "stages": [
5        {
6          "name": "Source",
7          "actions": [
8            {
9              "inputArtifacts": [],
10             "name": "Source",
11             "actionTypeId": {
12               "category": "Source",
13               "owner": "AWS",
14               "version": "1",
15               "provider": "S3"
16             },
17             "outputArtifacts": [
18               {
19                 "name": "MyApp"
20               }
21             ],
22             "configuration": {
23               "S3Bucket": "my-input-bucket-name",
```

170

```
 24                    "S3ObjectKey": "my-source-code-file-name.zip"
 25                  },
 26                  "runOrder": 1
 27                }
 28              ]
 29            },
 30            {
 31              "name": "Build",
 32              "actions": [
 33                {
 34                  "inputArtifacts": [
 35                    {
 36                      "name": "MyApp"
 37                    }
 38                  ],
 39                  "name": "Build",
 40                  "actionTypeId": {
 41                    "category": "Build",
 42                    "owner": "AWS",
 43                    "version": "1",
 44                    "provider": "AWS CodeBuild"
 45                  },
 46                  "outputArtifacts": [
 47                {
 48                      "name": "default"
 49                    }
 50              ],
 51                  "configuration": {
 52                    "ProjectName": "my-build-project-name"
 53                  },
 54                  "runOrder": 1
 55                }
 56              ]
 57            }
 58          ],
 59          "artifactStore": {
 60            "type": "S3",
 61            "location": "AWS-CodePipeline-internal-bucket-name"
 62          },
 63          "name": "my-pipeline-name",
 64          "version": 1
 65        }
 66    }
```

In this JSON-formatted data:

- The value of `roleArn` must match the ARN of the AWS CodePipeline service role you created or identified as part of the prerequisites.
- The values of `S3Bucket` and `S3ObjectKey` in `configuration` assume the source code is stored in an Amazon S3 bucket. For settings for other source code repository types, see the AWS CodePipeline Pipeline Structure Reference in the *AWS CodePipeline User Guide*.
- The value of `ProjectName` is the name of the AWS CodeBuild build project you created earlier in this procedure.
- The value of `location` is the name of the Amazon S3 bucket used by this pipeline. For more information, see Create a Policy for an Amazon S3 Bucket to Use as the Artifact Store for AWS

CodePipeline in the *AWS CodePipeline User Guide.*
- The value of **name** is the name of this pipeline. All pipeline names must be unique to your account.

Although this data describes only a source action and a build action, you can add actions for activities related to testing, deploying the build output artifact, invoking AWS Lambda functions, and more. For more information, see the AWS CodePipeline Pipeline Structure Reference in the *AWS CodePipeline User Guide.*

5. Switch to the folder that contains the JSON file, and then run the AWS CodePipeline [create\-pipeline](http://docs.aws.amazon.com/cli/latest/reference/codepipeline/create-pipeline.html) command, specifying the file name:

```
1 aws codepipeline create-pipeline --cli-input-json file://create-pipeline.json
```

Note
You must create the pipeline in an AWS region that supports AWS CodeBuild. For more information, see AWS CodeBuild in the "Regions and Endpoints" topic in the *Amazon Web Services General Reference.*

The JSON-formatted data appears in the output, and AWS CodePipeline creates the pipeline.

1. To get information about the pipeline's status, run the AWS CodePipeline [get\-pipeline\-state](http://docs.aws.amazon.com/cli/latest/reference/codepipeline/get-pipeline-state.html) command, specifying the name of the pipeline:

```
1 aws codepipeline get-pipeline-state --name my-pipeline-name
```

In the output, look for information that confirms the build was successful. Ellipses (...) are used to show data that has been omitted for brevity.

```
1  {
2    ...
3    "stageStates": [
4      ...
5      {
6        "actionStates": [
7          {
8            "actionName": "AWS CodeBuild",
9            "latestExecution": {
10             "status": "SUCCEEDED",
11             ...
12           },
13           ...
14         }
15       ]
16     }
17   ]
18 }
```

If you run this command too early, you might not see any information about the build action. You might need to run this command multiple times until the pipeline has finished running the build action.

2. After a successful build, follow these instructions to get the build output artifact. Open the Amazon S3 console at https://console.aws.amazon.com/s3/. **Note**
You can also get the build output artifact by choosing the **Build artifacts** link on the related build details page in the AWS CodeBuild console. To get to this page, skip the rest of the steps in this procedure, and see View Build Details (Console).

3. In the list of buckets, open the bucket used by the pipeline. The name of the bucket should follow the format **codepipeline-region-ID-random-number.** You can get the bucket name from the **create-**

`pipeline.json` file or you can run the AWS CodePipeline `get-pipeline` command to get the bucket's name.

```
1 aws codepipeline get-pipeline --name my-pipeline-name
```

In the output, the `pipeline` object contains an `artifactStore` object, which contains a `location` value with the name of the bucket.

4. Open the folder that matches the name of your pipeline (for example, `my-pipeline-name`).

5. In that folder, open the folder named `default`.

6. Extract the contents of the file. If there are multiple files in that folder, extract the contents of the file with the latest **Last Modified** timestamp. (You might need to give the file a `.zip` extension so that you can work with it in your system's ZIP utility.) The build output artifact will be in the extracted contents of the file.

Add an AWS CodeBuild Build Action to a Pipeline (AWS CodePipeline Console)

1. Open the AWS CodePipeline console at https://console.aws.amazon.com/codepipeline.

   You should have already signed in to the AWS Management Console by using one of the following:

   - Your AWS root account. This is not recommended. For more information, see The Account Root User in the *IAM User Guide*.

   - An administrator IAM user in your AWS account. For more information, see Creating Your First IAM Admin User and Group in the *IAM User Guide*.

   - An IAM user in your AWS account with permission to perform the following minimum set of actions:
   ```
   1  codepipeline:*
   2  iam:ListRoles
   3  iam:PassRole
   4  s3:CreateBucket
   5  s3:GetBucketPolicy
   6  s3:GetObject
   7  s3:ListAllMyBuckets
   8  s3:ListBucket
   9  s3:PutBucketPolicy
   10 codecommit:ListBranches
   11 codecommit:ListRepositories
   12 codedeploy:GetApplication
   13 codedeploy:GetDeploymentGroup
   14 codedeploy:ListApplications
   15 codedeploy:ListDeploymentGroups
   16 elasticbeanstalk:DescribeApplications
   17 elasticbeanstalk:DescribeEnvironments
   18 lambda:GetFunctionConfiguration
   19 lambda:ListFunctions
   20 opsworks:DescribeStacks
   21 opsworks:DescribeApps
   22 opsworks:DescribeLayers
   ```

2. In the AWS region selector, choose the region where your pipeline is located. This region must also support AWS CodeBuild. For more information, see AWS CodeBuild in the "Regions and Endpoints" topic in the *Amazon Web Services General Reference*.

3. On the **All Pipelines** page, choose the name of the pipeline.

4. On the pipeline details page, in the **Source** action, rest your mouse pointer on the tooltip. Make a note of the value for **Output artifact** (for example, **MyApp**):

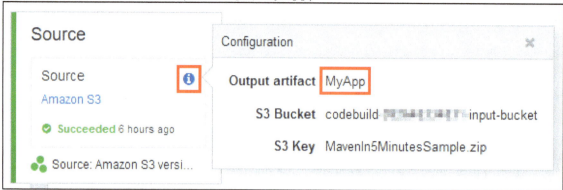

Note

This procedure assumes you want to add a build action inside of a build stage between the **Source** and **Beta** stages. If you want to add the build action somewhere else, rest your mouse pointer on the action just before the place where you want to add the build action, and make a note of the value for **Output artifact**.

5. Choose **Edit**.

6. Between the **Source** and **Beta** stages, choose the add symbol (+) next to **Stage**. **Note**
   This procedure assumes you want to add a new build stage to your pipeline. To add a build action to an existing stage, choose the edit (pencil) icon in the existing stage, and then skip to step 8 of this procedure. This procedure also assumes you want to add a build stage between the **Source** and **Beta** stages. To add the build stage somewhere else, choose the add symbol in the desired place.

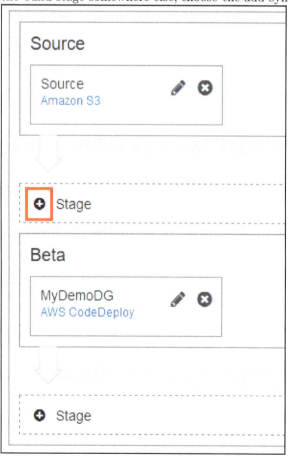

7. For **Enter stage name**, type the name of the build stage (for example, **Build**). If you choose a different name, use it throughout this procedure.

8. Inside of the selected stage, choose the add symbol (+) next to **Action**. **Note**
   This procedure assumes you want to add the build action inside of a build stage. To add the build action somewhere else, choose the add symbol in the desired place. You might first need to choose the edit (pencil) icon in the existing stage where you want to add the build action.

9. In the **Add action** pane, for **Action category**, choose **Build**.

10. In **Build actions**, for **Action name**, type a name for the action (for example, **AWS CodeBuild**). If you choose a different name, use it throughout this procedure.

11. For **Build provider**, choose **AWS CodeBuild**.

12. If you already have a build project in AWS CodeBuild, choose **Select an existing build project**. For **Project name**, choose the name of the build project, and then skip to step 21 of this procedure. **Note**
    If you choose an existing build project, it must have build output artifact settings already defined (even though AWS CodePipeline will override them). For more information, see the description of **Artifacts: Where to put the artifacts from this build project** in Create a Build Project (Console) or Change a Build Project's Settings (Console). **Important**
    If you enable webhooks for an AWS CodeBuild project, and the project is used as a build step in AWS CodePipeline, then two identical builds will be created for each commit. One build is triggered through webhooks; and one through AWS CodePipeline. Because billing is on a per-build basis, you will be billed for both builds. Therefore, if you are using AWS CodePipeline, we recommend that you disable webhooks in CodeBuild. In the AWS CodeBuild console, uncheck the webhook box. For more information, see step 9 in Change a Build Project's Settings (Console)

13. Choose **Create a new build project**.

14. For **Project name**, type a name for this build project. Build project names must be unique across each AWS account.

15. (Optional) Type a description in the **Description** box.

16. For **Environment image**, do one of the following:

    - To use a build environment based on a Docker image that is managed by AWS CodeBuild, choose **Use an image managed by AWS CodeBuild**. Make your selections from the **Operating system**, **Runtime**, and **Version** drop-down lists. For more information, see Docker Images Provided by AWS CodeBuild.

    - To use a build environment based on a Docker image in an Amazon ECR repository in your AWS account, choose **Specify a Docker image**. For **Custom image type**, choose **Amazon ECR**. Use the **Amazon ECR repository** and **Amazon ECR image** drop-down lists to specify the desired Amazon ECR repository and Docker image in that repository.

    - To use a build environment based on a Docker image in Docker Hub, choose **Specify a Docker image**. For **Custom image type**, choose **Other**. In the **Custom image ID** box, type the Docker image ID, using the format `docker-repo-name/docker-image-name:tag`.

17. For **Build specification**, do one of the following:

- If your source code includes a build spec file, choose **Use the buildspec.yml in the source code root directory**.
- If your source code does not include a build spec file, choose **Insert build commands**. For **Build command**, type the commands you want to run during the build phase in the build environment; for multiple commands, separate each command with **&&** for Linux-based build environments or ; for Windows-based build environments. For **Output files**, type the paths to the build output files in the build environment that you want to send to AWS CodePipeline; for multiple files, separate each file path with a comma. For more information, see the tooltips in the console.

18. For **AWS CodeBuild service role**, do one of the following:

- If you do not have an AWS CodeBuild service role in your AWS account, choose **Create a service role in your account**. In the **Role name** box, type a name for the service role or leave the suggested name. (Service role names must be unique across your AWS account.) **Note**
  If you use the console to create an AWS CodeBuild service role, by default this service role works with this build project only. If you use the console to associate this service role with another build project, this role will be updated to work with the other build project. A single AWS CodeBuild service role can work with up to ten build projects.
- If you have an AWS CodeBuild service role in your AWS account, choose **Choose an existing service role from your account**. In the **Role name** box, choose the name of the service role.

19. Expand **Advanced**.

To specify a build timeout other than 60 minutes (the default), use the **hours** and **minutes** boxes to specify a timeout between 5 and 480 minutes (8 hours).

For **Compute**, choose one of the available options.

Select the **Privileged** check box only if you plan to use this build project to build Docker images, and the build environment image you chose is not one provided by AWS CodeBuild with Docker support. Otherwise, all associated builds that attempt to interact with the Docker daemon will fail. Note that you must also start the Docker daemon so that your builds can interact with it as needed. One way to do this is to initialize the Docker daemon in the `install` phase of your build spec by running the following build commands. (Do not run the following build commands if you chose a build environment image provided by AWS CodeBuild with Docker support.)

```
1 - nohup /usr/local/bin/dockerd --host=unix:///var/run/docker.sock --host=tcp
      ://127.0.0.1:2375 --storage-driver=overlay&
2 - timeout -t 15 sh -c "until docker info; do echo .; sleep 1; done"
```

For **Environment variables**, use **Name** and **Value** to specify any optional environment variables for the build environment to use. To add more environment variables, choose **Add row. Important**
We strongly discourage using environment variables to store sensitive values, especially AWS access key IDs and secret access keys. Environment variables can be displayed in plain text using tools such as the AWS CodeBuild console and the AWS CLI.
To store and retrieve sensitive values, we recommend your build commands use the AWS CLI to interact with the Amazon EC2 Systems Manager Parameter Store. The AWS CLI comes preinstalled and preconfigured on all build environments provided by AWS CodeBuild. For more information, see Systems Manager Parameter Store and Systems Manager Parameter Store CLI Walkthrough in the *Amazon EC2 Systems Manager User Guide*

20. Choose **Save build project**.

21. For **Input artifact #1**, type the value of **Output artifact** that you noted in step 4 of this procedure.

22. For **Output artifact #1**, type a name for the output artifact (for example, **MyAppBuild**).

23. Choose **Add action**.

24. Choose **Save pipeline changes**, and then choose **Save and continue**.

25. Choose **Release change**.

26. After the pipeline runs successfully, you can get the build output artifact. With the pipeline displayed in the AWS CodePipeline console, in the **Build** action, rest your mouse pointer on the tooltip. Make a note of the value for **Output artifact** (for example, **MyAppBuild**). **Note**
You can also get the build output artifact by choosing the **Build artifacts** link on the build details page in the AWS CodeBuild console. To get to this page, see View Build Details (Console), and then skip to step 31 of this procedure.

27. Open the Amazon S3 console at https://console.aws.amazon.com/s3/.

28. In the list of buckets, open the bucket used by the pipeline. The name of the bucket should follow the format **codepipeline-region-ID-random-number**. You can use the AWS CLI to run the AWS CodePipeline **get-pipeline** command to get the name of the bucket:

```
1 aws codepipeline get-pipeline --name my-pipeline-name
```

In the output, the `pipeline` object contains an `artifactStore` object, which contains a `location` value with the name of the bucket.

29. Open the folder that matches the name of your pipeline (depending on the length of the pipeline's name, the folder name might be truncated), and then open the folder matching the value for **Output artifact** that you noted in step 26 of this procedure.

30. Extract the contents of the file. If there are multiple files in that folder, extract the contents of the file with the latest **Last Modified** timestamp. (You might need to give the file the `.zip` extension so that you can work with it in your system's ZIP utility.) The build output artifact will be in the extracted contents of the file.

31. If you instructed AWS CodePipeline to deploy the build output artifact, use the deployment provider's instructions to get to the build output artifact on the deployment targets.

Add an AWS CodeBuild Test Action to a Pipeline (AWS CodePipeline Console)

1. Open the AWS CodePipeline console at https://console.aws.amazon.com/codepipeline.

   You should have already signed in to the AWS Management Console by using one of the following:

   - Your AWS root account. This is not recommended. For more information, see The Account Root User in the *IAM User Guide*.

   - An administrator IAM user in your AWS account. For more information, see Creating Your First IAM Admin User and Group in the *IAM User Guide*.

   - An IAM user in your AWS account with permission to perform the following minimum set of actions:

```
1  codepipeline:*
2  iam:ListRoles
3  iam:PassRole
4  s3:CreateBucket
5  s3:GetBucketPolicy
6  s3:GetObject
7  s3:ListAllMyBuckets
8  s3:ListBucket
9  s3:PutBucketPolicy
10 codecommit:ListBranches
11 codecommit:ListRepositories
12 codedeploy:GetApplication
```

```
13 codedeploy:GetDeploymentGroup
14 codedeploy:ListApplications
15 codedeploy:ListDeploymentGroups
16 elasticbeanstalk:DescribeApplications
17 elasticbeanstalk:DescribeEnvironments
18 lambda:GetFunctionConfiguration
19 lambda:ListFunctions
20 opsworks:DescribeStacks
21 opsworks:DescribeApps
22 opsworks:DescribeLayers
```

2. In the AWS region selector, choose the region where your pipeline is located. This region must also support AWS CodeBuild. For more information, see AWS CodeBuild in the "Regions and Endpoints" topic in the *Amazon Web Services General Reference*.

3. On the **All Pipelines** page, choose the name of the pipeline.

4. On the pipeline details page, in the **Source** action, rest your mouse pointer on the tooltip. Make a note of the value for **Output artifact** (for example, **MyApp**):

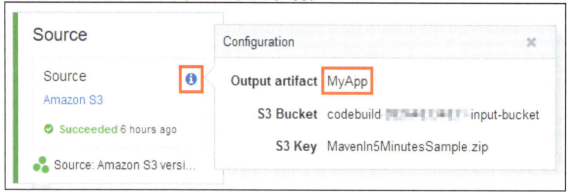

Note

This procedure assumes you want to add a test action inside of a test stage between the **Source** and **Beta** stages. If you want to add the test action somewhere else, rest your mouse pointer on the action just before, and make a note of the value for **Output artifact**.

5. Choose **Edit**.

6. Immediately after the **Source** stage, choose add (+) next to **Stage**. **Note**
This procedure assumes you want to add a test stage to your pipeline. To add a test action to an existing stage, choose the edit (pencil) icon in the existing stage, and then skip to step 8 of this procedure.
This procedure also assumes you want to add a test stage immediately after the **Source** stage. To add the test stage somewhere else, choose the add symbol in the desired place.

7. For **Enter stage name**, type the name of the test stage (for example, **Test**). If you choose a different name, use it throughout this procedure.

8. Inside of the selected stage, choose add (**+**) next to **Action**. **Note**
This procedure assumes you want to add the test action inside of a test stage. To add the test action somewhere else, choose the add symbol in the desired place. You might first need to choose the edit (pencil) icon in the existing stage where you want to add the test action.

9. In the **Add action** pane, for **Action category**, choose **Test**.

10. In **Test actions**, for **Action name**, type a name for the action (for example, **Test**). If you choose a different name, use it throughout this procedure.

11. For **Test provider**, choose **AWS CodeBuild**.

12. If you already have a build project in AWS CodeBuild, choose **Select an existing build project**. For **Project name**, choose the name of the build project, and then skip to step 21 of this procedure. **Important**
If you enable webhooks for an AWS CodeBuild project, and the project is used as a build step in AWS CodePipeline, then two identical builds will be created for each commit. One build is triggered through webhooks; and one through AWS CodePipeline. Because billing is on a per-build basis, you will be billed for both builds. Therefore, if you are using AWS CodePipeline, we recommend that you disable webhooks in CodeBuild. In the AWS CodeBuild console, clear the webhook box. For more information, see step 9 in Change a Build Project's Settings (Console)

13. Choose **Create a new build project**.

14. For **Project name**, type a name for this build project. Build project names must be unique across each AWS account.

15. (Optional) Type a description in the **Description** box.

16. For **Environment image**, do one of the following:

179

- To use a build environment based on a Docker image that is managed by AWS CodeBuild, choose **Use an image managed by AWS CodeBuild**. Make your selections from the **Operating system**, **Runtime**, and **Version** drop-down lists. For more information, see Docker Images Provided by AWS CodeBuild.
- To use a build environment based on a Docker image in an Amazon ECR repository in your AWS account, choose **Specify a Docker image**. For **Custom image type**, choose **Amazon ECR**. Use the **Amazon ECR repository** and **Amazon ECR image** drop-down lists to specify the desired Amazon ECR repository and Docker image in that repository.
- To use a build environment based on a Docker image in Docker Hub, choose **Specify a Docker image**. For **Custom image type**, choose **Other**. In the **Custom image ID** box, type the Docker image ID, using the format `docker-repo-name/docker-image-name:tag`.

17. For **Build specification**, do one of the following:

   - If your source code includes a build spec file, choose **Use the buildspec.yml in the source code root directory**.
   - If your source code does not include a build spec file, choose **Insert build commands**. For **Build command**, type the commands you want to run during the build phase in the build environment. For multiple commands, separate each command with **&&** for Linux-based build environments or ; for Windows-based build environments. For **Output files**, type the paths to the build output files in the build environment that you want to send to AWS CodePipeline. For multiple files, separate each file path with a comma. For more information, see the tooltips in the console.

18. For **AWS CodeBuild service role**, do one of the following:

   - If you do not have an AWS CodeBuild service role in your AWS account, choose **Create a service role in your account**. In the **Role name** box, type a name for the service role or leave the suggested name. (Service role names must be unique across your AWS account.) **Note**
     If you use the console to create an AWS CodeBuild service role, by default, this service role works with this build project only. If you use the console to associate this service role with another build project, this role will be updated to work with the other build project. A single AWS CodeBuild service role can work with up to ten build projects.
   - If you have an AWS CodeBuild service role in your AWS account, choose **Choose an existing service role from your account**. In the **Role name** box, choose the name of the service role.

19. (Optional) Expand **Advanced**.

   To specify a build timeout other than 60 minutes (the default), use the **hours** and **minutes** boxes to specify a timeout between 5 and 480 minutes (8 hours).

   Select the **Privileged** check box only if you plan to use this build project to build Docker images, and the build environment image you chose is not one provided by AWS CodeBuild with Docker support. Otherwise, all associated builds that attempt to interact with the Docker daemon will fail. Note that you must also start the Docker daemon so that your builds can interact with it as needed. One way to do this is to initialize the Docker daemon in the `install` phase of your build spec by running the following build commands. (Do not run the following build commands if you chose a build environment image provided by AWS CodeBuild with Docker support.)

```
1 - nohup /usr/local/bin/dockerd --host=unix:///var/run/docker.sock --host=tcp
      ://127.0.0.1:2375 --storage-driver=overlay&
2 - timeout -t 15 sh -c "until docker info; do echo .; sleep 1; done"
```

   For **Compute**, choose one of the available options.

   For **Environment variables**, use **Name** and **Value** to specify any optional environment variables for the build environment to use. To add more environment variables, choose **Add row**. **Important**
   We strongly discourage using environment variables to store sensitive values, especially AWS access key IDs and secret access keys. Environment variables can be displayed in plain text using tools such as the AWS CodeBuild console and the AWS CLI.

To store and retrieve sensitive values, we recommend your build commands use the AWS CLI to interact with the Amazon EC2 Systems Manager Parameter Store. The AWS CLI comes preinstalled and preconfigured on all build environments provided by AWS CodeBuild. For more information, see Systems Manager Parameter Store and Systems Manager Parameter Store CLI Walkthrough in the *Amazon EC2 Systems Manager User Guide*

20. Choose **Save build project**.

21. For **Input artifacts #1**, type the **Output artifact** value you noted in step 4 of this procedure.

22. (Optional) If you want your test action to produce an output artifact, and you set up your build spec accordingly, then for **Output artifact #1**, type the value you want to assign to the output artifact.

23. Choose **Add action**.

24. Choose **Save pipeline changes**, and then choose **Save and continue**.

25. Choose **Release change**.

26. After the pipeline runs successfully, you can get the test results. In the pipeline's **Test** stage, choose the **AWS CodeBuild** hyperlink to open the related build project page in the AWS CodeBuild console.

27. On the build project page, in the **Build history** area, choose the related **Build run** hyperlink.

28. On the build run page, in the **Build logs** area, choose the **View entire log** hyperlink to open the related build log in the Amazon CloudWatch console.

29. Scroll through the build log to view the test results.

Use AWS CodeBuild with Jenkins

The Jenkins plugin for AWS CodeBuild enables you to integrate AWS CodeBuild with your Jenkins build jobs. Instead of sending your build jobs to Jenkins build nodes, you use the plugin to send your build jobs to AWS CodeBuild. This eliminates the need for you to provision, configure, and manage Jenkins build nodes.

Setting Up Jenkins

For information about setting up Jenkins with the AWS CodeBuild plugin, see the Simplify Your Jenkins Builds with AWS CodeBuild blog post on the AWS DevOps Blog. You can download the AWS CodeBuild Jenkins from https://github.com/awslabs/aws-codebuild-jenkins-plugin.

Installing the Plugin

If you already have a Jenkins set up and would like to only install the AWS CodeBuild plugin, then on your Jenkins instance, in the Plugin Manager, search for "AWS CodeBuild Plugin for Jenkins" .

Using the Plugin

To use AWS CodeBuild with sources from outside of an Amazon VPC

1. Create a project in the AWS CodeBuild console. For more information, see Create a Build Project (Console).

   - Choose the region where you want to run the build.
   - (Optional) Set the Amazon VPC configuration to allow the AWS CodeBuild build container to access resources in your Amazon VPC.
   - Write down the name of your project. You need it in step 3.
   - (Optional) If your source repository is not natively supported by AWS CodeBuild, you can set Amazon S3 as the input source type for your project.

2. In the IAMconsole, create an IAM user to be used by the Jenkins plugin.

   - When you create credentials for the user, choose **Programmatic Access**.

   - Create a policy similar to the following and then attach the policy to your user.

```
1  {
2    "Version": "2012-10-17",
3    "Statement": [
4        {
5            "Effect": "Allow",
6            "Resource": ["arn:aws:logs:{{region}}:{{awsAccountId}}:log-group:/aws/
                  codebuild/{{projectName}}:*"],
7            "Action": ["logs:GetLogEvents"]
8        },
9        {
10           "Effect": "Allow",
11           "Resource": ["arn:aws:s3:::{{inputBucket}}"],
12           "Action": ["s3:GetBucketVersioning"]
13       },
14       {
15           "Effect": "Allow",
16           "Resource": ["arn:aws:s3:::{{inputBucket}}/{{inputObject}}"],
```

```
17        "Action": ["s3:PutObject"]
18    },
19    {
20        "Effect": "Allow",
21        "Resource": ["arn:aws:s3:::{{outputBucket}}/*"],
22        "Action": ["s3:GetObject"]
23    },
24    {
25        "Effect": "Allow",
26        "Resource": ["arn:aws:codebuild:{{region}}:{{awsAccountId}}:project/{{
               projectName}}"],
27        "Action": ["codebuild:StartBuild",
28                   "codebuild:BatchGetBuilds",
29                   "codebuild:BatchGetProjects"]
30    }
31    ]
32    }
```

3. Create a freestyle project in Jenkins.

   - On the **Configure** page, choose **Add build step**, and then choose **Run build on AWS CodeBuild**.
   - Configure your build step.
     - Provide values for **Region**, **Credentials**, and **Project Name**.
     - Choose **Use Project source**.
     - Save the configuration and run a build from Jenkins.

4. For **Source Code Management**, choose how you want to retrieve your source. You might need to install the GitHub plugin (or the Jenkins plugin for your source repository provider) on your Jenkins server.

   - On the **Configure** page, choose **Add build step**, and then choose **Run build on AWS CodeBuild**.
   - Configure your build step.
     - Provide values for **Region**, **Credentials**, and **Project Name**.
     - Choose **Use Jenkins source**.
     - Save the configuration and run a build from Jenkins.

To use the AWS CodeBuild plugin with the Jenkins Pipeline plugin

   - On your Jenkins pipeline project page, use the snippet generator to generate a pipeline script that adds AWS CodeBuild as a step in your pipeline. It should generate a script similar to this:

```
1 awsCodeBuild projectName: 'project', credentialsType: 'keys', region: 'us-west-2',
    sourceControlType: 'jenkins'
```

Working with Build Projects and Builds in AWS CodeBuild

To get started, follow the steps in Create a Build Project, and then follow the steps in Run a Build. For more information about build projects and builds, see the following topics.

Topics

- Working with Build Projects
- Working with Builds in AWS CodeBuild

Working with Build Projects

A *build project* defines how AWS CodeBuild will run a build. It includes information such as where to get the source code, the build environment to use, the build commands to run, and where to store the build output.

You can perform these tasks when working with build projects:

Topics

- Create a Build Project in AWS CodeBuild
- View a List of Build Project Names in AWS CodeBuild
- View a Build Project's Details in AWS CodeBuild
- Create AWS CodeBuild Triggers
- Edit AWS CodeBuild Triggers
- Change a Build Project's Settings in AWS CodeBuild
- Delete a Build Project in AWS CodeBuild

Create a Build Project in AWS CodeBuild

You can use the AWS CodeBuild console, AWS CLI, or AWS SDKs to create a build project.

Topics

- Prerequisites
- Create a Build Project (Console)
- Create a Build Project (AWS CLI)
- Create a Build Project (AWS SDKs)
- Create a Build Project (AWS CloudFormation)

Prerequisites

Answer the questions in Plan a Build.

Create a Build Project (Console)

1. Open the AWS CodeBuild console at https://console.aws.amazon.com/codebuild/.

2. If a welcome page is displayed, choose **Get started**.

   If a welcome page is not displayed, on the navigation pane, choose **Build projects**, and then choose **Create project**.

3. On the **Configure your project** page, for **Project name**, type a name for this build project. Build project names must be unique across each AWS account.

4. (Optional) Choose **Add description**, and type a description in the **Description** box.

5. In **Source: What to build**, for **Source provider**, choose the source code provider type. Use the following table to make selections appopropriate for your source provider:

   _____

[See the AWS documentation website for more details]

1. In **Environment: How to build**:

   For **Environment image**, do one of the following:

   - To use a Docker image managed by AWS CodeBuild, choose **Use an image managed by AWS CodeBuild**, and then make selections from **Operating system**, **Runtime**, and **Version**.
   - To use another Docker image, choose **Specify a Docker image**. For **Custom image type**, choose **Other** or **Amazon ECR**. If you choose **Other**, then for **Custom image ID**, type the name and tag of the Docker image in Docker Hub, using the format `repository-name/image-name:image-tag`. If you choose **Amazon ECR**, then use **Amazon ECR repository** and **Amazon ECR image** to choose the Docker image in your AWS account.

   For **Build specification**, do one of the following:

   - If your source code includes a build spec file, choose **Use the buildspec.yml in the source code root directory**.
   - If your source code does not include a build spec file, or if you want to run build commands different from the ones specified for the `build` phase in the `buildspec.yml` file in the source code's root directory, choose **Insert build commands**. For **Build command**, type the commands you want to run in the `build` phase. For multiple commands, separate each command by **&&** (for example, `mvn test && mvn package`). To run commands in other phases, or if you have a long list of commands

for the `build` phase, add a `buildspec.yml` file to the source code root directory, add the commands to the file, and then choose **Use the buildspec.yml in the source code root directory**.

For more information, see the Build Spec Reference.

2. In **Artifacts: Where to put the artifacts from this build project**, for **Artifacts type**, do one of the following:

   - If you do not want to create any build output artifacts, choose **No artifacts**. You might want to do this if you're only running build tests or you want to push a Docker image to an Amazon ECR repository.
   - To store the build output in an Amazon S3 bucket, choose **Amazon S3**, and then do the following:
     - If you want to use your project name for the build output ZIP file or folder, leave **Artifacts name** blank. Otherwise, type the name in the **Artifacts name** box. (If you want to output a ZIP file, and you want the ZIP file to have a file extension, be sure to include it after the ZIP file name.)
     - For **Bucket name**, choose the name of the output bucket.
     - If you chose **Insert build commands** earlier in this procedure, then for **Output files**, type the locations of the files from the build that you want to put into the build output ZIP file or folder. For multiple locations, separate each location with a comma (for example, `appspec.yml, target/my-app.jar`). For more information, see the description of `files` in Build Spec Syntax.

3. In **Cache**, do one of the following:

   - If you do not want to use a cache, choose **No cache**.
   - To use a cache, choose **Amazon S3**, and then do the following:
     - For **Bucket**, choose the name of the Amazon S3 bucket where the cache is stored.
     - (Optional) For **Path prefix**, type an Amazon S3 path prefix. The **Path prefix** value is similar to a directory name that enables you to store the cache under the same directory in a bucket. **Important**
       Do not append "/" to the end of **Path prefix**.

Using a cache saves considerable build time because reusable pieces of the build environment are stored in the cache and used across builds. For information about specifying a cache in the build spec file, see Build Spec Syntax.

4. In **Service role**, do one of the following:

   - If you do not have an AWS CodeBuild service role, choose **Create a service role in your account**. In **Role name**, accept the default name or type your own.
   - If you have an AWS CodeBuild service role, choose **Choose an service existing role from your account**. In **Role name**, choose the service role. **Note**
     When you use the console to create or update a build project, you can create an AWS CodeBuild service role at the same time. By default, the role works with that build project only. If you use the console to associate this service role with another build project, the role is updated to work with the other build project. A service role can work with up to 10 build projects.

5. In **VPC**, do one of the following:

   - If you are not using a VPC for your project, choose **No VPC**.
   - If you are using want AWS CodeBuild to work with your VPC:
     - For **VPC**, choose the VPC ID that AWS CodeBuild uses.
     - For **Subnets**, choose the subnets that include resources that AWS CodeBuild uses.
     - For **Security Groups**, choose the security groups that AWS CodeBuild uses to allow access to resources in the VPCs.

For more information, see Use AWS CodeBuild with Amazon Virtual Private Cloud.

6. Expand **Show advanced settings**. **Note**

If you arrived at this page by choosing **Get started** from a welcome page, then the **Show advanced settings** section is not displayed. Skip to step 20 of this procedure. For information about changing default settings, see Change a Build Project's Settings (Console).

7. (Optional) For **Timeout**, specify a value between 5 minutes and 480 minutes (8 hours) after which AWS CodeBuild stops the build if it is not complete. If **hours** and **minutes** are left blank, the default value of 60 minutes is used.

8. (Optional) For **Encryption key**, do one of the following:

   - To use the AWS-managed customer master key (CMK) for Amazon S3 in your account to encrypt the build output artifacts, leave **Encryption key** blank. This is the default.
   - To use a customer-managed CMK to encrypt the build output artifacts, in **Encryption key**, type the ARN of the CMK. Use the format `arn:aws:kms:region-ID:account-ID:key/key-ID`.

9. (Optional) Select **Privileged** only if you plan to use this build project to build Docker images, and the build environment image you chose is not provided by AWS CodeBuild with Docker support. Otherwise, all associated builds that attempt to interact with the Docker daemon fail. You must also start the Docker daemon so that your builds can interact with it. One way to do this is to initialize the Docker daemon in the `install` phase of your build spec by running the following build commands. Do not run these commands if you chose a build environment image provided by AWS CodeBuild with Docker support.

```
1 - nohup /usr/local/bin/dockerd --host=unix:///var/run/docker.sock --host=tcp
      ://127.0.0.1:2375 --storage-driver=overlay&
2 - timeout -t 15 sh -c "until docker info; do echo .; sleep 1; done"
```

10. (Optional) If you chose **Amazon S3** for **Artifacts type** earlier in this procedure, then for **Artifacts packaging**, do one of the following:

    - To have AWS CodeBuild create a ZIP file containing the build output, choose **Zip**.
    - To have AWS CodeBuild create a folder containing the build output, choose **None**. (This is the default.)

11. For **Compute type**, choose one of the available options.

12. For **Environment variables**, type the name, value, and type of each environment variable for builds to use. Use **Add row** to add an environment variable. **Note**
AWS CodeBuild will set the environment variable for your AWS region automatically. If you do not add them to your buildspec.yml, then the following environment variables must be set:
AWS_ACCOUNT_ID IMAGE_REPO_NAME IMAGE_TAG

Others can see environment variables by using the AWS CodeBuild console and the AWS CLI. If you have no concerns about the visibility of your environment variable, set the **Name** and **Value** fields, and then set **Type** to **Plaintext**.

We recommend that you store an environment variable with a sensitive value, such as an AWS access key ID, an AWS secret access key, or a password as a parameter in Amazon EC2 Systems Manager Parameter Store. For **Type**, choose **Parameter Store**. For **Name**, type an identifier for AWS CodeBuild to reference. For **Value**, type the parameter's name as stored in Amazon EC2 Systems Manager Parameter Store. Using a parameter named `/CodeBuild/dockerLoginPassword` as an example, for **Type**, choose **Parameter Store**. For **Name**, type `LOGIN_PASSWORD`. For **Value**, type `/CodeBuild/dockerLoginPassword`. **Important**
We recommend that you store parameters in Amazon EC2 Systems Manager Parameter Store with parameter names that start with `/CodeBuild/` (for example, `/CodeBuild/dockerLoginPassword`). You can use the AWS CodeBuild console to create a parameter in Amazon EC2 Systems Manager. Choose **Create a parameter**, and then follow the instructions in the dialog box. (In that dialog box, for **KMS key**, you can optionally specify the ARN of an AWS KMS key in your account. Amazon EC2 Systems Manager uses this key to encrypt the parameter's value during storage and decrypt during retrieval.) If you use the AWS CodeBuild console to create a parameter, the console starts the parameter name with `/CodeBuild/` as it is being stored. For more information, see Systems Manager Parameter Store and Systems Manager

Parameter Store Console Walkthrough in the *Amazon EC2 Systems Manager User Guide*.

If your build project refers to parameters stored in Amazon EC2 Systems Manager Parameter Store, the build project's service role must allow the `ssm:GetParameters` action. If you chose **Create a service role in your account** earlier, then AWS CodeBuild includes this action in the default service role for your build project automatically. However, if you chose **Choose an existing service role from your account**, then you must include this action to your service role separately.

If your build project refers to parameters stored in Amazon EC2 Systems Manager Parameter Store with parameter names that do not start with `/CodeBuild/`, and you chose **Create a service role in your account**, then you must update that service role to allow access to parameter names that do not start with `/CodeBuild/`. This is because that service role allows access only to parameter names that start with `/CodeBuild/`.

Environment variables you set replace existing environment variables. For example, if the Docker image already contains an environment variable named `MY_VAR` with a value of `my_value`, and you set an environment variable named `MY_VAR` with a value of `other_value`, then `my_value` is replaced by `other_value`. Similarly, if the Docker image already contains an environment variable named `PATH` with a value of `/usr/local/sbin:/usr/local/bin`, and you set an environment variable named `PATH` with a value of `$PATH:/usr/share/ant/bin`, then `/usr/local/sbin:/usr/local/bin` is replaced by the literal value `$PATH:/usr/share/ant/bin`.

Do not set any environment variable with a name that begins with `CODEBUILD_`. This prefix is reserved for internal use.

If an environment variable with the same name is defined in multiple places, the value is determined as follows:

The value in the start build operation call takes highest precedence. The value in the build project definition takes next precedence. The value in the build spec declaration takes lowest precedence.

13. (Optional) For **Tags**, type the name and value of any tags you want supporting AWS services to use. Use **Add row** to add a tag. You can add up to 50 tags.

14. Choose **Continue**.

15. On the **Review** page, do one of the following:

    - To run a build, choose **Save and build**.
    - To finish creating the build project without running a build, choose **Save**.

Create a Build Project (AWS CLI)

For information about using the AWS CLI with AWS CodeBuild, see the Command Line Reference.

1. Run the `create-project` command:

```
1 aws codebuild create-project --generate-cli-skeleton
```

JSON-formatted data appears in the output. Copy the data to a file (for example, `create-project.json`) in a location on the local computer or instance where the AWS CLI is installed. Modify the copied data as follows, and save your results.

```
1 {
2   "name": "project-name",
3   "description": "description",
4   "source": {
5     "type": "source-type",
6     "location": "source-location",
7     "gitCloneDepth": "gitCloneDepth",
8     "buildspec": "buildspec",
9     "badgeEnabled": "badgeEnabled",
10    "InsecureSsl": "InsecureSsl",
```

```
11      "auth": {
12        "type": "auth-type",
13        "resource": "resource"
14      }
15    },
16    "artifacts": {
17      "type": "artifacts-type",
18      "location": "artifacts-location",
19      "path": "path",
20      "namespaceType": "namespaceType",
21      "name": "artifacts-name",
22      "packaging": "packaging"
23    },
24    "cache": {
25      "type": "cache-type",
26      "location": "cache-location"
27    },
28    "serviceRole": "serviceRole",
29    "vpcConfig": {
30      "securityGroupIds": [
31          "security-group-id"
32      ],
33      "subnets": [
34          "subnet-id"
35      ],
36      "vpcId": "vpc-id"
37    },
38    "timeoutInMinutes": timeoutInMinutes,
39    "encryptionKey": "encryptionKey",
40    "tags": [
41      {
42        "key": "tag-key",
43        "value": "tag-value"
44      }
45    ],
46    "environment": {
47      "type": "environment-type",
48      "image": "image",
49      "computeType": "computeType",
50      "certificate": "certificate",
51      "environmentVariables": [
52        {
53          "name": "environmentVariable-name",
54          "value": "environmentVariable-value",
55          "type": "environmentVariable-type"
56        }
57      ],
58      "privilegedMode": privilegedMode
59    }
60 }
```

Replace the following:

- *project-name*: Required value. The name for this build project. This name must be unique across all
  of the build projects in your AWS account.

- *description*: Optional value. The description for this build project.
- For the required `source` object, information about this build project's source code settings. These settings include the following:
  - *source-type*: Required value. The type of repository that contains the source code to build. Valid values include `CODECOMMIT`, `CODEPIPELINE`, `GITHUB`, `GITHUB_ENTERPRISE`, `BITBUCKET`, and `S3`.
  - *source-location*: Required value (unless you set *source-type* to `CODEPIPELINE`). The location of the source code for the specified repository type.
    - For AWS CodeCommit, the HTTPS clone URL to the repository that contains the source code and the build spec (for example, `https://git-codecommit.region-id.amazonaws.com/v1/repos/repo-name`).
    - For Amazon S3, the build input bucket name, followed by a forward slash (/), followed by the name of the ZIP file that contains the source code and the build spec (for example, `bucket-name/object-name.zip`). This assumes that the ZIP file is in the root of the build input bucket. (If the ZIP file is in a folder inside of the bucket, use `bucket-name/path/to/object-name.zip` instead.)
    - For GitHub, the HTTPS clone URL to the repository that contains the source code and the build spec. Also, you must connect your AWS account to your GitHub account. To do this, use the AWS CodeBuild console to create a build project. When you use the console to connect (or reconnect) with GitHub, on the GitHub **Authorize application** page, for **Organization access**, choose **Request access** next to each repository you want AWS CodeBuild to be able to access. Choose **Authorize application**. (After you have connected to your GitHub account, you do not need to finish creating the build project. You can close the AWS CodeBuild console.) To instruct AWS CodeBuild to use this connection, in the `source` object, set the `auth` object's `type` value to `OAUTH`.
    - For GitHub Enterprise, the HTTP or HTTPS clone URL to the repository that contains the source code and the build spec. You must also connect your AWS account to your GitHub Enterprise account. To do this, use the AWS CodeBuild console to create a build project. First, create a personal access token in GitHub Enterprise. Copy this token to your clipboard, so that it can be used when creating your AWS CodeBuild project. For more information, see Creating a Personal Access Token in GitHub Enterprise on the GitHub Help website. When you use the console to create your AWS CodeBuild project, in **Source: What to build**, for **Source provider**, choose **GitHub Enterprise**. For **Personal Access Token**, paste the token that was copied to your clipboard. Choose **Save Token**. Your AWS CodeBuild account is now connected to your GitHub Enterprise account.
    - For Bitbucket, the HTTPS clone URL to the repository that contains the source code and the build spec. You must also connect your AWS account to your Bitbucket account. To do this, use the AWS CodeBuild console to create a build project. When you use the console to connect (or reconnect) with Bitbucket, on the Bitbucket **Confirm access to your account** page, choose **Grant access**. (After you have connected to your Bitbucket account, you do not need to finish creating the build project. You can close the AWS CodeBuild console.) To instruct AWS CodeBuild to use this connection, in the `source` object, set the `auth` object's `type` value to `OAUTH`.
    - For AWS CodePipeline, do not specify a `location` value for `source`. It is ignored by AWS CodePipeline because when you create a pipeline in AWS CodePipeline, you specify the source code location in the Source stage of the pipeline.
  - *gitCloneDepth*: Optional value. The depth of history to download. Minimum value is 0. If this value is 0, greater than 25, or not provided, then the full history is downloaded with each build project. If your source type is Amazon S3, this value is not supported.
  - *buildspec*: Optional value. The build specification definition or file to use. If this value is set, it can be either an inline build spec definition or the path to an alternate build spec file relative to the value of the built-in `CODEBUILD_SRC_DIR` environment variable. If this value is not provided or is set to an empty string, then the source code must contain a `buildspec.yml` file in its root directory. For more information, see Build Spec File Name and Storage Location.
  - *auth*: This object is used only by the AWS CodeBuild console. Do not specify values for *auth-type*

(unless *source-type* is set to `GITHUB`, as described previously) or *resource*.

- *badgeEnabled*: Optional value. To include build badges with your AWS CodeBuild project, you must specify *badgeEnabled* with a value of `true`. For more information, see Build Badges Sample with AWS CodeBuild.
- *InsecureSsl*: Optional value. This is used with GitHub Enterprise only. Set this value to `true` to ignore SSL warnings while connecting to your GitHub Enterprise project repository. The default value is `false`. *InsecureSsl* should be used for testing purposes only. It should not be used in a production environment.

- For the required `artifacts` object, information about this build project's output artifact settings. These settings include the following:
  - *artifacts-type*: Required value. The type of build output artifact. Valid values include `CODEPIPELINE`, `NO_ARTIFACTS`, and `S3`.
  - *artifacts-location*: Required value (unless you set *artifacts-type* to `CODEPIPELINE` or `NO_ARTIFACTS`). The location of the build output artifact:
    - If you specified `CODEPIPELINE` for *artifacts-type*, do not specify a `location` for `artifacts`.
    - If you specified `NO_ARTIFACTS` for *artifacts-type*, do not specify a `location` for `artifacts`.
    - If you specified `S3` for *artifacts-type*, then this is name of the output bucket you created or identified in the prerequisites.
  - *path*: Optional value. The path and name of the build output ZIP file or folder:
    - If you specified `CODEPIPELINE` for *artifacts-type*, then do not specify a `path` for `artifacts`.
    - If you specified `NO_ARTIFACTS` for *artifacts-type*, do not specify a `path` for `artifacts`.
    - If you specified `S3` for *artifacts-type*, then this is the path inside of *artifacts-location* to the build output ZIP file or folder. If you do not specify a value for *path*, then AWS CodeBuild uses *namespaceType* (if specified) and *artifacts-name* to determine the path and name of the build output ZIP file or folder. For example, if you specify `MyPath` for *path* and `MyArtifact.zip` for *artifacts-name*, then the path and name would be `MyPath/MyArtifact.zip`.
  - *namespaceType*: Optional value. The path and name of the build output ZIP file or folder:
    - If you specified `CODEPIPELINE` for *artifacts-type*, do not specify a `namespaceType` for `artifacts`.
    - If you specified `NO_ARTIFACTS` for *artifacts-type*, do not specify a `namespaceType` for `artifacts`.
    - If you specified `S3` for *artifacts-type*, valid values include `BUILD_ID` and `NONE`. Use `BUILD_ID` to insert the build ID into the path of the build output ZIP file or folder. Otherwise, use `NONE`. If you do not specify a value for *namespaceType*, AWS CodeBuild uses *path* (if specified) and *artifacts-name* to determine the path and name of the build output ZIP file or folder. For example, if you specify `MyPath` for *path*, `BUILD_ID` for *namespaceType*, and `MyArtifact.zip` for *artifacts-name*, then the path and name would be `MyPath/build-ID/MyArtifact.zip`.
  - *artifacts-name*: Required value (unless you set *artifacts-type* to `CODEPIPELINE` or `NO_ARTIFACTS`). The path and name of the build output ZIP file or folder:
    - If you specified `CODEPIPELINE` for *artifacts-type*, do not specify a `name` for `artifacts`.
    - If you specified `NO_ARTIFACTS` for *artifacts-type*, do not specify a `name` for `artifacts`.
    - If you specified `S3` for *artifacts-type*, then this is the name of the build output ZIP file or folder inside of *artifacts-location*. For example, if you specify `MyPath` for *path* and `MyArtifact.zip` for *artifacts-name*, then the path and name would be `MyPath/MyArtifact.zip`.
  - *packaging*: Optional value. The type of build output artifact to create:
    - If you specified `CODEPIPELINE` for *artifacts-type*, do not specify a `packaging` for `artifacts`.
    - If you specified `NO_ARTIFACTS` for *artifacts-type*, do not specify a `packaging` for `artifacts`.
    - If you specified `S3` for *artifacts-type*, valid values include `ZIP` and `NONE`. To create a ZIP file that contains the build output, use `ZIP`. To create a folder that contains the build output, use `NONE`. The default value is `NONE`.

- For the required *cache* object, information about this build project's cache settings. These settings include the following:
  - *CacheType*: Required value. Valid values are `S3` or `NO_CACHE`.
  - *CacheLocation*: Required value unless you set *CacheType* to `NONE`. If you specified S3 for

CacheType, then this is the ARN of the S3 bucket and the path prefix. For example, if your Amazon S3 bucket name is `my-bucket`, and your path prefix is `build-cache`, then acceptable formats for your *CacheLocation* are `my-bucket/build-cache` or `aws:s3:::my-bucket/build-cache`.

- *serviceRole*: Required value. The ARN of the service role AWS CodeBuild uses to interact with services on behalf of the IAM user (for example, `arn:aws:iam::account-id:role/role-name`).
- For the optional *vpcConfig* object, information about your VPC configuration. These settings include:
  - *vpcId*: Required value. The VPC ID that AWS CodeBuild uses. To get a list of all Amazon VPC IDs in your region, run this command:

```
1 aws ec2 describe-vpcs
```

  - *subnets*: Required value. The subnet IDs that include resources used by AWS CodeBuild. To obtain these IDs, run this command:

```
1 aws ec2 describe-subnets --filters "Name=vpc-id,Values=<vpc-id>" --region us-east-1
```

Note

If you are using a region other than us-east-1, be sure to use it when you run the command. + *securityGroupIds*: Required value. The security group IDs used by AWS CodeBuild to allow access to resources in the VPCs. To obtain these IDs, run this command:

```
1   ```
2   aws ec2 describe-security-groups --filters "Name=vpc-id,Values=<vpc-id>" --region us-east-1
3   ```
```

Note

If you are using a region other than us-east-1, be sure to use it when you run the command.

- For the required **environment** object, information about this project's build environment settings. These settings include:
  - *environment-type*: Required value. The type of build environment. Valid values are `LINUX_CONTAINER` and `WINDOWS_CONTAINER`.
  - *image*: Required value. The Docker image identifier used by this build environment. Typically, this identifier is expressed as *image-name:tag*. For example, in the Docker repository that AWS CodeBuild uses to manage its Docker images, this could be `aws/codebuild/java:openjdk-8`. In Docker Hub, `maven:3.3.9-jdk-8`. In Amazon ECR, `account-id.dkr.ecr.region-id.amazonaws.com/your-Amazon-ECR-repo-name:tag`. For more information, see Docker Images Provided by AWS CodeBuild.
  - *computeType*: Required value. A category corresponding to the number of CPU cores and memory used by this build environment. Allowed values include `BUILD_GENERAL1_SMALL`, `BUILD_GENERAL1_MEDIUM`, and `BUILD_GENERAL1_LARGE`.
  - *certificate*: Optional value. The ARN of the AWS S3 bucket, path prefix and object key containing the PEM encoded certificate. The object key can be either just the .pem file or a .zip file containing the pem encoded certificate. For example, if your Amazon S3 bucket name is my-bucket, your path prefix is cert, and your object key name is certificate.pem, then acceptable formats for your *certificate* are my-bucket/cert/certificate.pem or arn:aws:s3:::my-bucket/cert/certificate.pem.
  - For the optional **environmentVariables** array, information about any environment variables you want to specify for this build environment. Each environment variable is expressed as an object containing a **name**, **value**, and **type** of *environmentVariable-name*, *environmentVariable-value*, and *environmentVariable-type*.

    Others can see an environment variable by using the AWS CodeBuild console and the AWS CLI. If you have no concerns about the visibility of your environment variable, set *environmentVariable-name* and *environmentVariable-value*, and then set *environmentVariable-type* to `PLAINTEXT`.

    We recommend you store an environment variable with a sensitive value, such as an AWS access key ID, an AWS secret access key, or a password as a parameter in Amazon EC2 Systems Manager Parameter Store. For *environmentVariable-name*, for that stored parameter, set an identifier for AWS

CodeBuild to reference. For *environmentVariable-value*, set the parameter's name as stored in Amazon EC2 Systems Manager Parameter Store. Set *environmentVariable-type* to `PARAMETER_STORE`. Using a parameter named `/CodeBuild/dockerLoginPassword` as an example, set *environmentVariable-name* to `LOGIN_PASSWORD`. Set *environmentVariable-value* to `/CodeBuild/dockerLoginPassword`. Set *environmentVariable-type* to `PARAMETER_STORE`. **Important**

If your build project refers to parameters stored in Amazon EC2 Systems Manager Parameter Store, the build project's service role must allow the `ssm:GetParameters` action. If you chose **Create a service role in your account** earlier, then AWS CodeBuild includes this action in the default service role for your build project automatically. However, if you chose **Choose an existing service role from your account**, then you must include this action to your service role separately.

If your build project refers to parameters stored in Amazon EC2 Systems Manager Parameter Store with parameter names that do not start with `/CodeBuild/`, and you chose **Create a service role in your account**, then you must update that service role to allow access to parameter names that do not start with `/CodeBuild/`. This is because that service role allows access only to parameter names that start with `/CodeBuild/`.

Any environment variables you set replace existing environment variables. For example, if the Docker image already contains an environment variable named `MY_VAR` with a value of `my_value`, and you set an environment variable named `MY_VAR` with a value of `other_value`, then `my_value` is replaced by `other_value`. Similarly, if the Docker image already contains an environment variable named `PATH` with a value of `/usr/local/sbin:/usr/local/bin`, and you set an environment variable named `PATH` with a value of `$PATH:/usr/share/ant/bin`, then `/usr/local/sbin:/usr/local/bin` is replaced by the literal value `$PATH:/usr/share/ant/bin`.

Do not set any environment variable with a name that begins with `CODEBUILD_`. This prefix is reserved for internal use.

If an environment variable with the same name is defined in multiple places, the value is determined as follows:

The value in the start build operation call takes highest precedence. The value in the build project definition takes next precedence. The value in the build spec declaration takes lowest precedence.

- You must specify *privilegedMode* with a value of `true` only if you plan to use this build project to build Docker images, and the build environment image you specified is not provided by AWS CodeBuild with Docker support. Otherwise, all associated builds that attempt to interact with the Docker daemon fail. You must also start the Docker daemon so that your builds can interact with it. One way to do this is to initialize the Docker daemon in the `install` phase of your build spec by running the following build commands. Do not run these commands if you specified a build environment image provided by AWS CodeBuild with Docker support.

```
1 - nohup /usr/local/bin/dockerd --host=unix:///var/run/docker.sock --host=tcp
        ://127.0.0.1:2375 --storage-driver=overlay&
2 - timeout -t 15 sh -c "until docker info; do echo .; sleep 1; done"
```

- *timeoutInMinutes*: Optional value. The number of minutes, between 5 to 480 (8 hours), after which AWS CodeBuild stops the build if it is not complete. If not specified, the default of 60 is used. To determine if and when AWS CodeBuild stopped a build due to a timeout, run the `batch-get-builds` command. To determine if the build has stopped, look in the output for a `buildStatus` value of `FAILED`. To determine when the build timed out, look in the output for the `endTime` value associated with a `phaseStatus` value of `TIMED_OUT`.
- *encryptionKey*: Optional value. The alias or ARN of the AWS KMS customer master key (CMK) AWS CodeBuild uses to encrypt the build output. If you specify an alias, use the format `arn:aws:kms:region-ID:account-ID:key/key-ID` or, if an alias exists, use the format `alias/key-alias`. If not specified, the AWS-managed CMK for Amazon S3 is used.
- For the optional *tags* array, information about any tags you want to associate with this build project. You can specify up to 50 tags. These tags can be used by any AWS service that supports AWS CodeBuild build project tags. Each tag is expressed as an object containing a `key` and `value` value of *tag-key* and *tag-value*.

For an example, see To create the build project (AWS CLI).

1. Switch to the directory that contains the file you just saved, and run the `create-project` command again:

```
1 aws codebuild create-project --cli-input-json file://create-project.json
```

2. If successful, data similar to the following appears in the output:

```
1  {
2    "project": {
3      "name": "project-name",
4      "description": "description",
5      "serviceRole": "serviceRole",
6      "tags": [
7        {
8          "key": "tags-key",
9          "value": "tags-value"
10       }
11     ],
12     "artifacts": {
13       "namespaceType": "namespaceType",
14       "packaging": "packaging",
15       "path": "path",
16       "type": "artifacts-type",
17       "location": "artifacts-location",
18       "name": "artifacts-name"
19     },
20     "lastModified": lastModified,
21     "timeoutInMinutes": timeoutInMinutes,
22     "created": created,
23     "environment": {
24       "computeType": "computeType",
25       "image": "image",
26       "type": "environment-type",
27       "environmentVariables": [
28         {
29           "name": "environmentVariable-name",
30           "value": "environmentVariable-value",
31           "type": "environmentVariable-type"
32         }
33       ]
34     },
35     "source": {
36       "type": "source-type",
37       "location": "source-location",
38       "buildspec": "buildspec",
39       "auth": {
40         "type": "auth-type",
41         "resource": "resource"
42       }
43     },
44     "encryptionKey": "encryptionKey",
45     "arn": "arn"
46   }
47 }
```

- The project object contains information about the new build project:
  - The lastModified value represents the time, in Unix time format, when information about the build project was last changed.

195

- The `created` value represents the time, in Unix time format, when the build project was created.
- The `arn` value represents the ARN of the build project.

Note

Except for the build project name, you can change any of the build project's settings later. For more information, see Change a Build Project's Settings (AWS CLI).

To start running a build, see Run a Build (AWS CLI).

If your source code is stored in a GitHub repository, and you want AWS CodeBuild to rebuild the source code every time a code change is pushed to the repository, see Start Running Builds Automatically (AWS CLI).

Create a Build Project (AWS SDKs)

For information about using AWS CodeBuild with the AWS SDKs, see the AWS SDKs and Tools Reference.

Create a Build Project (AWS CloudFormation)

For information about using AWS CodeBuild with AWS CloudFormation, see the AWS CloudFormation template for AWS CodeBuild in the *AWS CloudFormation User Guide*.

View a List of Build Project Names in AWS CodeBuild

To view a list of build projects in AWS CodeBuild, you can use the AWS CodeBuild console, AWS CLI, or AWS SDKs.

Topics

- View a List of Build Project Names (Console)
- View a List of Build Project Names (AWS CLI)
- View a List of Build Project Names (AWS SDKs)

View a List of Build Project Names (Console)

1. Open the AWS CodeBuild console at https://console.aws.amazon.com/codebuild/.

2. In the navigation pane, choose **Build projects. Note**
   By default, only the ten most recent build projects are displayed. To view more build projects, select a different value for **Projects per page** or select the back and forward arrows for **Viewing projects**.

View a List of Build Project Names (AWS CLI)

Run the `list-projects` command:

```
1 aws codebuild list-projects --sort-by sort-by --sort-order sort-order --next-token next-token
```

In the preceding command, replace the following placeholders:

- *sort-by*: Optional string. The criterion to be used to list build project names. Valid values include:
  - `CREATED_TIME`: List the build project names based on when each build project was created.
  - `LAST_MODIFIED_TIME`: List the build project names based on when information about each build project was last changed.
  - `NAME`: List the build project names based on each build project's name.
- *sort-order*: Optional string. The order in which to list build projects, based on *sort-by*. Valid values include `ASCENDING` and `DESCENDING`.
- *next-token*: Optional string. During a previous run, if there were more than 100 items in the list, only the first 100 items are returned, along with a unique string called a *next token*. To get the next batch of items in the list, run this command again, adding the next token to the call. To get all of the items in the list, keep running this command with each subsequent next token, until no more next tokens are returned.

For example, if you run this command:

```
1 aws codebuild list-projects --sort-by NAME --sort-order ASCENDING
```

A result similar to the following might appear in the output:

```
1 {
2   "nextToken": "Ci33ACF6...The full token has been omitted for brevity...U+AkMx8=",
3   "projects": [
4     "codebuild-demo-project",
5     "codebuild-demo-project2",
6     ... The full list of build project names has been omitted for brevity ...
7     "codebuild-demo-project99"
8   ]
9 }
```

If you run this command again:

```
1 aws codebuild list-projects  --sort-by NAME --sort-order ASCENDING --next-token Ci33ACF6...The
    full token has been omitted for brevity...U+AkMx8=
```

A result similar to the following might appear in the output:

```
1 {
2   "projects": [
3     "codebuild-demo-project100",
4     "codebuild-demo-project101",
5     ... The full list of build project names has been omitted for brevity ...
6     "codebuild-demo-project122"
7   ]
8 }
```

View a List of Build Project Names (AWS SDKs)

For more information about using AWS CodeBuild with the AWS SDKs, see the AWS SDKs and Tools Reference.

View a Build Project's Details in AWS CodeBuild

To view the details of a build project in AWS CodeBuild, you can use the AWS CodeBuild console, AWS CLI, or AWS SDKs.

Topics

- View a Build Project's Details (Console)
- View a Build Project's Details (AWS CLI)
- View a Build Project's Details (AWS SDKs)

View a Build Project's Details (Console)

1. Open the AWS CodeBuild console at https://console.aws.amazon.com/codebuild/.

2. In the navigation pane, choose **Build projects**. **Note**
   By default, only the ten most recent build projects are displayed. To view more build projects, select a different value for **Projects per page** or select the back and forward arrows for **Viewing projects**.

3. In the list of build projects, in the **Project** column, choose the link that corresponds to the build project.

4. On the **Build project:** *project-name* page, expand **Project details**.

View a Build Project's Details (AWS CLI)

For more information about using the AWS CLI with AWS CodeBuild, see the Command Line Reference.

Run the `batch-get-projects` command:

```
1 aws codebuild batch-get-projects --names names
```

In the preceding command, replace the following placeholder:

- *names*: Required string. One or more build project names to view details about. To specify more than one build project, separate each build project's name with a space. You can specify up to 100 build project names. To get a list of build projects, see View a List of Build Project Names (AWS CLI).

For example, if you run this command:

```
1 aws codebuild batch-get-projects --names codebuild-demo-project codebuild-demo-project2 my-other
    -demo-project
```

A result similar to the following might appear in the output. Ellipses (...) represent data omitted for brevity.

```
1  {
2    "projectsNotFound": [
3      "my-other-demo-project"
4    ],
5    "projects": [
6      {
7        ...
8        "name": codebuild-demo-project,
9        ...
10     },
11     {
12       ...
13       "name": codebuild-demo-project2",
14       ...
```

```
15      }
16    ]
17 }
```

In the preceding output, the `projectsNotFound` array lists any build project names that were specified, but no information was found. The `projects` array lists details for each build project where information was found. Build project details have been omitted from the preceding output for brevity. For more information, see the output of Create a Build Project (AWS CLI).

View a Build Project's Details (AWS SDKs)

For more information about using AWS CodeBuild with the AWS SDKs, see the AWS SDKs and Tools Reference.

Create AWS CodeBuild Triggers

You can create a trigger on a project to schedule a build once every hour, day, or week. You can also create a trigger using a custom rule with an Amazon CloudWatch cron expression. For example, using a cron expression, you can schedule a build at a specific time every weekday.

You create a trigger after you create a project.

To create a trigger

1. Open the AWS CodeBuild console at https://console.aws.amazon.com/codebuild/.

2. In the navigation pane, choose **Build projects**.

3. Choose the link for the build project to which you want to add a trigger, and then choose the **Build triggers** tab. **Note**
By default, the 100 most recent build projects are displayed. To view more build projects, choose a different value for **Projects per page** or choose the back and forward arrows for **Viewing projects**.

4. Choose **Create trigger**.

5. Type a name in **Trigger name**.

6. From the **Frequency** drop-down list, choose the frequency for your trigger. If you want to create a frequency using a cron expression, choose **Custom**.

7. Specify the parameters for the frequency of your trigger. You can type the first few characters of your selections in the text box to filter drop-down menu items. **Note**
Start hours and minutes are zero-based. The start minute is a number between zero and 59. The start hour is a number between zero and 23. For example, a daily trigger that starts every day at 12:15 P.M. has a start hour of 12 and a start minute of 15. A daily trigger that starts every day at midnight has a start hour of zero and a start minute of zero. A daily trigger that starts every day at 11:59 P.M. has a start hour of 23 and a start minute of 59.

[See the AWS documentation website for more details]

1. Select **Enable this trigger** to enable the trigger.

2. (Optional) In **Source version**, type a version of your source.

- For Amazon S3, type the version ID that corresponds to the version of the input artifact you want to build. If **Source version** is left blank, the latest version is used.
- For AWS CodeCommit, type a commit ID. If **Source version** is left blank, the default branch's HEAD commit ID is used.
- For GitHub or GitHub Enterprise, type a commit ID, a pull request ID, a branch name, or a tag name that corresponds to the version of the source code you want to build. If you specify a pull request ID, it must use the format `pr/pull-request-ID` (for example, `pr/25`). If you specify a branch name, the branch's HEAD commit ID is used. If **Source version** is blank, the default branch's HEAD commit ID is used.
- For Bitbucket, type a commit ID, a branch name, or a tag name that corresponds to the version of the source code you want to build. If you specify a branch name, the branch's HEAD commit ID is used. If **Source version** is blank, the default branch's HEAD commit ID is used.

1. (Optional) Specify a timeout between 5 minutes and 480 minutes (8 hours). This value specifies how long AWS CodeBuild attempts a build before it stops. If **hours** and **minutes** is left blank, the default timeout value specified in the project is used.

Edit AWS CodeBuild Triggers

You can edit a trigger on a project to schedule a build once every hour, day, or week. You can also edit a trigger to use a custom rule with an Amazon CloudWatch cron expression. For example, using a cron expression, you can schedule a build at a specific time on every weekday. For information about creating a trigger, see Create AWS CodeBuild Triggers.

To edit a trigger:

1. Open the AWS CodeBuild console at https://console.aws.amazon.com/codebuild/.

2. In the navigation pane, choose **Build projects**.

3. Choose the link for the build project you want to change, and then choose **Edit project**. **Note** By default, the 100 most recent build projects are displayed. To view more build projects, choose a different value for **Projects per page** or choose the back and forward arrows for **Viewing projects**.

4. Do one of the following:

   - Choose the radio button next to the trigger you want to change, choose **Actions**, and then choose **Edit**.
   - Choose the link for the trigger you want to change.

5. From the **Frequency** drop-down list, choose the frequency for your trigger. If you want to create a frequency using a cron expression, choose **Custom**.

6. Specify the parameters for the frequency of your trigger. You can type the first few characters of your selections in the text box to filter drop-down menu items. **Note** Start hours and minutes are zero-based. The start minute is a number between zero and 59. The start hour is a number between zero and 23. For example, a daily trigger that starts every day at 12:15 P.M. has a start hour of 12 and a start minute of 15. A daily trigger that starts every day at midnight has a start hour of zero and a start minute of zero. A daily trigger that starts every day at 11:59 P.M. has a start hour of 23 and a start minute of 59.

[See the AWS documentation website for more details]

1. Select **Enable this trigger** to enable the trigger.

Note
You can use the Amazon CloudWatch console at https://console.aws.amazon.com/cloudwatch/ to edit source version, timeout, and other options that are not available in AWS CodeBuild.

Change a Build Project's Settings in AWS CodeBuild

To change a build project's settings in AWS CodeBuild, you can use the AWS CodeBuild console, AWS CLI, or AWS SDKs.

Topics

- Change a Build Project's Settings (Console)
- Change a Build Project's Settings (AWS CLI)
- Change a Build Project's Settings (AWS SDKs)

Change a Build Project's Settings (Console)

1. Open the AWS CodeBuild console at https://console.aws.amazon.com/codebuild/.

2. In the navigation pane, choose **Build projects**.

3. Do one of the following:

   - Choose the radio button next to the build project you want to change, choose **Actions**, and then choose **Update**.
   - Choose the link for the build project you want to change, and then choose **Edit project**. **Note** By default, the 100 most recent build projects are displayed. To view more build projects, choose a different value for **Projects per page** or choose the back and forward arrows for **Viewing projects**.

4. On the project details page, type a description in **Description**.

   For more information about settings referred to in this procedure, see Create a Build Project (Console).

5. To change information about the source code location, in the **Source: What to build** area, choose **Update source**. Use the following table to make selections appopropriate for your source provider:

[See the AWS documentation website for more details]

1. To change information about the build environment, in **Environment: How to build**, choose **Update image**. Make changes appropriate for the build environment type (for example, **Environment image**, **Operating system**, **Runtime**, **Version**, **Custom image type**, **Custom image ID**, **Amazon ECR repository**, or **Amazon ECR image**).

2. Do one of the following:

   - If your source code previously did not include a buildspec.yml file but does now, choose **Update build specification**, and then choose **Use buildspec.yml from source code**.
   - If your source code previously included a buildspec.yml file but now does not, choose **Update build specification**, then choose **Insert build commands**, and then type the commands in **Build commands**.

3. To change information about the build output artifact location and name, in **Artifacts: Where to put the artifacts from this build project**, change the values of **Artifacts type**, **Artifact name**, **Bucket name**, or **Output files**.

4. To change information about the cache, in **Cache**, do one of the following:

   - If you previously chose a cache but now you do not want to use a cache, choose **No cache**.
   - If you previously chose **No cache** but now you want to use a cache, choose **Amazon S3**, and then do the following:
     - For **Bucket**, choose the name of the Amazon S3 bucket where the cache is stored.

- (Optional) For **Path prefix**, type an Amazon S3 path prefix. The **Path prefix** value is similar to a directory name that enables you to store the cache under the same directory in a bucket. **Important** Do not append "/" to the end of **Path prefix**.

Using a cache saves considerable build time because reusable pieces of the build environment are stored in the cache and used across builds. For information about specifying a cache in the build spec file, see Build Spec Syntax.

5. To change information about the AWS CodeBuild service role, in **Service role**, change the values of **Create a role, Choose an existing service role from your account,** or **Role name. Note** When you use the console to create or update a build project, you can create an AWS CodeBuild service role at the same time. By default, the role works with that build project only. If you use the console to associate this service role with another build project, the role is updated to work with the other build project. A service role can work with up to 10 build projects.

6. In **VPC**, do one of the following:

   - If you are not using a VPC for your project, choose **No VPC**.
   - If you want AWS CodeBuild to work with your VPC:
     - For **VPC**, choose the VPC ID that AWS CodeBuild uses.
     - For **Subnets**, choose the subnets that include resources that AWS CodeBuild uses.
     - For **Security Groups**, choose the security groups that AWS CodeBuild uses to allow access to resources in the VPCs.

   For more information, see Use AWS CodeBuild with Amazon Virtual Private Cloud.

7. To change information about the build timeout, in **Show advanced settings**, for **Timeout**, change the values of **hours** and **minutes**. If **hours** and **minutes** are left blank, the default value is 60 minutes.

8. To change information about the AWS KMS customer master key (CMK), in **Show advanced settings**, change the value of **Encryption key. Important** If you leave **Encryption key** blank, AWS CodeBuild uses the AWS-managed CMK for Amazon S3 in your AWS account instead.

9. If you plan to use this build project to build Docker images and the specified build environment is not provided by AWS CodeBuild with Docker support, in **Show advanced settings**, select **Privileged**. Otherwise, all associated builds that attempt to interact with the Docker daemon fail. You must also start the Docker daemon so that your builds can interact with it as needed. One way to do this is to initialize the Docker daemon in the `install` phase of your build spec by running the following build commands. (Do not run the following build commands if the specified build environment image is provided by AWS CodeBuild with Docker support.)

```
1 - nohup /usr/local/bin/dockerd --host=unix:///var/run/docker.sock --host=tcp
      ://127.0.0.1:2375 --storage-driver=overlay&
2 - timeout -t 15 sh -c "until docker info; do echo .; sleep 1; done"
```

10. To change information about the way build output artifacts are stored, in **Show advanced settings**, change the value of **Artifacts packaging**.

11. To change the amount of memory and vCPUs that are used to run builds, in **Show advanced settings**, change the value of **Compute type**.

12. To change information about environment variables you want builds to use, in **Show advanced settings**, for **Environment variables**, change the values for **Name, Value,** and **Type**. Use **Add row** to add an environment variable. Choose the delete (**X**) button next to an environment variable you no longer want to use.

   Others can see environment variables by using the AWS CodeBuild console and the AWS CLI. If you have no concerns about the visibility of your environment variable, set the **Name** and **Value** fields, and then set **Type** to **Plaintext**.

We recommend that you store an environment variable with a sensitive value, such as an AWS access key ID, an AWS secret access key, or a password as a parameter in Amazon EC2 Systems Manager Parameter Store. For **Type**, choose **Parameter Store**. For **Name**, type an identifier for AWS CodeBuild to reference. For **Value**, type the parameter's name as stored in Amazon EC2 Systems Manager Parameter Store. Using a parameter named /CodeBuild/dockerLoginPassword as an example, for **Type** choose **Parameter Store**. For **Name**, type LOGIN_PASSWORD. For **Value**, type /CodeBuild/dockerLoginPassword. **Important**
We recommend that you store parameters in Amazon EC2 Systems Manager Parameter Store with parameter names that start with /CodeBuild/ (for example, /CodeBuild/dockerLoginPassword). You can use the AWS CodeBuild console to create a parameter in Amazon EC2 Systems Manager. Choose **Create a parameter**, and then follow the instructions in the dialog box. (In that dialog box, for **KMS key**, you can optionally specify the ARN of an AWS KMS key in your account. Amazon EC2 Systems Manager uses this key to encrypt the parameter's value during storage and decrypt during retrieval.) If you use the AWS CodeBuild console to create a parameter, the console starts the parameter name with /CodeBuild/ as it is being stored. For more information, see Systems Manager Parameter Store and Systems Manager Parameter Store Console Walkthrough in the *Amazon EC2 Systems Manager User Guide*.

If your build project refers to parameters stored in Amazon EC2 Systems Manager Parameter Store, the build project's service role must allow the ssm:GetParameters action. If you chose **Create a service role in your account** earlier, then AWS CodeBuild includes this action in the default service role for your build project automatically. However, if you chose **Choose an existing service role from your account**, then you must include this action to your service role separately.

If your build project refers to parameters stored in Amazon EC2 Systems Manager Parameter Store with parameter names that do not start with /CodeBuild/, and you chose **Create a service role in your account**, then you must update that service role to allow access to parameter names that do not start with /CodeBuild/. This is because that service role allows access only to parameter names that start with /CodeBuild/.

Environment variables you set replace existing environment variables. For example, if the Docker image already contains an environment variable named MY_VAR with a value of my_value, and you set an environment variable named MY_VAR with a value of other_value, then my_value is replaced by other_value. Similarly, if the Docker image already contains an environment variable named PATH with a value of /usr/local/sbin:/usr/local/bin, and you set an environment variable named PATH with a value of $PATH:/usr/share/ant/bin, then /usr/local/sbin:/usr/local/bin is replaced by the literal value $PATH:/usr/share/ant/bin.

Do not set any environment variable with a name that begins with CODEBUILD_. This prefix is reserved for internal use.

If an environment variable with the same name is defined in multiple places, its value is determined as follows:

The value in the start build operation call takes highest precedence. The value in the build project definition takes next precedence. The value in the build spec declaration takes lowest precedence.

13. To change information about tags for this build project, in **Show advanced settings**, for **Tags**, change the values of **Name** and **Value**. Use **Add row** to add a tag. You can add up to 50 tags. Choose the delete (**X**) icon next to a tag you no longer want to use.

14. Choose **Update**.

Change a Build Project's Settings (AWS CLI)

For more information about using the AWS CLI with AWS CodeBuild, see the Command Line Reference.

1. Run the update-project command as follows:

```
1 aws codebuild update-project --generate-cli-skeleton
```

JSON-formatted data appears in the output. Copy the data to a file (for example, update-project.json) in a location on the local computer or instance where the AWS CLI is installed. Then modify the copied data as described in Create a Build Project (AWS CLI), and save your results. **Note**

In the JSON-formatted data, you must provide the name of the build project that you want to change settings for. All other settings are optional. You cannot change the build project's name, but you can change any of its other settings.

2. Switch to the directory containing the file you just saved, and run the `update-project` command again.

```
1 aws codebuild update-project --cli-input-json file://update-project.json
```

3. If successful, data similar to that as described in Create a Build Project (AWS CLI) appears in the output.

Change a Build Project's Settings (AWS SDKs)

For information about using AWS CodeBuild with the AWS SDKs, see the AWS SDKs and Tools Reference.

Delete a Build Project in AWS CodeBuild

You can use the AWS CodeBuild console, AWS CLI, or AWS SDKs to delete a build project in AWS CodeBuild.

Warning
If you delete a build project, it cannot be recovered. All information about builds will also be deleted and cannot be recovered.

Topics

- Delete a Build Project (Console)
- Delete a Build Project (AWS CLI)
- Delete a Build Project (AWS SDKs)

Delete a Build Project (Console)

1. Open the AWS CodeBuild console at https://console.aws.amazon.com/codebuild/.

2. In the navigation pane, choose **Build projects**.

3. Do one of the following:

   - Choose the radio button next to the build project you want to delete, choose **Actions**, and then choose **Delete**.
   - Choose the link for the build project you want to delete, and then choose **Delete**. **Note**
     Only the most recent 10 build projects are displayed by default. To view more build projects, select a different value for **Projects per page** or select the back and forward arrows for **Viewing projects**.

Delete a Build Project (AWS CLI)

For more information about using the AWS CLI with AWS CodeBuild, see the Command Line Reference.

1. Run the `delete-project` command:

```
1 aws codebuild delete-project --name name
```

   Replace the following placeholder:

   - *name*: Required string. The name of the build project to delete. To get a list of available build projects, run the `list-projects` command. For more information, see View a List of Build Project Names (AWS CLI).

2. If successful, no data and no errors appear in the output.

Delete a Build Project (AWS SDKs)

For more information about using AWS CodeBuild with the AWS SDKs, see the AWS SDKs and Tools Reference.

Working with Builds in AWS CodeBuild

A *build* represents a set of actions performed by AWS CodeBuild to create output artifacts (for example, a JAR file) based on a set of input artifacts (for example, a collection of Java class files).

You can perform these tasks when working with builds:

Topics

- Run a Build in AWS CodeBuild
- View Build Details in AWS CodeBuild
- View a List of Build IDs in AWS CodeBuild
- View a List of Build IDs for a Build Project in AWS CodeBuild
- Stop a Build in AWS CodeBuild
- Delete Builds in AWS CodeBuild

Run a Build in AWS CodeBuild

You can use the AWS CodeBuild console, AWS CLI, or AWS SDKs to run a build in AWS CodeBuild.

Topics

- Run a Build (Console)
- Run a Build (AWS CLI)
- Start Running Builds Automatically (AWS CLI)
- Stop Running Builds Automatically (AWS CLI)
- Run a Build (AWS SDKs)

Run a Build (Console)

To use AWS CodePipeline to run a build with AWS CodeBuild, skip these steps and follow the instructions in Use AWS CodePipeline with AWS CodeBuild.

1. Open the AWS CodeBuild console at https://console.aws.amazon.com/codebuild/.

2. Do one of the following:

   - If you just finished creating a build project, the **Build project:** *project-name* page should be displayed. Choose **Start build**.
   - If you created a build project earlier, in the navigation pane, choose **Build projects**. Choose the build project, and then choose **Start build**.

3. On the **Start new build** page, do one of the following:

   - For Amazon S3, for the optional **Source version** value, type the version ID that corresponds to the version of the input artifact you want to build. If **Source version** is left blank, the latest version will be used.
   - For AWS CodeCommit, for the optional **Source version** value, for **Branch**, choose the name of the branch that contains the version of the source code you want to build. For **Source version**, accept the displayed HEAD commit ID or type a different one. If **Source version** is blank, the default branch's HEAD commit ID is used. You cannot type a tag name for **Source version**. To specify a tag, type the tag's commit ID. Change the value for **Git clone depth**. This will create a shallow clone with a history truncated to the specified number of commits. If you want a full clone, choose **Full**.
   - For GitHub or GitHub Enterprise, for the optional **Source version** value, type a commit ID, a pull request ID, a branch name, or a tag name that corresponds to the version of the source code you want to build. If you specify a pull request ID, it must use the format `pr/pull-request-ID` (for example, `pr/25`). If you specify a branch name, the branch's HEAD commit ID is used. If **Source version** is blank, the default branch's HEAD commit ID is used. Change the value for **Git clone depth**. This creates a shallow clone with a history truncated to the specified number of commits. If you want a full clone, choose **Full**.
   - For Bitbucket, for the optional **Source version** value, type a commit ID, a branch name, or a tag name that corresponds to the version of the source code you want to build. If you specify a branch name, the branch's HEAD commit ID is used. If **Source version** is blank, the default branch's HEAD commit ID is used. Change the value for **Git clone depth**. This creates a shallow clone with a history truncated to the specified number of commits. If you want a full clone, choose **Full**.

4. Expand **Show advanced options**.

   - If you want to change the output artifacts type for this build only, choose the replacement type in **Artifacts type**.
   - If you want to change the name of the output artifact for this build only, type the replacement name in **Artifacts name**.

- If you want to change the name of the output bucket for this build only, choose the replacement name in **Bucket name**.
- If you want to change the way output artifacts are packaged for this build only, choose the replacement packaging type in **Artifacts packaging**.
- If you want to change the build timeout for this build only, specify the new value in **Timeout**.

5. Expand **Environment variables**.

If you want to change the environment variables for this build only, change the values for **Name**, **Value**, and **Type**. Use **Add row** to add a new environment variable for this build only. Choose the delete (**X**) button next to an environment variable you do not want to use in this build.

Others can see an environment variable by using the AWS CodeBuild console and the AWS CLI. If you have no concerns about the visibility of your environment variable, set the **Name** and **Value** fields, and then set **Type** to **Plaintext**.

We recommend that you store an environment variable with a sensitive value, such as an AWS access key ID, an AWS secret access key, or a password as a parameter in Amazon EC2 Systems Manager Parameter Store. For **Type**, choose **Parameter Store**. For **Name**, type an identifier for AWS CodeBuild to reference. For **Value**, type the parameter's name as stored in Amazon EC2 Systems Manager Parameter Store. Using a parameter named `/CodeBuild/dockerLoginPassword` as an example, for **Type**, choose **Parameter Store**. For **Name**, type `LOGIN_PASSWORD`. For **Value**, type `/CodeBuild/dockerLoginPassword`. **Important** We recommend that you store parameters in Amazon EC2 Systems Manager Parameter Store with parameter names that start with `/CodeBuild/` (for example, `/CodeBuild/dockerLoginPassword`). You can use the AWS CodeBuild console to create a parameter in Amazon EC2 Systems Manager. Choose **Create a parameter**, and then follow the instructions in the dialog box. (In that dialog box, for **KMS key**, you can optionally specify the ARN of an AWS KMS key in your account. Amazon EC2 Systems Manager uses this key to encrypt the parameter's value during storage and decrypt during retrieval.) If you use the AWS CodeBuild console to create a parameter, the console starts the parameter with `/CodeBuild/` as it is being stored. For more information, see Systems Manager Parameter Store and Systems Manager Parameter Store Console Walkthrough in the *Amazon EC2 Systems Manager User Guide*.
If your build project refers to parameters stored in Amazon EC2 Systems Manager Parameter Store, the build project's service role must allow the `ssm:GetParameters` action. If you chose **Create a service role in your account** earlier, then AWS CodeBuild includes this action in the default service role for your build project automatically. However, if you chose **Choose an existing service role from your account**, then you must include this action in your service role separately.
If your build project refers to parameters stored in Amazon EC2 Systems Manager Parameter Store with parameter names that do not start with `/CodeBuild/`, and you chose **Create a service role in your account**, then you must update that service role to allow access to parameter names that do not start with `/CodeBuild/`. This is because that service role allows access only to parameter names that start with `/CodeBuild/`.
Any environment variables you set replace existing environment variables. For example, if the Docker image already contains an environment variable named `MY_VAR` with a value of `my_value`, and you set an environment variable named `MY_VAR` with a value of `other_value`, then `my_value` is replaced by `other_value`. Similarly, if the Docker image already contains an environment variable named `PATH` with a value of `/usr/local/sbin:/usr/local/bin`, and you set an environment variable named `PATH` with a value of `$PATH:/usr/share/ant/bin`, then `/usr/local/sbin:/usr/local/bin` is replaced by the literal value `$PATH:/usr/share/ant/bin`.
Do not set any environment variable with a name that begins with `CODEBUILD_`. This prefix is reserved for internal use.
If an environment variable with the same name is defined in multiple places, its value is determined as follows:
The value in the start build operation call takes highest precedence. The value in the build project definition takes next precedence. The value in the build spec declaration takes lowest precedence.

6. Choose **Start build**.

For detailed information about this build, see View Build Details (Console).

Run a Build (AWS CLI)

Note

To use AWS CodePipeline to run a build with AWS CodeBuild, skip these steps and follow the instructions in Create a Pipeline that Uses AWS CodeBuild (AWS CLI).

For more information about using the AWS CLI with AWS CodeBuild, see the Command Line Reference.

1. Run the `start-build` command in one of the following ways:

```
1 aws codebuild start-build --project-name project-name
```

Use this if you want to run a build that uses the latest version of the build input artifact and the build project's existing settings.

```
1 aws codebuild start-build --generate-cli-skeleton
```

Use this if you want to run a build with an earlier version of the build input artifact or if you want to override the settings for the build output artifacts, environment variables, build spec, or default build timeout period.

2. If you run the `start-build` command with the `--project-name` option, replace *project-name* with the name of the build project, and then skip to step 6 of this procedure. To get a list of build projects, see View a List of Build Project Names.

3. If you run the `start-build` command with the `--idempotency-token` option, a unique case sensitive identifier, or token, is included with the `start-build` request. The token is valid for 12 hours after the request. If you repeat the `start-build` request with the same token, but change a parameter, AWS CodeBuild returns a parameter mismatch error.

4. If you run the `start-build` command with the `--generate-cli-skeleton` option, JSON-formatted data appears in the output. Copy the data to a file (for example, `start-build.json`) in a location on the local computer or instance where the AWS CLI is installed. Modify the copied data to match the following format, and save your results:

```
1  {
2    "projectName": "projectName",
3    "sourceVersion": "sourceVersion",
4    "artifactsOverride": {
5      "type": "type",
6      "location": "location",
7      "path": "path",
8      "namespaceType": "namespaceType",
9      "name": "artifactsOverride-name",
10     "packaging": "packaging"
11   },
12   "buildspecOverride": "buildspecOverride",
13   "cacheOverride": {
14       "location": "cacheOverride-location",
15       "type": "cacheOverride-type",
16   },
17   "certificateOverride": "certificateOverride",
18   "computeTypeOverride": "computeTypeOverride",
19   "environmentTypeOverride": "environmentTypeOverride",
20   "environmentVariablesOverride": {
21       "name": "environmentVariablesOverride-name",
```

```
22        "value": "environmentVariablesValue",
23        "type": "environmentVariablesOverride-type"
24    },
25    "gitCloneDepthOverride": "gitCloneDepthOverride",
26    "imageOverride": "imageOverride",
27    "idempotencyToken": "idempotencyToken",
28    "insecureSslOverride": "insecureSslOverride",
29    "privilegedModeOverride": "privilegedModeOverride",
30    "timeoutInMinutesOverride": timeoutInMinutesOverride",
31    "sourceAuthOverride": "sourceAuthOverride",
32    "sourceLocationOverride": "sourceLocationOverride",
33    "serviceRoleOverride": "serviceRoleOverride",
34    "sourceTypeOverride": "sourceTypeOverride"
35 }
```

Replace the following placeholders:

- *projectName*: Required string. The name of the build project to use for this build.
- *sourceVersion*: Optional string. A version of the source code to be built, as follows:
  - For Amazon S3, the version ID that corresponds to the version of the input ZIP file you want to build. If *sourceVersion* is not specified, then the latest version is used.
  - For AWS CodeCommit, the commit ID that corresponds to the version of the source code you want to build. If *sourceVersion* is not specified, the default branch's HEAD commit ID is used. (You cannot specify a tag name for *sourceVersion*, but you can specify the tag's commit ID.)
  - For GitHub, the commit ID, pull request ID, branch name, or tag name that corresponds to the version of the source code you want to build. If a pull request ID is specified, it must use the format `pr/pull-request-ID` (for example, `pr/25`). If a branch name is specified, the branch's HEAD commit ID is used. If *sourceVersion* is not specified, the default branch's HEAD commit ID is used.
  - For Bitbucket, the commit ID, branch name, or tag name that corresponds to the version of the source code you want to build. If a branch name is specified, the branch's HEAD commit ID is used. If *sourceVersion* is not specified, the default branch's HEAD commit ID is used.
- The following placeholders are for `artifactsOveride`.
  - *type*: Optional string. The build output artifact type that overrides for this build the one defined in the build project.
  - *location*: Optional string. The build output artifact location that overrides for this build the one defined in the build project.
  - *path*: Optional string. The build output artifact path that overrides for this build the one defined in the build project.
  - *namespaceType*: Optional string. The build output artifact path type that overrides for this build the one defined in the build project.
  - *name*: Optional string. The build output artifact name that overrides for this build the one defined in the build project.
  - *packaging*: Optional string. The build output artifact packaging type that overrides for this build the one defined in the build project.
- *buildspecOverride*: Optional string. A build spec declaration that overrides for this build the one defined in the build project. If this value is set, it can be either an inline build spec definition or the path to an alternate build spec file relative to the value of the built-in `CODEBUILD_SRC_DIR` environment variable.
- The following placeholders are for `cacheOveride`.
  - *cacheOverride-location*: Optional string. The location of a `ProjectCache` object for this build that overrides the `ProjectCache` object specified in the build project. `cacheOverride` is optional and takes a `ProjectCache` object. `location` is required in a `ProjectCache` object.
  - *cacheOverride-type*: Optional string. The type of a `ProjectCache` object for this build that overrides the `ProjectCache` object specified in the build project. `cacheOverride` is optional and

212

takes a `ProjectCache` object. `type` is required in a `ProjectCache` object.

- *certificateOverride*: Optional string. The name of a certificate for this build that overrides the one specified in the build project.
- *environmentTypeOverride*: Optional string. A container type for this build that overrides the one specified in the build project. The current valid string is `LINUX_CONTAINER`.
- The following placeholders are for `environmentVariablesOveride`.
    - *environmentVariablesOverride-name*: Optional string. The name of an environment variable in the build project whose value you want to override for this build.
    - *environmentVariablesOverride-type*: Optional string. The type of environment variable in the build project whose value you want to override for this build.
    - *environmentVariablesValue*: Optional string. The value of the environment variable defined in the build project that you want to override for this build.
- *gitCloneDepthOverride*: Optional string. The value of the **Git clone depth** in the build project whose value you want to override for this build. If your source type is Amazon S3, this value is not supported.
- *imageOverride*: Optional string. The name of an image for this build that overrides the one specified in the build project.
- *idempotencyToken*: Optional string. A string that serves as a token to specify that the build request is idempotent. You can choose any string that is 64 characters or less. The token is valid for 12 hours after the start-build request. If you repeat the start-build request with the same token, but change a parameter, AWS CodeBuild returns a parameter mismatch error.
- *insecureSslOverride*: Optional boolean that specifies whether to override the insecure SSL setting specified in the build project. The insecure SSL setting determines whether to ignore SSL warnings while connecting to the project source code. This override applies only if the build's source is GitHub Enterprise.
- *privilegedModeOverride*: Optional boolean. If set to true, the build overrides privileged mode in the build project.
- *sourceAuthOverride*: Optional string. An authorization type for this build that overrides the one defined in the build project. This override applies only if the build project's source is BitBucket or GitHub.
- *sourceLocationOverride*: Optional string. A location that overrides for this build the source location for the one defined in the build project.
- *serviceRoleOverride*: Optional string. The name of a service role for this build that overrides the one specified in the build project.
- *sourceTypeOverride*: Optional string. A source input type for this build that overrides the source input defined in the build project. Valid strings are `NO_SOURCE`, `CODECOMMIT`, `CODEPIPELINE`, `GITHUB`, `S3`, `BITBUCKET`, and `GITHUB_ENTERPRISE`.
- *timeoutInMinutesOverride*: Optional number. The number of build timeout minutes that overrides for this build the one defined in the build project. **Important**
We recommend that you store an environment variable with a sensitive value, such as an AWS access key ID, an AWS secret access key, or a password as a parameter in Amazon EC2 Systems Manager Parameter Store. AWS CodeBuild can use a parameter stored in Amazon EC2 Systems Manager Parameter Store only if that parameter's name starts with `/CodeBuild/` (for example, `/CodeBuild/dockerLoginPassword`). You can use the AWS CodeBuild console to create a parameter in Amazon EC2 Systems Manager. Choose **Create a parameter**, and then follow the instructions in the dialog box. (In that dialog box, for **KMS key**, you can optionally specify the ARN of an AWS KMS key in your account. Amazon EC2 Systems Manager uses this key to encrypt the parameter's value during storage and decrypt during retrieval.) If you use the AWS CodeBuild console to create a parameter, the console starts the parameter with `/CodeBuild/` as it is being stored. However, if you use the Amazon EC2 Systems Manager Parameter Store console to create a parameter, you must start the parameter's name with `/CodeBuild/`, and you must set **Type** to **Secure String**. For more information, see Systems Manager Parameter Store and Systems Manager Parameter Store Console Walkthrough in the *Amazon EC2 Systems Manager User Guide*.
If your build project refers to parameters stored in Amazon EC2 Systems Manager Parameter Store,

the build project's service role must allow the `ssm:GetParameters` action. If you chose **Create a new service role in your account** earlier, then AWS CodeBuild includes this action in the default service role for your build project automatically. However, if you chose **Choose an existing service role from your account**, then you must include this action in your service role separately.

Environment variables you set replace existing environment variables. For example, if the Docker image already contains an environment variable named `MY_VAR` with a value of `my_value`, and you set an environment variable named `MY_VAR` with a value of `other_value`, then `my_value` is replaced by `other_value`. Similarly, if the Docker image already contains an environment variable named `PATH` with a value of `/usr/local/sbin:/usr/local/bin`, and you set an environment variable named `PATH` with a value of `$PATH:/usr/share/ant/bin`, then `/usr/local/sbin:/usr/local/bin` is replaced by the literal value `$PATH:/usr/share/ant/bin`.

Do not set any environment variable with a name that begins with `CODEBUILD_`. This prefix is reserved for internal use.

If an environment variable with the same name is defined in multiple places, the environment variable's value is determined as follows:

The value in the start build operation call takes highest precedence. The value in the build project definition takes next precedence. The value in the build spec declaration takes lowest precedence.

For information about valid values for these placeholders, see Create a Build Project (AWS CLI). For a list of the latest settings for a build project, see View a Build Project's Details.

5. Switch to the directory that contains the file you just saved, and run the `start-build` command again.

```
1 aws codebuild start-build --cli-input-json file://start-build.json
```

6. If successful, data similar to that described in the To run the build (AWS CLI) procedure appears in the output.

To work with detailed information about this build, make a note of the `id` value in the output, and then see View Build Details (AWS CLI).

Start Running Builds Automatically (AWS CLI)

If your source code is stored in a GitHub or a GitHub Enterprise repository, you can use GitHub webhooks to have AWS CodeBuild rebuild your source code whenever a code change is pushed to the repository.

Run the `create-webhook` command as follows:

```
1 aws codebuild create-webhook --project-name
```

- where *project-name* is the name of the build project that contains the source code to be rebuilt.

For GitHub, information similar to the following appears in the output:

```
1 {
2   "webhook": {
3     "url": "url"
4   }
5 }
```

- where *url* is the URL to the GitHub webhook.

For GitHub Enterprise, information similar to the following appears in the output:

```
{
    "webhook": {
        "secret": "YRV4JYAGFsekJiirp5ytx86oZpyhUdySNSDTLNuXoXX1c7aZ6XYDf37-ZFyY02rs4JSE7OmLW3w-gh-ryoVB8OSSSC1aAtBtuPkHw
YuncCCmdogCVCfniQ7ukYX2_xM--nlDma5EngIg_Bi_N465yi33zyTUNPoQlxCpLO-BwghcVa9lAurwR77-uY7i-_XCJFahwMx1f4ubOgBBSmMT2A16apqjq
QJoKSb61XVKyZy1Giuy4nliAXfv9WNn76CaCsndb3fVIE78fpygfo41xYxSQ6vpo6LRTKtPzbyeTHbVXGda1PJvnkBlnKmJDo0RTgI1m2oYr17dWziQlrrvo
CoNgy1SOO_7LKfA-nNXFc_f1SiFy0AqeMB43-dOOcdkzybHncE81QTRwEUCFfmX-AJCwmLXVOkg0G67T92Sjbpz0fRlkh5pwIFl93_bB_jOHDinK6iOiPpf2
dIDAIZgGMagqZeWb-axDeTAbopoU8J6gFI1yKo5aq9ql51zC1PERUsMgJFtJr_a-Z-L_kylr-4hSSxasSJNuJ43_XOBRWqT51xqvH-A69bVO7KbVT_Kc6wxk
SHyYCEMoa_Pfa7ZQgyfY6B00ogMNj31yFbjthORNL1cDo6-3J-McDLoyrRtSEOV9QnxvsG5zu1N5-z20rkJtg_MOfNwocfUutFXb7vrGTduHlR1dzXLRusHu
xOVVuDUWm9vhWMr-hUkeGo_1kDKyk4E2QFvZXpjYw0vFfV-dwxFRR_mifzxW1wyfmt2iFtLkp_YZj_4WeFAckGefr-ilNaYvsZpzXj78Ae1adVoLf48AmDdN
2pWsWJjatU9zt942gLisFFmKakcvJuy5yxXHaxxbhUyC8NHYiESUWPfcfnqrMsr8op3P4AUCHlpiZCYYuiwI_cac-pIUBO0Xaur_lu_fyFghgOJc7cfTnA36
rv5X5DnFDM8P3HNBeLjaF9QZ6AijegPEwTHIkJON3AUDwpkz_hwTXyUoAU8MdZfPTXbBoT6N5Z5THBHsYxR",
        "payloadUrl": "https://codebuild.us-east-2.amazonaws.com/webhooks?t=eyJlbmNyeXB0ZWREYXRhIjoiUmFqMmJERGRQbGhwLzNT
Nld3R0VGRjZZOTNwLzlZVG1NZlpIR1E0RUsxdzhGeWhnVFFqWTR0WEFwT2dJRnNmRHc3S3RNc0xYMENncXFTakg1cE1nSy9zPSIsIml2UGFyYW11dGVyU3Bl
YyI6IndSQ1Qrc2VPQjBCZzhPeVYiLCJtYXRlcmlhbFNldFNlcmlhbCI6MX0%3D&v=1"
    }
}
```

Copy the secret key and payload URL from the output. You need them to add a webhook in GitHub Enterprise. In GitHub Enterprise, choose the repository where your AWS CodeBuild project is stored, choose **Settings**, choose **Hooks & services**, and then choose **Add webhook**. Enter the payload URL and secret key, accept the defaults for the other fields, and then choose **Add webhook**.

Stop Running Builds Automatically (AWS CLI)

If your source code is stored in a GitHub or a GitHub Enterprise repository, you can set up GitHub webhooks to have AWS CodeBuild rebuild your source code whenever a code change is pushed to the respository. For more information, see Start Running Builds Automatically (AWS CLI).

If you have enabled this behavior, you can turn it off by running the `delete-webhook` command as follows:

```
1 aws codebuild delete-webhook --project-name
```

- where *project-name* is the name of the build project that contains the source code to be rebuilt.

If this command is successful, no information and no errors appear in the output.

Note
This deletes the webhook from your AWS CodeBuild project only. You should also delete the webhook from your GitHub or GitHub Enterprise repository.

Run a Build (AWS SDKs)

To use AWS CodePipeline to run a build with AWS CodeBuild, skip these steps and follow the instructions in Use AWS CodePipeline with AWS CodeBuild to Test Code and Run Builds instead.

For information about using AWS CodeBuild with the AWS SDKs, see the AWS SDKs and Tools Reference.

View Build Details in AWS CodeBuild

To view details about builds managed by AWS CodeBuild, you can use the AWS CodeBuild console, AWS CLI, or AWS SDKs.

Topics

- View Build Details (Console)
- View Build Details (AWS CLI)
- View Build Details (AWS SDKs)
- Build Phase Transitions

View Build Details (Console)

1. Open the AWS CodeBuild console at https://console.aws.amazon.com/codebuild/.

2. Do one of the following:

   - In the navigation pane, choose **Build history**. In the list of builds, in the **Build run** column, choose the link that corresponds to the build.
   - In the navigation pane, choose **Build projects**. In the list of build projects, in the **Project** column, choose the link that corresponds to the name of the build project. Then, in the list of builds, in the **Build run** column, choose the link that corresponds to the build. **Note**
     By default, only the ten most recent builds or build projects are displayed. To view more builds or build projects, select a different value for **Builds per page** or **Projects per page** or select the back and forward arrows for **Viewing builds** or **Viewing projects**.

View Build Details (AWS CLI)

For more information about using the AWS CLI with AWS CodeBuild, see the Command Line Reference.

Run the `batch-get-builds` command:

```
1 aws codebuild batch-get-builds --ids ids
```

Replace the following placeholder:

- *ids*: Required string. One or more build IDs to view details about. To specify more than one build ID, separate each build ID with a space. You can specify up to 100 build IDs. To get a list of build IDs, see one or more of the following topics:
  - View a List of Build IDs (AWS CLI)
  - View a List of Build IDs for a Build Project (AWS CLI)

For example, if you run this command:

```
1 aws codebuild batch-get-builds --ids codebuild-demo-project:e9c4f4df-3f43-41d2-ab3a-60fe2EXAMPLE
    codebuild-demo-project:815e755f-bade-4a7e-80f0-efe51EXAMPLE my-other-project:813bb6c6-891b
    -426a-9dd7-6d8a3EXAMPLE
```

If the command is successful, data similar to that described in the To view summarized build information (AWS CLI) procedure in Getting Started will appear in the output.

View Build Details (AWS SDKs)

For more information about using AWS CodeBuild with the AWS SDKs, see the AWS SDKs and Tools Reference.

Build Phase Transitions

Builds in AWS CodeBuild proceed in phases:

An important point to note here is that the `UPLOAD_ARTIFACTS` phase is always attempted, even if the `BUILD` phase fails.

View a List of Build IDs in AWS CodeBuild

To view a list of build IDs for builds managed by AWS CodeBuild, you can use the AWS CodeBuild console, AWS CLI, or AWS SDKs.

Topics

- View a List of Build IDs (Console)
- View a List of Build IDs (AWS CLI)
- View a List of Build IDs (AWS SDKs)

View a List of Build IDs (Console)

1. Open the AWS CodeBuild console at https://console.aws.amazon.com/codebuild/.

2. In the navigation pane, choose **Build history**. **Note**
   By default, only the ten most recent builds are displayed. To view more builds, select a different value for **Builds per page** or select the back and forward arrows for **Viewing builds**.

View a List of Build IDs (AWS CLI)

For more information about using the AWS CLI with AWS CodeBuild, see the Command Line Reference.

- Run the `list-builds` command:

```
1 aws codebuild list-builds --sort-order sort-order --next-token next-token
```

In the preceding command, replace the following placeholders:

- *sort-order*: Optional string. How to list the build IDs. Valid values include `ASCENDING` and `DESCENDING`.

- *next-token*: Optional string. During a previous run, if there were more than 100 items in the list, only the first 100 items would be returned, along with a unique string called a *next token*. To get the next batch of items in the list, run this command again, adding the next token to the call. To get all of the items in the list, keep running this command with each subsequent next token, until no more next tokens are returned.

For example, if you run this command:

```
1 aws codebuild list-builds --sort-order ASCENDING
```

A result similar to the following might appear in the output:

```
1 {
2   "nextToken": "4AEA6u7J...The full token has been omitted for brevity...MzY2OA==",
3   "ids": [
4     "codebuild-demo-project:815e755f-bade-4a7e-80f0-efe51EXAMPLE"
5     "codebuild-demo-project:84a7f3d1-d40e-4956-b4cf-7a9d4EXAMPLE"
6     ... The full list of build IDs has been omitted for brevity ...
7     "codebuild-demo-project:931d0b72-bf6f-4040-a472-5c707EXAMPLE"
8   ]
9 }
```

If you run this command again:

```
1 aws codebuild list-builds --sort-order ASCENDING --next-token 4AEA6u7J...The full token has
    been omitted for brevity...MzY2OA==
```

A result similar to the following might appear in the output:

```
1 {
2    "ids": [
3        "codebuild-demo-project:49015049-21cf-4b50-9708-df115EXAMPLE",
4        "codebuild-demo-project:543e7206-68a3-46d6-a4da-759abEXAMPLE",
5        ... The full list of build IDs has been omitted for brevity ...
6        "codebuild-demo-project:c282f198-4582-4b38-bdc0-26f96EXAMPLE"
7    ]
8 }
```

View a List of Build IDs (AWS SDKs)

For more information about using AWS CodeBuild with the AWS SDKs, see the AWS SDKs and Tools Reference.

View a List of Build IDs for a Build Project in AWS CodeBuild

You can use the AWS CodeBuild console, AWS CLI, or AWS SDKs to view a list of build IDs for a build project in AWS CodeBuild.

Topics

- View a List of Build IDs for a Build Project (Console)
- View a List of Build IDs for a Build Project (AWS CLI)
- View a List of Build IDs for a Build Project (AWS SDKs)

View a List of Build IDs for a Build Project (Console)

1. Open the AWS CodeBuild console at https://console.aws.amazon.com/codebuild/.

2. In the navigation pane, choose **Build projects**. In the list of build projects, in the **Project** column, choose the build project.

Note

By default, only the ten most recent builds or build projects are displayed. To view more builds or build projects, select a different value for **Builds per page** or **Projects per page** or select the back and forward arrows for **Viewing builds** or **Viewing projects**.

View a List of Build IDs for a Build Project (AWS CLI)

For more information about using the AWS CLI with AWS CodeBuild, see the Command Line Reference.

Run the `list-builds-for-project` command, as follows:

```
1 aws codebuild list-builds-for-project --project-name project-name --sort-order sort-order --next
    -token next-token
```

In the preceding command, replace the following placeholders:

- *project-name*: Required string. The name of the build project to list builds IDs for. To get a list of build projects, see View a List of Build Project Names (AWS CLI).
- *sort-order*: Optional string. How to list the build IDs. Valid values include `ASCENDING` and `DESCENDING`.
- *next-token*: Optional string. During a previous run, if there were more than 100 items in the list, only the first 100 items are returned, along with a unique string called a *next token*. To get the next batch of items in the list, run this command again, adding the next token to the call. To get all of the items in the list, keep running this command with each subsequent next token that is returned, until no more next tokens are returned.

For example, if you run this command similar to this:

```
1 aws codebuild list-builds-for-project --project-name codebuild-demo-project --sort-order
    ASCENDING
```

A result like the following might appear in the output:

```
1 {
2   "nextToken": "4AEA6u7J...The full token has been omitted for brevity...MzY2OA==",
3   "ids": [
4     "codebuild-demo-project:9b175d16-66fd-4e71-93a0-50a08EXAMPLE"
5     "codebuild-demo-project:a9d1bd09-18a2-456b-8a36-7d65aEXAMPLE"
6     ... The full list of build IDs has been omitted for brevity ...
7     "codebuild-demo-project:fe70d102-c04f-421a-9cfa-2dc15EXAMPLE"
```

```
8    ]
9 }
```

If you run this command again:

```
1 aws codebuild list-builds-for-project --project-name codebuild-demo-project --sort-order
      ASCENDING --next-token 4AEA6u7J...The full token has been omitted for brevity...MzY2OA==
```

A result like the following might be output:

```
1 {
2   "ids": [
3     "codebuild-demo-project:98253670-7a8a-4546-b908-dc890EXAMPLE"
4     "codebuild-demo-project:ad5405b2-1ab3-44df-ae2d-fba84EXAMPLE"
5     ... The full list of build IDs has been omitted for brevity ...
6     "codebuild-demo-project:f721a282-380f-4b08-850a-e0ac1EXAMPLE"
7   ]
8 }
```

View a List of Build IDs for a Build Project (AWS SDKs)

For more information about using AWS CodeBuild with the AWS SDKs, see the AWS SDKs and Tools Reference.

Stop a Build in AWS CodeBuild

To stop a build in AWS CodeBuild, you can use the AWS CodeBuild console, AWS CLI,or AWS SDKs.

Topics

- Stop a Build (Console)
- Stop a Build (AWS CLI)
- Stop a Build (AWS SDKs)

Stop a Build (Console)

1. Open the AWS CodeBuild console at https://console.aws.amazon.com/codebuild/.

2. Do one of the following:

   - If the ***build-project-name:build-ID*** page is displayed, choose **Stop**.
   - In the navigation pane, choose **Build history**. In the list of builds, choose the box that corresponds to the build, and then choose **Stop**.
   - In the navigation pane, choose **Build projects**. In the list of build projects, in the **Project** column, choose the link that corresponds to the build project's name. In the list of builds, choose the box that corresponds to the build, and then choose **Stop**.

Note
By default, only the most recent 10 builds or build projects are displayed. To view more builds or build projects, select a different value for **Builds per page** or **Projects per page** or select the back and forward arrows for **Viewing builds** or **Viewing projects**.
If AWS CodeBuild cannot successfully stop a build (for example, the build process is already complete), the **Stop** button will be disabled or may be missing altogether.

Stop a Build (AWS CLI)

- Run the `stop-build` command:

```
1 aws codebuild stop-build --id id
```

   In the preceding command, replace the following placeholder:

   - *id*: Required string. The ID of the build to stop. To get a list of build IDs, see the following topics:
     - View a List of Build IDs (AWS CLI)
     - View a List of Build IDs for a Build Project (AWS CLI)

   If AWS CodeBuild successfully stops the build, the `buildStatus` value in the `build` object in the output will be `STOPPED`.

   If AWS CodeBuild cannot successfully stop the build (for example, the build is already complete), the `buildStatus` value in the `build` object in the output will be the final build status (for example, `SUCCEEDED`).

Stop a Build (AWS SDKs)

For more information about using AWS CodeBuild with the AWS SDKs, see the AWS SDKs and Tools Reference.

Delete Builds in AWS CodeBuild

To delete builds in AWS CodeBuild, you can use the AWS CLI, or the AWS SDKs.

Delete Builds (AWS CLI)

Run the `batch-delete-builds` command:

```
1 aws codebuild batch-delete-builds --ids ids
```

In the preceding command, replace the following placeholder:

- *ids*: Required string. The IDs of the builds to delete. To specify multiple builds, separate each build ID with a space. To get a list of build IDs, see the following topics:
  - View a List of Build IDs (AWS CLI)
  - View a List of Build IDs for a Build Project (AWS CLI)

If successful, a `buildsDeleted` array appears in the output, containing the Amazon Resource Name (ARN) of each build that was successfully deleted. Information about builds that were not successfully deleted appears in output within a `buildsNotDeleted` array.

For example, if you run this command:

```
1 aws codebuild batch-delete-builds --ids my-demo-build-project:f8b888d2-5e1e-4032-8645-
    b115195648EX my-other-demo-build-project:a18bc6ee-e499-4887-b36a-8c90349c7eEX
```

Information similar to the following appears in the output:

```
1  {
2    "buildsNotDeleted": [
3      {
4        "id": "arn:aws:codebuild:us-west-2:123456789012:build/my-demo-build-project:f8b888d2-5e1e
            -4032-8645-b115195648EX",
5        "statusCode": "BUILD_IN_PROGRESS"
6      }
7    ],
8    "buildsDeleted": [
9      "arn:aws:codebuild:us-west-2:123456789012:build/my-other-demo-build-project:a18bc6ee-e499
          -4887-b36a-8c90349c7eEX"
10   ]
11 }
```

Delete Builds (AWS SDKs)

For information about using AWS CodeBuild with the AWS SDKs, see the AWS SDKs and Tools Reference.

Advanced Topics

This section includes several advanced topics that are useful to more experienced AWS CodeBuild users.

Topics

- Advanced Setup
- Command Line Reference for AWS CodeBuild
- AWS SDKs and Tools Reference for AWS CodeBuild
- Specify the AWS CodeBuild Endpoint
- Authentication and Access Control for AWS CodeBuild
- Logging AWS CodeBuild API Calls with AWS CloudTrail

Advanced Setup

If you follow the steps in Getting Started to access AWS CodeBuild for the first time, most likely you will not need to reference the information in this topic. However, as you continue using AWS CodeBuild, you will want to do things such as give IAM groups and users in your organization access to AWS CodeBuild, modify existing service roles in IAM or customer master keys in AWS KMS to access AWS CodeBuild, or set up the AWS CLI across your organization's workstations to access AWS CodeBuild. This topic describes how to complete the related setup steps.

We assume you already have an AWS account. However, if you do not already have one, go to http://aws.amazon.com, choose **Sign In to the Console**, and follow the online instructions.

Topics

- Add AWS CodeBuild Access Permissions to an IAM Group or IAM User
- Create an AWS CodeBuild Service Role
- Create and Configure an AWS KMS CMK for AWS CodeBuild
- Install and Configure the AWS CLI

Add AWS CodeBuild Access Permissions to an IAM Group or IAM User

To access AWS CodeBuild with an IAM group or IAM user, you must add access permissions. This section describes how to do this with the IAM console or the AWS CLI.

If you will access AWS CodeBuild with your AWS root account (not recommended) or an administrator IAM user in your AWS account, then you do not need to follow these instructions.

For information about AWS root accounts and administrator IAM users, see The Account Root User and Creating Your First IAM Admin User and Group in the *IAM User Guide*.

To add AWS CodeBuild access permissions to an IAM group or IAM user (console)

1. Open the IAM console at https://console.aws.amazon.com/iam/.

   You should have already signed in to the AWS Management Console by using one of the following:

   - Your AWS root account. This is not recommended. For more information, see The Account Root User in the *IAM User Guide*.

   - An administrator IAM user in your AWS account. For more information, see Creating Your First IAM Admin User and Group in the *IAM User Guide*.

   - An IAM user in your AWS account with permission to perform the following minimum set of actions:

     1 `iam:AttachGroupPolicy`
     2 `iam:AttachUserPolicy`
     3 `iam:CreatePolicy`
     4 `iam:ListAttachedGroupPolicies`
     5 `iam:ListAttachedUserPolicies`
     6 `iam:ListGroups`
     7 `iam:ListPolicies`
     8 `iam:ListUsers`

     For more information, see Overview of IAM Policies in the *IAM User Guide*.

2. In the navigation pane, choose **Policies**.

3. To add a custom set of AWS CodeBuild access permissions to an IAM group or IAM user, skip ahead to step 4 in this procedure.

To add a default set of AWS CodeBuild access permissions to an IAM group or IAM user, choose **Policy Type**, **AWS Managed**, and then do the following:

- To add full access permissions to AWS CodeBuild, select the box named **AWSCodeBuildAdminAccess**. Then choose **Policy Actions**, **Attach**. Select the box next to the target IAM group or IAM user, and then choose **Attach Policy**. Repeat this for the policies named **AmazonS3ReadOnlyAccess** and **IAMFullAccess**.
- To add access permissions to AWS CodeBuild for everything except build project administration, select the box named **AWSCodeBuildDeveloperAccess**. Then choose **Policy Actions**, **Attach**. Select the box next to the target IAM group or IAM user, and then choose **Attach Policy**. Repeat this for the policy named **AmazonS3ReadOnlyAccess**.
- To add read-only access permissions to AWS CodeBuild, select the boxes named **AWSCodeBuildReadOnlyAccess**. Select the box next to the target IAM group or IAM user, and then choose **Attach Policy**. Repeat this for the policy named **AmazonS3ReadOnlyAccess**.

You have now added a default set of AWS CodeBuild access permissions to an IAM group or IAM user. Skip the rest of the steps in this procedure.

4. Choose **Create Policy**.

5. On the **Create Policy** page, next to **Create Your Own Policy**, choose **Select**.

6. On the **Review Policy** page, for **Policy Name**, type a name for the policy (for example, **CodeBuildAccessPolicy**). If you use a different name, substitute it throughout this procedure.

7. For **Policy Document**, type the following, and then choose **Create Policy**.

```
{
  "Version": "2012-10-17",
  "Statement": [
    {
      "Sid": "CodeBuildDefaultPolicy",
      "Effect": "Allow",
      "Action": [
        "codebuild:*",
        "iam:PassRole"
      ],
      "Resource": "*"
    },
    {
      "Sid": "CloudWatchLogsAccessPolicy",
      "Effect": "Allow",
      "Action": [
        "logs:FilterLogEvents",
        "logs:GetLogEvents"
      ],
      "Resource": "*"
    },
    {
      "Sid": "S3AccessPolicy",
      "Effect": "Allow",
      "Action": [
        "s3:CreateBucket",
        "s3:GetObject",
        "s3:List*",
        "s3:PutObject"
      ],
      "Resource": "*"
```

```
32        }
33    ]
34 }
```

Note

This policy allows access to all AWS CodeBuild actions and to a potentially large number of AWS resources. To restrict permissions to specific AWS CodeBuild actions, change the value of `codebuild:*` in the AWS CodeBuild policy statement. For more information, see Authentication and Access Control. To restrict access to specific AWS resources, change the value of the `Resource` object. For more information, see Authentication and Access Control.

1. In the navigation pane, choose **Groups** or **Users**.

2. In the list of groups or users, choose the name of the IAM group or IAM user to which you want to add AWS CodeBuild access permissions.

3. For a group, on the group settings page, on the **Permissions** tab, expand **Managed Policies**, and choose **Attach Policy**.

   For a user, on the user settings page, on the **Permissions** tab, choose **Add permissions**.

4. For a group, on the **Attach Policy** page, select **CodeBuildAccessPolicy**, and then choose **Attach Policy**.

   For a user, on the **Add permisions** page, choose **Attach existing policies directly**. Select **CodeBuildAccessPolicy**, choose **Next: Reivew**, and then choose **Add permissions**.

To add AWS CodeBuild access permissions to an IAM group or IAM user (AWS CLI)

1. Make sure you have configured the AWS CLI with the AWS access key and AWS secret access key that correspond to one of the IAM entities, as described in the previous procedure. For more information, see Getting Set Up with the AWS Command Line Interface in the *AWS Command Line Interface User Guide*.

2. To add a custom set of AWS CodeBuild access permissions to an IAM group or IAM user, skip ahead to step 3 in this procedure.

   To add a default set of AWS CodeBuild access permissions to an IAM group or IAM user, do the following:

   Run one of the following commands, depending on whether you want to add permissions to an IAM group or IAM user:

```
1 aws iam attach-group-policy --group-name group-name --policy-arn policy-arn
2
3 aws iam attach-user-policy --user-name user-name --policy-arn policy-arn
```

   You must run the command three times, replacing *group-name* or *user-name* with the IAM group name or IAM user name, and replacing *policy-arn* once for each of the following policy Amazon Resource Names (ARNs):

   - To add full access permissions to AWS CodeBuild, use the following policy ARNs:
     - `arn:aws:iam::aws:policy/AWSCodeBuildAdminAccess`
     - `arn:aws:iam::aws:policy/AmazonS3ReadOnlyAccess`
     - `arn:aws:iam::aws:policy/IAMFullAccess`
   - To add access permissions to AWS CodeBuild for everything except build project administration, use the following policy ARNs:
     - `arn:aws:iam::aws:policy/AWSCodeBuildDeveloperAccess`
     - `arn:aws:iam::aws:policy/AmazonS3ReadOnlyAccess`
   - To add read-only access permissions to AWS CodeBuild, use the following policy ARNs:
     - `arn:aws:iam::aws:policy/AWSCodeBuildReadOnlyAccess`
     - `arn:aws:iam::aws:policy/AmazonS3ReadOnlyAccess`

227

You have now added a default set of AWS CodeBuild access permissions to an IAM group or IAM user. Skip the rest of the steps in this procedure.

3. In an empty directory on the local workstation or instance where the AWS CLI is installed, create a file named `put-group-policy.json` or `put-user-policy.json`. If you use a different file name, substitute it throughout this procedure.

```
1  {
2    "Version": "2012-10-17",
3    "Statement": [
4      {
5        "Sid": "CodeBuildAccessPolicy",
6        "Effect": "Allow",
7        "Action": [
8          "codebuild:*",
9          "iam:PassRole"
10       ],
11       "Resource": "*"
12     },
13     {
14       "Sid": "CloudWatchLogsAccessPolicy",
15       "Effect": "Allow",
16       "Action": [
17         "logs:FilterLogEvents",
18         "logs:GetLogEvents"
19       ],
20       "Resource": "*"
21     },
22     {
23       "Sid": "S3AccessPolicy",
24       "Effect": "Allow",
25       "Action": [
26         "s3:CreateBucket",
27         "s3:GetObject",
28         "s3:List*",
29         "s3:PutObject"
30       ],
31       "Resource": "*"
32     }
33   ]
34 }
```

Note
This policy allows access to all AWS CodeBuild actions and to a potentially large number of AWS resources. To restrict permissions to specific AWS CodeBuild actions, change the value of `codebuild:*` in the AWS CodeBuild policy statement. For more information, see Authentication and Access Control. To restrict access to specific AWS resources, change the value of the related `Resource` object. For more information, see Authentication and Access Control or the specific AWS service's security documentation.

1. Switch to the directory where you saved the file, and then run one of the following commands. You can use different values for `CodeBuildGroupAccessPolicy` and `CodeBuildUserAccessPolicy`. If you use different values, substitute them here.

   For an IAM group:

```
1  aws iam put-group-policy --group-name group-name --policy-name CodeBuildGroupAccessPolicy
       --policy-document file://put-group-policy.json
```

For an IAM user:

```
1 aws iam put-user-policy --user-name user-name --policy-name CodeBuildUserAccessPolicy --
      policy-document file://put-user-policy.json
```

In the preceding commands, replace *group-name* or *user-name* with the name of the target IAM group or IAM user.

Create an AWS CodeBuild Service Role

You need an AWS CodeBuild service role so that AWS CodeBuild can interact with dependent AWS services on your behalf. You can create an AWS CodeBuild service role by using the AWS CodeBuild or AWS CodePipeline consoles. For information, see:

- Create a Build Project (Console)
- Create a Pipeline that Uses AWS CodeBuild (AWS CodePipeline Console)
- Add an AWS CodeBuild Build Action to a Pipeline (AWS CodePipeline Console)
- Change a Build Project's Settings (Console)

If you do not plan to use these consoles, this section describes how to create an AWS CodeBuild service role with the IAM console or the AWS CLI.

Note

The service role described on this page contains a policy that grants the minimum permissions required to use AWS CodeBuild. You might need to add additional permissions depending on your use case. For example, if you want to use AWS CodeBuild with Amazon Virtual Private Cloud, then the service role you create requires the permissions in the following policy: Create an AWS CodeBuild Service Role.

To create an AWS CodeBuild service role (console)

1. Open the IAM console at https://console.aws.amazon.com/iam/.

   You should have already signed in to the console by using one of the following:

   - Your AWS root account. This is not recommended. For more information, see The Account Root User in the *IAM User Guide*.

   - An administrator IAM user in your AWS account. For more information, see Creating Your First IAM Admin User and Group in the *IAM User Guide*.

   - An IAM user in your AWS account with permission to perform the following minimum set of actions:

   ```
    1 iam:AddRoleToInstanceProfile
    2 iam:AttachRolePolicy
    3 iam:CreateInstanceProfile
    4 iam:CreatePolicy
    5 iam:CreateRole
    6 iam:GetRole
    7 iam:ListAttachedRolePolicies
    8 iam:ListPolicies
    9 iam:ListRoles
   10 iam:PassRole
   11 iam:PutRolePolicy
   12 iam:UpdateAssumeRolePolicy
   ```

   For more information, see Overview of IAM Policies in the *IAM User Guide*.

2. In the navigation pane, choose **Policies**.

3. Choose **Create Policy**.

4. On the **Create Policy** page, choose **JSON**.

5. For the JSON Policy, type the following, and then choose **Review Policy**:

```
1  {
2    "Version": "2012-10-17",
3    "Statement": [
4      {
5        "Sid": "CloudWatchLogsPolicy",
6        "Effect": "Allow",
7        "Action": [
8          "logs:CreateLogGroup",
9          "logs:CreateLogStream",
10         "logs:PutLogEvents"
11       ],
12       "Resource": [
13         "*"
14       ]
15     },
16     {
17       "Sid": "CodeCommitPolicy",
18       "Effect": "Allow",
19       "Action": [
20         "codecommit:GitPull"
21       ],
22       "Resource": [
23         "*"
24       ]
25     },
26     {
27       "Sid": "S3GetObjectPolicy",
28       "Effect": "Allow",
29       "Action": [
30         "s3:GetObject",
31         "s3:GetObjectVersion"
32       ],
33       "Resource": [
34         "*"
35       ]
36     },
37     {
38       "Sid": "S3PutObjectPolicy",
39       "Effect": "Allow",
40       "Action": [
41         "s3:PutObject"
42       ],
43       "Resource": [
44         "*"
45       ]
46     }
47   ]
48 }
```

Note

This policy contains statements that allow access to a potentially large number of AWS resources. To restrict AWS CodeBuild to access specific AWS resources, change the value of the `Resource` array. For more information, see the security documentation for the AWS service.

1. On the **Review Policy** page, for **Policy Name**, type a name for the policy (for example, **CodeBuild-ServiceRolePolicy**), and then choose **Create policy. Note**
If you use a different name, substitute it throughout this procedure.

2. In the navigation pane, choose **Roles**.

3. Choose **Create role**.

4. On the **Create role** page, with **AWS Service** already selected, choose **CodeBuild**, as the service that will use this role, and then choose **Next:Permissions**.

5. On the **Attach permissions policies** page, select **CodeBuildServiceRolePolicy**, and then choose **Next: Review**.

6. On the **Create role and review** page, for **Role name**, type a name for the role (for example, **Code-BuildServiceRole**), and then choose **Create role**.

To create an AWS CodeBuild service role (AWS CLI)

1. Make sure you have configured the AWS CLI with the AWS access key and AWS secret access key that correspond to one of the IAM entities, as described in the previous procedure. For more information, see Getting Set Up with the AWS Command Line Interface in the *AWS Command Line Interface User Guide*.

2. In an empty directory on the local workstation or instance where the AWS CLI is installed, create two files named `create-role.json` and `put-role-policy.json`. If you choose different file names, substitute them throughout this procedure.

`create-role.json`:

```
1  {
2    "Version": "2012-10-17",
3    "Statement": [
4      {
5        "Effect": "Allow",
6        "Principal": {
7          "Service": "codebuild.amazonaws.com"
8        },
9        "Action": "sts:AssumeRole"
10     }
11   ]
12 }
```

`put-role-policy.json`:

```
1  {
2    "Version": "2012-10-17",
3    "Statement": [
4      {
5        "Sid": "CloudWatchLogsPolicy",
6        "Effect": "Allow",
7        "Action": [
8          "logs:CreateLogGroup",
9          "logs:CreateLogStream",
10         "logs:PutLogEvents"
11       ],
12       "Resource": [
13         "*"
14       ]
15     },
```

```
16    {
17       "Sid": "CodeCommitPolicy",
18       "Effect": "Allow",
19       "Action": [
20         "codecommit:GitPull"
21       ],
22       "Resource": [
23         "*"
24       ]
25    },
26    {
27       "Sid": "S3GetObjectPolicy",
28       "Effect": "Allow",
29       "Action": [
30         "s3:GetObject",
31         "s3:GetObjectVersion"
32       ],
33       "Resource": [
34         "*"
35       ]
36    },
37    {
38       "Sid": "S3PutObjectPolicy",
39       "Effect": "Allow",
40       "Action": [
41         "s3:PutObject"
42       ],
43       "Resource": [
44         "*"
45       ]
46    }
47  ]
48 }
```

Note

This policy contains statements that allow access to a potentially large number of AWS resources. To restrict AWS CodeBuild to access specific AWS resources, change the value of the `Resource` array. For more information, see the security documentation for the AWS service.

1. Switch to the directory where you saved the preceding files, and then run the following two commands, one at a time, in this order. You can use different values for `CodeBuildServiceRole` and `CodeBuildServiceRolePolicy`, but be sure to substitute them here.

```
1 aws iam create-role --role-name CodeBuildServiceRole --assume-role-policy-document file://
    create-role.json
```

```
1 aws iam put-role-policy --role-name CodeBuildServiceRole --policy-name
    CodeBuildServiceRolePolicy --policy-document file://put-role-policy.json
```

Create and Configure an AWS KMS CMK for AWS CodeBuild

For AWS CodeBuild to encrypt its build output artifacts, it needs access to an AWS KMS customer master key (CMK). By default, AWS CodeBuild uses the AWS-managed CMK for Amazon S3 in your AWS account.

If you do not want to use this CMK, you must create and configure a customer-managed CMK yourself. This section describes how to do this with the IAM console.

For information about CMKs, see AWS Key Management Service Concepts and Creating Keys in the *AWS KMS Developer Guide*.

To configure a CMK for use by AWS CodeBuild, follow the instructions in the "How to Modify a Key Policy" section of Modifying a Key Policy in the *AWS KMS Developer Guide*. Then add the following statements (between *### BEGIN ADDING STATEMENTS HERE ###* and *### END ADDING STATEMENTS HERE ###*) to the key policy. Ellipses (...) are used for brevity and to help you locate where to add the statements. Do not remove any statements, and do not type these ellipses into the key policy.

```
1  {
2    "Version": "2012-10-17",
3    "Id": "...",
4    "Statement": [
5      ### BEGIN ADDING STATEMENTS HERE ###
6      {
7        "Sid": "Allow access through Amazon S3 for all principals in the account that are
               authorized to use Amazon S3",
8        "Effect": "Allow",
9        "Principal": {
10         "AWS": "*"
11       },
12       "Action": [
13         "kms:Encrypt",
14         "kms:Decrypt",
15         "kms:ReEncrypt*",
16         "kms:GenerateDataKey*",
17         "kms:DescribeKey"
18       ],
19       "Resource": "*",
20       "Condition": {
21         "StringEquals": {
22           "kms:ViaService": "s3.region-ID.amazonaws.com",
23           "kms:CallerAccount": "account-ID"
24         }
25       }
26     },
27     {
28       "Effect": "Allow",
29       "Principal": {
30         "AWS": "arn:aws:iam::account-ID:role/CodeBuild-service-role"
31       },
32       "Action": [
33         "kms:Encrypt",
34         "kms:Decrypt",
35         "kms:ReEncrypt*",
36         "kms:GenerateDataKey*",
37         "kms:DescribeKey"
38       ],
39       "Resource": "*"
40     },
41     ### END ADDING STATEMENTS HERE ###
42     {
43       "Sid": "Enable IAM User Permissions",
```

```
44        ...
45      },
46      {
47        "Sid": "Allow access for Key Administrators",
48        ...
49      },
50      {
51        "Sid": "Allow use of the key",
52        ...
53      },
54      {
55        "Sid": "Allow attachment of persistent resources",
56        ...
57      }
58    ]
59 }
```

- *region-ID* represents the ID of the AWS region where the Amazon S3 buckets associated with AWS CodeBuild are located (for example, `us-east-1`).
- *account-ID* represents the ID of the of the AWS account that owns the CMK.
- *CodeBuild-service-role* represents the name of the AWS CodeBuild service role you created or identified earlier in this topic.

Note
To create or configure a CMK through the IAM console, you must first sign in to the AWS Management Console by using one of the following:
Your AWS root account. This is not recommended. For more information, see The Account Root User in the *IAM User Guide.* An administrator IAM user in your AWS account. For more information, see Creating Your First IAM Admin User and Group in the *IAM User Guide.* An IAM user in your AWS account with permission to create or modify the CMK. For more information, see Permissions Required to Use the AWS KMS Console in the *AWS KMS Developer Guide.*

Install and Configure the AWS CLI

To access AWS CodeBuild, you can use the AWS CLI with—or instead of—the AWS CodeBuild console, the AWS CodePipeline console, or the AWS SDKs. To install and configure the AWS CLI, see Getting Set Up with the AWS Command Line Interface in the *AWS Command Line Interface User Guide.*

1. Run the following command to confirm whether your installation of the AWS CLI supports AWS CodeBuild:

```
1 aws codebuild list-builds
```

   If successful, information similar to the following will appear in the output:

```
1 {
2    "ids": []
3 }
```

   The empty square brackets indicate that you have not yet run any builds.

2. If an error is output, you must uninstall your current version of the AWS CLI and then install the latest version. For more information, see Uninstalling the AWS CLI and Installing the AWS Command Line Interface in the *AWS Command Line Interface User Guide.*

Command Line Reference for AWS CodeBuild

The AWS CLI provides commands for automating AWS CodeBuild. Use the information in this topic as a supplement to the AWS Command Line Interface User Guide and the AWS CLI Reference for AWS CodeBuild.

Not what you're looking for? If you want to use the AWS SDKs to call AWS CodeBuild, see the AWS SDKs and Tools Reference.

To use the information in this topic, you should have already installed the AWS CLI and configured it for use with AWS CodeBuild, as described in Install and Configure the AWS CLI.

To use the AWS CLI to specify the endpoint for AWS CodeBuild, see Specify the AWS CodeBuild Endpoint (AWS CLI).

Run this command to get a list of AWS CodeBuild commands.

```
1  aws codebuild help
```

Run this command to get information about a AWS CodeBuild command, where *command-name* is the name of the command.

```
1  aws codebuild command-name help
```

AWS CodeBuild commands include:

- `batch-delete-builds`: Deletes one or more builds in AWS CodeBuild. For more information, see Delete Builds (AWS CLI).
- `batch-get-builds`: Gets information about multiple builds in AWS CodeBuild. For more information, see View Build Details (AWS CLI).
- `batch-get-projects`: Gets information about one or more specified build projects. For more information, see View a Build Project's Details (AWS CLI).
- `create-project`: Creates a build project. For more information, see Create a Build Project (AWS CLI).
- `delete-project`: Deletes a build project. For more information, see Delete a Build Project (AWS CLI).
- `list-builds`: Lists Amazon Resource Names (ARNs) for builds in AWS CodeBuild. For more information, see View a List of Build IDs (AWS CLI).
- `list-builds-for-project`: Gets a list of build IDs that are associated with a specified build project. For more information, see View a List of Build IDs for a Build Project (AWS CLI).
- `list-curated-environment-images`: Gets a list of Docker images managed by AWS CodeBuild that you can use for your builds. For more information, see Docker Images Provided by AWS CodeBuild.
- `list-projects`: Gets a list of build project names. For more information, see View a List of Build Project Names (AWS CLI).
- `start-build`: Starts running a build. For more information, see Run a Build (AWS CLI).
- `stop-build`: Attempts to stop the specified build from running. For more information, see Stop a Build (AWS CLI).
- `update-project`: Changes information about the specified build project. For more information, see Change a Build Project's Settings (AWS CLI).

AWS SDKs and Tools Reference for AWS CodeBuild

To use one the AWS SDKs or tools to automate AWS CodeBuild, see the following resources.

If you want to use the AWS CLI to run AWS CodeBuild, see the Command Line Reference.

Supported AWS SDKs and Tools for AWS CodeBuild

The following AWS SDKs and tools support AWS CodeBuild:

- The AWS SDK for C++. For more information, see the Aws::CodeBuild namespace section of the *AWS SDK for C++ API Reference.*
- The AWS SDK for Go. For more information, see the codebuild section of the *AWS SDK for Go API Reference.*
- The AWS SDK for Java. For more information, see the `com.amazonaws.services.codebuild` and `com.amazonaws.services.codebuild.model` sections of the AWS SDK for Java API Reference.
- The AWS SDK for JavaScript in the Browser and the AWS SDK for JavaScript in Node.js. For more information, see the Class: AWS.AWS CodeBuild section of the *AWS SDK for JavaScript API Reference.*
- The AWS SDK for .NET. For more information, see the Amazon.CodeBuild and Amazon.CodeBuild.Model namespace sections of the *AWS SDK for .NET API Reference.*
- The AWS SDK for PHP. For more information, see the Namespace Aws\CodeBuild section of the *AWS SDK for PHP API Reference.*
- The AWS SDK for Python (Boto3). For more information, see the CodeBuild section of the *Boto 3 Documentation.*
- The AWS SDK for Ruby. For more information, see the Module: Aws::CodeBuild section of the *AWS SDK for Ruby API Reference.*
- The AWS Tools for PowerShell. For more information, see the AWS CodeBuild section of the *AWS Tools for PowerShell Cmdlet Reference.*

Specify the AWS CodeBuild Endpoint

You can use the AWS Command Line Interface (AWS CLI) or one of the AWS SDKs to specify the endpoint used by AWS CodeBuild. There is an endpoint for each region in which AWS CodeBuild is available. In addition to a regional endpoint, four regions also have a Federal Information Processing Standards (FIPS) endpoint. For more information about FIPS endpoints, see FIPS 140-2 Overview.

Specifying an endpoint is optional. If you don't explicitly tell AWS CodeBuild which endpoint to use, the service uses the endpoint associated with the region your AWS account uses. AWS CodeBuild never defaults to a FIPS endpoint. If you want to use a FIPS endpoint, you must associate AWS CodeBuild with it using one of the following methods.

Note
You can use an alias or region name to specify an endpoint using an AWS SDK. If you use the AWS CLI, then you must use the full endpoint name.

For endpoints that can be used with AWS CodeBuild, see AWS CodeBuild Regions and Endpoints.

Topics

- Specify the AWS CodeBuild Endpoint (AWS CLI)
- Specify the AWS CodeBuild Endpoint (AWS SDK)

Specify the AWS CodeBuild Endpoint (AWS CLI)

You can use the AWS CLI to specify the endpoint through which AWS CodeBuild is accessed by using the `--endpoint-url` argument in any AWS CodeBuild command. For example, run this command to get a list of project build names using the Federal Information Processing Standards (FIPS) endpoint in the US East (N. Virginia) Region:

```
1 aws codebuild list-projects --endpoint-url https://codebuild-fips.us-east-1.amazonaws.com
```

Include the `https://` at the begining of the endpoint.

The `--endpoint-url` AWS CLI argument is available to all AWS services. For more information about this and other AWS CLI arguments, see AWS CLI Command Reference.

Specify the AWS CodeBuild Endpoint (AWS SDK)

You can use an AWS SDK to specify the endpoint through which AWS CodeBuild is accessed. Although this example uses the AWS SDK for Java, you can specify the endpoint with the other AWS SDKs.

Use the `withEndpointConfiguration` method when constructing the AWSCodeBuild client. Here is format to use:

```
1 AWSCodeBuild awsCodeBuild = AWSCodeBuildClientBuilder.standard().
2     withEndpointConfiguration(new AwsClientBuilder.EndpointConfiguration("endpoint", "region")).
3     withCredentials(new AWSStaticCredentialsProvider(sessionCredentials)).
4     build();
```

For information about `AWSCodeBuildClientBuilder`, see Class AWSCodeBuildClientBuilder.

The credentials used in `withCredentials` must be of type `AWSCredentialsProvider`. For more information, see Working with AWS Credentials.

Do not include `https://` at the begining of the endpoint.

If you want to specify a non-FIPS endpoint, you can use the region instead of the actual endpoint. For example, to specify the endpoint in the US East (N. Virginia) region, you can use `us-east-1` instead of the full endpoint name, `codebuild.us-east-1.amazonaws.com`.

If you want to specify a FIPS endpoint, you can use an alias to simplify your code. Only FIPS endpoints have an alias. Other endpoints must be specified using their region or full name.

The following table lists the alias for each of the four available FIPS endpoints:

———————————————————

[See the AWS documentation website for more details]

To specify use of the FIPS endpoint in the US West (Oregon) region using an alias:

```
1 AWSCodeBuild awsCodeBuild = AWSCodeBuildClientBuilder.standard().
2    withEndpointConfiguration(new AwsClientBuilder.EndpointConfiguration("us-west-2-fips", "us-
        west-2")).
3    withCredentials(new AWSStaticCredentialsProvider(sessionCredentials)).
4    build();
```

To specify use of the non-FIPS endpoint in the US East (N. Virginia) region:

```
1 AWSCodeBuild awsCodeBuild = AWSCodeBuildClientBuilder.standard().
2    withEndpointConfiguration(new AwsClientBuilder.EndpointConfiguration("us-east-1", "us-east
        -1")).
3    withCredentials(new AWSStaticCredentialsProvider(sessionCredentials)).
4    build();
```

To specify use of the non-FIPS endpoint in the Asia Pacific (Mumbai) region:

```
1 AWSCodeBuild awsCodeBuild = AWSCodeBuildClientBuilder.standard().
2    withEndpointConfiguration(new AwsClientBuilder.EndpointConfiguration("ap-south-1", "ap-south
        -1")).
3    withCredentials(new AWSStaticCredentialsProvider(sessionCredentials)).
4    build();
```

Authentication and Access Control for AWS CodeBuild

Access to AWS CodeBuild requires credentials. Those credentials must have permissions to access AWS resources, such as storing and retrieving build artifacts in Amazon S3 buckets and viewing Amazon CloudWatch Logs for builds. The following sections describe how you can use AWS Identity and Access Management (IAM) and AWS CodeBuild to help secure access to your resources:

- Authentication
- Access Control

Authentication

You can access AWS as any of the following types of identities:

- **AWS account root user** – When you sign up for AWS, you provide an email address and password that is associated with your AWS account. These are your *root credentials* and they provide complete access to all of your AWS resources. **Important**
  For security reasons, we recommend that you use the root credentials only to create an administrator user, which is an IAM user with full permissions to your AWS account. Then, you can use this administrator user to create other IAM users and roles with limited permissions. For more information, see IAM Best Practices and Creating an Admin User and Group in the *IAM User Guide Guide*.

- **IAM user** – An IAM user is simply an identity in your AWS account that has custom permissions (for example, permission to create build projects in AWS CodeBuild). You can use an IAM user name and password to sign in to secure AWS webpages like the AWS Management Console, AWS Discussion Forums, or the AWS Support Center.

  In addition to a user name and password, you can also generate access keys for each user. You can use these keys when you access AWS services programmatically, either through one of the AWS SDKs or by using the AWS Command Line Interface (AWS CLI). The AWS SDKs and AWS CLI tools use the access keys to cryptographically sign your request. If you don't use the AWS tools, you must sign the request yourself. AWS CodeBuild supports Signature Version 4, a protocol for authenticating inbound API requests. For more information about authenticating requests, see the Signature Version 4 Signing Process in the *AWS General Reference*.

- **IAM role** – An IAM role is similar to an IAM user, but it is not associated with a specific person. An IAM role enables you to obtain temporary access keys that can be used to access AWS services and resources. IAM roles with temporary credentials are useful in the following situations:

  - **Federated user access** – Instead of creating an IAM user, you can use preexisting user identities from AWS Directory Service, your enterprise user directory, or a web identity provider. These are known as federated users. AWS assigns a role to a federated user when access is requested through an identity provider. For more information about federated users, see Federated Users and Roles in the *IAM User Guide Guide*.
  - **Cross-account access** – You can use an IAM role in your account to grant another AWS account permissions to access your account's resources. For an example, see Tutorial: Delegate Access Across AWS Accounts Using IAM Roles in the *IAM User Guide Guide*.
  - **AWS service access** – You can use an IAM role in your account to grant permissions to an AWS service to access your account's resources. For example, you can create a role that allows Amazon Redshift to access an Amazon S3 bucket on your behalf and then load data stored in the bucket into an Amazon Redshift cluster. For more information, see Creating a Role to Delegate Permissions to an AWS Service in the *IAM User Guide Guide*.
  - **Applications running on Amazon EC2** – Instead of storing access keys in the Amazon EC2 instance for use by applications running on the instance and making AWS API requests, you can use an IAM role to manage temporary credentials for these applications. To assign an AWS role to an Amazon EC2 instance and make it available to all of its applications, you can create an instance

profile that is attached to the instance. An instance profile contains the role and enables programs running on the Amazon EC2 instance to get temporary credentials. For more information, see Using Roles for Applications on Amazon EC2 in the *IAM User Guide Guide*.

Access Control

You can have valid credentials to authenticate your requests, but unless you have permissions, you cannot create or access AWS CodeBuild resources. For example, you must have permissions to create, view, or delete build projects and to start, stop, or view builds.

The following sections describe how to manage permissions for AWS CodeBuild. We recommend that you read the overview first.

- Overview of Managing Access Permissions to Your AWS CodeBuild Resources
- Using Identity-Based Policies (IAM Policies) for AWS CodeBuild
- AWS CodeBuild Permissions Reference

Overview of Managing Access Permissions to Your AWS CodeBuild Resources

Every AWS resource is owned by an AWS account, and permissions to create or access a resource are governed by permissions policies. An account administrator can attach permissions policies to IAM identities (that is, users, groups, and roles).

Note

An account administrator (or administrator user) is a user with administrator privileges. For more information, see IAM Best Practices in the *IAM User Guide Guide*.

When you grant permissions, you decide who is getting the permissions, the resources they can access, and the actions that can be performed on those resources.

Topics

- AWS CodeBuild Resources and Operations
- Understanding Resource Ownership
- Managing Access to Resources
- Specifying Policy Elements: Actions, Effects, and Principals

AWS CodeBuild Resources and Operations

In AWS CodeBuild, the primary resource is a build project. In a policy, you use an Amazon Resource Name (ARN) to identify the resource the policy applies to. Builds are also resources and have ARNs associated with them. For more information, see Amazon Resource Names (ARN) and AWS Service Namespaces in the *Amazon Web Services General Reference*.

Resource type	ARN format
Build project	`arn:aws:codebuild:region-ID:account-ID:project/project-name`
Build	`arn:aws:codebuild:region-ID:account-ID:build/build-ID`
All AWS CodeBuild resources	`arn:aws:codebuild:*`
All AWS CodeBuild resources owned by the specified account in the specified region	`arn:aws:codebuild:region-ID:account-ID:*`

Note

Most AWS services treat a colon (:) or a forward slash (/) as the same character in ARNs. However, AWS CodeBuild uses an exact match in resource patterns and rules. Be sure to use the correct characters when you create event patterns so that they match the ARN syntax in the resource.

For example, you can indicate a specific build project (*myBuildProject*) in your statement using its ARN as follows:

```
1 "Resource": "arn:aws:codebuild:us-east-2:123456789012:project/myBuildProject"
```

To specify all resources, or if an API action does not support ARNs, use the wildcard character (*) in the `Resource` element as follows:

```
1 "Resource": "*"
```

Some AWS CodeBuild API actions accept multiple resources (for example, `BatchGetProjects`). To specify multiple resources in a single statement, separate their ARNs with commas, as follows:

241

```
1 "Resource": [
2   "arn:aws:codebuild:us-east-2:123456789012:project/myBuildProject",
3   "arn:aws:codebuild:us-east-2:123456789012:project/myOtherBuildProject"
4 ]
```

AWS CodeBuild provides a set of operations to work with the AWS CodeBuild resources. For a list, see AWS CodeBuild Permissions Reference.

Understanding Resource Ownership

The AWS account owns the resources that are created in the account, regardless of who created the resources. Specifically, the resource owner is the AWS account of the principal entity (that is, the root account, an IAM user, or an IAM role) that authenticates the resource creation request. The following examples illustrate how this works:

- If you use the root account credentials of your AWS account to create a rule, your AWS account is the owner of the AWS CodeBuild resource.
- If you create an IAM user in your AWS account and grant permissions to create AWS CodeBuild resources to that user, the user can create AWS CodeBuild resources. However, your AWS account, to which the user belongs, owns the AWS CodeBuild resources.
- If you create an IAM role in your AWS account with permissions to create AWS CodeBuild resources, anyone who can assume the role can create AWS CodeBuild resources. Your AWS account, to which the role belongs, owns the AWS CodeBuild resources.

Managing Access to Resources

A permissions policy describes who has access to which resources.

Note
This section discusses the use of IAM in AWS CodeBuild. It doesn't provide detailed information about the IAM service. For complete IAM documentation, see What Is IAM? in the *IAM User Guide Guide*. For information about IAM policy syntax and descriptions, see AWS IAM Policy Reference in the *IAM User Guide Guide*.

Policies attached to an IAM identity are referred to as identity-based policies (IAM policies). Policies attached to a resource are referred to as resource-based policies. AWS CodeBuild supports identity-based (IAM policies) only.

Identity-Based Policies (IAM Policies)

You can attach policies to IAM identities.

- **Attach a permissions policy to a user or a group in your account** – To grant a user permissions to view build projects and other AWS CodeBuild resources in the AWS CodeBuild console, you can attach a permissions policy to a user or group that the user belongs to.

- **Attach a permissions policy to a role (grant cross-account permissions)** – You can attach an identity-based permissions policy to an IAM role to grant cross-account permissions. For example, the administrator in Account A can create a role to grant cross-account permissions to another AWS account (for example, Account B) or an AWS service as follows:

  1. Account A administrator creates an IAM role and attaches a permissions policy to the role that grants permissions on resources in Account A.

  2. Account A administrator attaches a trust policy to the role identifying Account B as the principal who can assume the role.

3. Account B administrator can then delegate permissions to assume the role to any users in Account B. Doing this allows users in Account B to create or access resources in Account A. The principal in the trust policy must also be an AWS service principal if you want to grant an AWS service permissions to assume the role.

   For more information about using IAM to delegate permissions, see Access Management in the *IAM User Guide Guide*.

In AWS CodeBuild, identity-based policies are used to manage permissions to the resources related to the deployment process. For example, you can control access to build projects.

You can create IAM policies to restrict the calls and resources that users in your account have access to, and then attach those policies to IAM users. For more information about how to create IAM roles and to explore example IAM policy statements for AWS CodeBuild, see Overview of Managing Access Permissions to Your AWS CodeBuild Resources.

Specifying Policy Elements: Actions, Effects, and Principals

For each AWS CodeBuild resource, the service defines a set of API operations. To grant permissions for these API operations, AWS CodeBuild defines a set of actions that you can specify in a policy. Some API operations can require permissions for more than one action in order to perform the API operation. For more information, see AWS CodeBuild Resources and Operations and AWS CodeBuild Permissions Reference.

The following are the basic policy elements:

- **Resource** – You use an Amazon Resource Name (ARN) to identify the resource that the policy applies to.
- **Action** – You use action keywords to identify resource operations you want to allow or deny. For example, the `codebuild:CreateProject` permission gives the user permissions to perform the `CreateProject` operation.
- **Effect** – You specify the effect, either allow or deny, when the user requests the action. If you don't explicitly grant access to (allow) a resource, access is implicitly denied. You can also explicitly deny access to a resource. You might do this to make sure a user cannot access a resource, even if a different policy grants access.
- **Principal** – In identity-based policies (IAM policies), the user the policy is attached to is the implicit principal. For resource-based policies, you specify the user, account, service, or other entity that you want to receive permissions.

To learn more about IAM policy syntax and descriptions, see AWS IAM Policy Reference in the *IAM User Guide Guide*.

For a table showing all of the AWS CodeBuild API actions and the resources they apply to, see the AWS CodeBuild Permissions Reference.

Using Identity-Based Policies (IAM Policies) for AWS CodeBuild

This topic provides examples of identity-based policies that demonstrate how an account administrator can attach permissions policies to IAM identities (that is, users, groups, and roles) and thereby grant permissions to perform operations on AWS CodeBuild resources.

Important
We recommend that you first review the introductory topics that explain the basic concepts and options available to manage access to your AWS CodeBuild resources. For more information, see Overview of Managing Access Permissions to Your AWS CodeBuild Resources.

Topics

- Permissions Required to Use the AWS CodeBuild Console
- Permissions Required for the AWS CodeBuild Console to Connect to Source Providers Using OAuth
- AWS Managed (Predefined) Policies for AWS CodeBuild
- Customer-Managed Policy Examples

The following shows an example of a permissions policy that allows a user to get information about build projects only in the **us-east-2** region for account **123456789012** for any build project that starts with the name **my**:

```
1  {
2    "Version": "2012-10-17",
3    "Statement": [
4      {
5        "Effect": "Allow",
6        "Action": "codebuild:BatchGetProjects",
7        "Resource": "arn:aws:codebuild:us-east-2:123456789012:project/my*"
8      }
9    ]
10 }
```

Permissions Required to Use the AWS CodeBuild Console

A user who uses the AWS CodeBuild console must have a minimum set of permissions that allows the user to describe other AWS resources for the AWS account. You must have permissions from the following services:

- AWS CodeBuild
- Amazon CloudWatch
- AWS CodeCommit (if you are storing your source code in an AWS CodeCommit repository)
- Amazon Elastic Container Registry (Amazon ECR) (if you are using a build environment that relies on a Docker image in an Amazon ECR repository)
- Amazon Elastic Container Service (Amazon ECS) (if you are using a build environment that relies on a Docker image in an Amazon ECR repository)
- AWS Identity and Access Management (IAM)
- AWS Key Management Service (AWS KMS)
- Amazon Simple Storage Service (Amazon S3)

If you create an IAM policy that is more restrictive than the minimum required permissions, the console won't function as intended.

Permissions Required for the AWS CodeBuild Console to Connect to Source Providers Using OAuth

The AWS CodeBuild console uses the following API actions to connect to source providers (for example, GitHub repositories) using OAuth.

- `codebuild:ListConnectedOAuthAccounts`
- `codebuild:ListRepositories`
- `codebuild:PersistOAuthToken`

To associate source providers using OAuth (such as GitHub repositories) with your build projects, you must use the AWS CodeBuild console. To do this, you must first add the preceding API actions to IAM access policies associated with the IAM user you use to access the AWS CodeBuild console.

These API actions are not intended to be called by your code. Therefore, these API actions are not included in the AWS CLI and AWS SDKs.

AWS Managed (Predefined) Policies for AWS CodeBuild

AWS addresses many common use cases by providing standalone IAM policies that are created and administered by AWS. These AWS managed policies grant necessary permissions for common use cases so you can avoid having to investigate what permissions are needed. For more information, see AWS Managed Policies in the *IAM User Guide.*

The following AWS managed policies, which you can attach to users in your account, are specific to AWS CodeBuild.

- **AWSCodeBuildAdminAccess** – Provides full access to AWS CodeBuild including permissions to administrate AWS CodeBuild build projects.
- **AWSCodeBuildDeveloperAccess** – Provides access to AWS CodeBuild but does not allow build project administration.
- **AWSCodeBuildReadOnlyAccess** – Provides read-only access to AWS CodeBuild.

To access build output artifacts that AWS CodeBuild creates, you must also attach the AWS managed policy named **AmazonS3ReadOnlyAccess**.

To create and manage AWS CodeBuild service roles, you must also attach the AWS managed policy named **IAMFullAccess**.

You can also create your own custom IAM policies to allow permissions for AWS CodeBuild actions and resources. You can attach these custom policies to the IAM users or groups that require those permissions.

Customer-Managed Policy Examples

In this section, you can find example user policies that grant permissions for AWS CodeBuild actions. These policies work when you are using the AWS CodeBuild API, AWS SDKs, or AWS CLI. When you are using the console, you must grant additional permissions specific to the console. For information, see Permissions Required to Use the AWS CodeBuild Console.

You can use the following sample IAM policies to limit AWS CodeBuild access for your IAM users and roles.

Topics
- Allow a User to Get Information About Build Projects
- Allow a User to Create Build Projects
- Allow a User to Delete Build Projects
- Allow a User to Get a List of Build Project Names
- Allow a User to Change Information About Build Projects

- Allow a User to Get Information About Builds
- Allow a User to Get a List of Build IDs for a Build Project
- Allow a User to Get a List of Build IDs
- Allow a User to Begin Running Builds
- Allow a User to Attempt to Stop Builds
- Allow a User to Attempt to Delete Builds
- Allow a User to Get Information About Docker Images that Are Managed by AWS CodeBuild
- Allow AWS CodeBuild Access to AWS Services Required to Create a VPC Network Interface

Allow a User to Get Information About Build Projects

The following example policy statement allows a user to get information about build projects only in the us-east-2 region for account 123456789012 for any build project that starts with the name my:

```
1  {
2    "Version": "2012-10-17",
3    "Statement": [
4      {
5        "Effect": "Allow",
6        "Action": "codebuild:BatchGetProjects",
7        "Resource": "arn:aws:codebuild:us-east-2:123456789012:project/my*"
8      }
9    ]
10 }
```

Allow a User to Create Build Projects

The following example policy statement allows a user to create build projects with any name but only in the us-east-2 region for account 123456789012 and using only the specified AWS CodeBuild service role:

```
1  {
2    "Version": "2012-10-17",
3    "Statement": [
4      {
5        "Effect": "Allow",
6        "Action": "codebuild:CreateProject",
7        "Resource": "arn:aws:codebuild:us-east-2:123456789012:project/*"
8      },
9      {
10       "Effect": "Allow",
11       "Action": "iam:PassRole",
12       "Resource": "arn:aws:iam:123456789012:role/CodeBuildServiceRole"
13     }
14   ]
15 }
```

Allow a User to Delete Build Projects

The following example policy statement allows a user to delete build projects only in the us-east-2 region for account 123456789012 for any build project that starts with the name my:

```
1  {
2    "Version": "2012-10-17",
```

```
 3    "Statement": [
 4      {
 5        "Effect": "Allow",
 6        "Action": "codebuild:DeleteProject",
 7        "Resource": "arn:aws:codebuild:us-east-2:123456789012:project/my*"
 8      }
 9    ]
10  }
```

Allow a User to Get a List of Build Project Names

The following example policy statement allows a user to get a list of build project names for the same account:

```
 1  {
 2    "Version": "2012-10-17",
 3    "Statement": [
 4      {
 5        "Effect": "Allow",
 6        "Action": "codebuild:ListProjects",
 7        "Resource": "*"
 8      }
 9    ]
10  }
```

Allow a User to Change Information About Build Projects

The following example policy statement allows a user to change information about build projects with any name but only in the us-east-2 region for account 123456789012 and using only the specified AWS CodeBuild service role:

```
 1  {
 2    "Version": "2012-10-17",
 3    "Statement": [
 4      {
 5        "Effect": "Allow",
 6        "Action": "codebuild:UpdateProject",
 7        "Resource": "arn:aws:codebuild:us-east-2:123456789012:project/*"
 8      },
 9      {
10        "Effect": "Allow",
11        "Action": "iam:PassRole",
12        "Resource": "arn:aws:iam:123456789012:role/CodeBuildServiceRole"
13      }
14    ]
15  }
```

Allow a User to Get Information About Builds

The following example policy statement allows a user to get information about builds only in the us-east-2 region for account 123456789012 for the build projects named my-build-project and my-other-build-project:

```
1  {
2    "Version": "2012-10-17",
3    "Statement": [
4      {
5        "Effect": "Allow",
6        "Action": "codebuild:BatchGetBuilds",
7        "Resource": [
8          "arn:aws:codebuild:us-east-2:123456789012:project/my-build-project",
9          "arn:aws:codebuild:us-east-2:123456789012:project/my-other-build-project"
10       ]
11     }
12   ]
13 }
```

Allow a User to Get a List of Build IDs for a Build Project

The following example policy statement allows a user to get a list of build IDs only in the us-east-2 region for account 123456789012 for the build projects named my-build-project and my-other-build-project:

```
1  {
2    "Version": "2012-10-17",
3    "Statement": [
4      {
5        "Effect": "Allow",
6        "Action": "codebuild:ListBuildsForProject",
7        "Resource": [
8          "arn:aws:codebuild:us-east-2:123456789012:project/my-build-project",
9          "arn:aws:codebuild:us-east-2:123456789012:project/my-other-build-project"
10       ]
11     }
12   ]
13 }
```

Allow a User to Get a List of Build IDs

The following example policy statement allows a user to get a list of all build IDs for the same account:

```
1  {
2    "Version": "2012-10-17",
3    "Statement": [
4      {
5        "Effect": "Allow",
6        "Action": "codebuild:ListBuilds",
7        "Resource": "*"
8      }
9    ]
10 }
```

Allow a User to Begin Running Builds

The following example policy statement allows a user to run builds only in the us-east-2 region for account 123456789012 for build project that starts with the name my:

248

```
1  {
2    "Version": "2012-10-17",
3    "Statement": [
4      {
5        "Effect": "Allow",
6        "Action": "codebuild:StartBuild",
7        "Resource": "arn:aws:codebuild:us-east-2:123456789012:project/my*"
8      }
9    ]
10 }
```

Allow a User to Attempt to Stop Builds

The following example policy statement allows a user to attempt to stop running builds only in the us-east-2 region for account 123456789012 for any build project that starts with the name my:

```
1  {
2    "Version": "2012-10-17",
3    "Statement": [
4      {
5        "Effect": "Allow",
6        "Action": "codebuild:StopBuild",
7        "Resource": "arn:aws:codebuild:us-east-2:123456789012:project/my*"
8      }
9    ]
10 }
```

Allow a User to Attempt to Delete Builds

The following example policy statement allows a user to attempt to delete builds only in the us-east-2 region for account 123456789012 for any build project that starts with the name my:

```
1  {
2    "Version": "2012-10-17",
3    "Statement": [
4      {
5        "Effect": "Allow",
6        "Action": "codebuild:BatchDeleteBuilds",
7        "Resource": "arn:aws:codebuild:us-east-2:123456789012:project/my*"
8      }
9    ]
10 }
```

Allow a User to Get Information About Docker Images that Are Managed by AWS CodeBuild

The following example policy statement allows a user to get information about all Docker images that are managed by AWS CodeBuild:

```
1  {
2    "Version": "2012-10-17",
3    "Statement": [
4      {
5        "Effect": "Allow",
```

```
6        "Action": "codebuild:ListCuratedEnvironmentImages",
7        "Resource": "*"
8      }
9    ]
10 }
```

Allow AWS CodeBuild Access to AWS Services Required to Create a VPC Network Interface

The following example policy statement grants AWS CodeBuild permission to create a network interface in an Amazon VPC:

```
1  {
2      "Version": "2012-10-17",
3      "Statement": [
4          {
5              "Effect": "Allow",
6              "Action": [
7                  "ec2:CreateNetworkInterface",
8                  "ec2:DescribeDhcpOptions",
9                  "ec2:DescribeNetworkInterfaces",
10                 "ec2:DeleteNetworkInterface",
11                 "ec2:DescribeSubnets",
12                 "ec2:DescribeSecurityGroups",
13                 "ec2:DescribeVpcs"
14             ],
15             "Resource": "*"
16         },
17         {
18             "Effect": "Allow",
19             "Action": [
20                 "ec2:CreateNetworkInterfacePermission"
21             ],
22             "Resource": "arn:aws:ec2:{{region}}:{{account-id}}:network-interface/*",
23             "Condition": {
24                 "StringEquals": {
25                     "ec2:Subnet": [
26                         "arn:aws:ec2:{{region}}:{{account-id}}:subnet/[[subnets]]"
27                     ],
28                     "ec2:AuthorizedService": "codebuild.amazonaws.com"
29                 }
30             }
31         }
32     ]
33 }
```

AWS CodeBuild Permissions Reference

You can use the following table as a reference when you are setting up Access Control and writing permissions policies that you can attach to an IAM identity (identity-based policies).

You can use AWS-wide condition keys in your AWS CodeBuild policies to express conditions. For a list, see Available Keys in the *IAM User Guide*.

You specify the actions in the policy's `Action` field. To specify an action, use the `codebuild:` prefix followed by the API operation name (for example, `codebuild:CreateProject` and `codebuild:StartBuild`). To specify multiple actions in a single statement, separate them with commas (for example, `"Action": [ "codebuild: CreateProject", "codebuild:StartBuild" ]`).

Using Wildcard Characters

You specify an ARN, with or without a wildcard character (*), as the resource value in the policy's `Resource` field. You can use a wildcard to specify multiple actions or resources. For example, `codebuild:*` specifies all AWS CodeBuild actions and `codebuild:Batch*` specifies all AWS CodeBuild actions that begin with the word `Batch`. The following example grants access to all build project with names that begin with `my`:

```
1 arn:aws:codebuild:us-east-2:123456789012:project/my*
```

If you see an expand arrow () in the upper-right corner of the table, you can open the table in a new window. To close the window, choose the close button (**X**) in the lower-right corner.

AWS CodeBuild API Operations and Required Permissions for Actions

AWS CodeBuild API operations	Required permissions (API actions)	Resources
BatchDeleteBuilds	`codebuild: BatchDeleteBuilds` Required to delete builds.	`arn:aws:codebuild:region -ID:account-ID:project/ project-name`
BatchGetBuilds	`codebuild:BatchGetBuilds` Required to get information about builds.	`arn:aws:codebuild:region -ID:account-ID:project/ project-name`
BatchGetProjects	`codebuild: BatchGetProjects` Required to get information about build projects.	`arn:aws:codebuild:region -ID:account-ID:project/ project-name`
CreateProject	`codebuild:CreateProject iam:PassRole` Required to create build projects.	`arn:aws:codebuild:region -ID:account-ID:project/ project-name arn:aws:iam :account-ID:role/role- name`
DeleteProject	`codebuild:DeleteProject` Required to delete build projects.	`arn:aws:codebuild:region -ID:account-ID:project/ project-name`
ListBuilds	`codebuild:ListBuilds`Required to get a list of build IDs.	`*`
ListBuildsForProject	`codebuild: ListBuildsForProject` Required to get a list of build IDs for a build project.	`arn:aws:codebuild:region -ID:account-ID:project/ project-name`

251

AWS CodeBuild API operations	Required permissions (API actions)	Resources
ListCuratedEnvironmentImages	`codebuild:` `ListCuratedEnvironmentImag` Required to get information about all Docker images that are managed by AWS CodeBuild.	* (required, but does not refer to an addressable AWS resource)
ListProjects	`codebuild:ListProjects` Required to get a list of build project names.	*
StartBuild	`codebuild:StartBuild` Required to start running builds.	`arn:aws:codebuild:region` `-ID:account-ID:project/` `project-name`
StopBuild	`codebuild:StopBuild` Required to attempt to stop running builds.	`arn:aws:codebuild:region` `-ID:account-ID:project/` `project-name`
UpdateProject	`codebuild:UpdateProject` `iam:PassRole` Required to change information about builds.	`arn:aws:codebuild:region` `-ID:account-ID:project/` `project-name arn:aws:iam` `:account-ID:role/role-` `name`

Logging AWS CodeBuild API Calls with AWS CloudTrail

AWS CodeBuild is integrated with CloudTrail, a service that captures API calls made by or on behalf of AWS CodeBuild in your AWS account and delivers the log files to an Amazon S3 bucket you specify. CloudTrail captures API calls from the AWS CodeBuild console, the AWS CLI, and the AWS SDKs. Using the information collected by CloudTrail, you can determine which request was made to AWS CodeBuild, the source IP address from which the request was made, who made the request, when it was made, and so on. To learn more about CloudTrail, including how to configure and enable it, see the AWS CloudTrail User Guide.

AWS CodeBuild Information in CloudTrail

When CloudTrail logging is enabled in your AWS account, calls made to AWS CodeBuild actions are tracked in log files. AWS CodeBuild records are written together with other AWS service records in a log file. CloudTrail determines when to create and write to a new file based on a time period and file size.

All of the AWS CodeBuild actions are logged and documented in the Command Line Reference. For example, calls to create build projects and run builds generate entries in CloudTrail log files.

Every log entry contains information about who generated the request. The user identity information in the log helps you determine whether the request was made with root or IAM user credentials, with temporary security credentials for a role or federated user, or by another AWS service. For more information, see the `userIdentity` field in the CloudTrail Event Reference.

You can store your log files in your bucket for as long as you want, but you can also define Amazon S3 lifecycle rules to archive or delete log files automatically. By default, Amazon S3 server-side encryption (SSE) is used to encrypt your log files.

You can have CloudTrail publish Amazon SNS notifications when new log files are delivered. For more information, see Configuring Amazon SNS Notifications for CloudTrail.

You can also aggregate AWS CodeBuild log files from multiple AWS regions and multiple AWS accounts into a single Amazon S3 bucket. For more information, see Receiving CloudTrail Log Files from Multiple Regions.

Understanding AWS CodeBuild Log File Entries

CloudTrail log files can contain one or more log entries where each entry is made up of multiple JSON-formatted events. A log entry represents a single request from any source and includes information about the requested action, any parameters, the date and time of the action, and so on. The log entries are not guaranteed to be in any particular order. That is, they are not an ordered stack trace of the public calls.

The following example shows a CloudTrail log entry that demonstrates creating a build project in AWS CodeBuild:

```
1  {
2    "eventVersion": "1.05",
3    "userIdentity": {
4      "type": "FederatedUser",
5      "principalId": "account-ID:user-name",
6      "arn": "arn:aws:sts::account-ID:federated-user/user-name",
7      "accountId": "account-ID",
8      "accessKeyId": "access-key-ID",
9      "sessionContext": {
10       "attributes": {
11         "mfaAuthenticated": "false",
12         "creationDate": "2016-09-06T17:59:10Z"
13       },
14       "sessionIssuer": {
```

```
15      "type": "IAMUser",
16      "principalId": "access-key-ID",
17      "arn": "arn:aws:iam::account-ID:user/user-name",
18      "accountId": "account-ID",
19      "userName": "user-name"
20    }
21  }
22 },
23 "eventTime": "2016-09-06T17:59:11Z",
24 "eventSource": "codebuild.amazonaws.com",
25 "eventName": "CreateProject",
26 "awsRegion": "region-ID",
27 "sourceIPAddress": "127.0.0.1",
28 "userAgent": "user-agent",
29 "requestParameters": {
30    "awsActId": "account-ID"
31 },
32 "responseElements": {
33    "project": {
34      "environment": {
35        "image": "image-ID",
36        "computeType": "BUILD_GENERAL1_SMALL",
37        "type": "LINUX_CONTAINER",
38        "environmentVariables": []
39      },
40      "name": "codebuild-demo-project",
41      "description": "This is my demo project",
42      "arn": "arn:aws:codebuild:region-ID:account-ID:project/codebuild-demo-project:project-ID",
43      "encryptionKey": "arn:aws:kms:region-ID:key-ID",
44      "timeoutInMinutes": 10,
45      "artifacts": {
46        "location": "arn:aws:s3:::codebuild-region-ID-account-ID-output-bucket",
47        "type": "S3",
48        "packaging": "ZIP",
49        "outputName": "MyOutputArtifact.zip"
50      },
51      "serviceRole": "arn:aws:iam::account-ID:role/CodeBuildServiceRole",
52      "lastModified": "Sep 6, 2016 10:59:11 AM",
53      "source": {
54        "type": "GITHUB",
55        "location": "https://github.com/my-repo.git"
56      },
57      "created": "Sep 6, 2016 10:59:11 AM"
58    }
59 },
60 "requestID": "9d32b228-745b-11e6-98bb-23b67EXAMPLE",
61 "eventID": "581f7dd1-8d2e-40b0-aeee-0dbf7EXAMPLE",
62 "eventType": "AwsApiCall",
63 "recipientAccountId": "account-ID"
64 }
```

Troubleshooting AWS CodeBuild

Use the information in this topic to help you identify, diagnose, and address issues.

Topics

- Error: "CodeBuild is not authorized to perform: sts:AssumeRole" When Creating or Updating a Build Project
- Error: "The bucket you are attempting to access must be addressed using the specified endpoint..." When Running a Build
- Error: "Failed to upload artifacts: Invalid arn" When Running a Build
- Error: "Unable to Locate Credentials"
- Earlier Commands in Build Specs Are Not Recognized by Later Commands
- Apache Maven Builds Reference Artifacts from the Wrong Repository
- Build Commands Run as root by Default
- The Bourne Shell (sh) Must Exist in Build Images
- Error: "AWS CodeBuild is experiencing an issue" When Running a Build
- Error: "BUILD_CONTAINER_UNABLE_TO_PULL_IMAGE" When Using a Custom Build Image
- Builds May Fail When File Names Have Non-US English Characters
- Builds May Fail When Getting Parameters from Amazon EC2 Parameter Store
- "Access denied" Error Message When Attempting to Download Cache
- Error: "Unable to download cache: RequestError: send request failed caused by: x509: failed to load system roots and no roots provided"
- Error: "Unable to download certificate from S3. AccessDenied"
- Error: "Git Clone Failed: unable to access 'your-repository-URL': SSL certificate problem: self signed certificate"
- Error: "The policy's default version was not created by enhanced zero click role creation or was not the most recent version created by enhanced zero click role creation."

Error: "CodeBuild is not authorized to perform: sts:AssumeRole" When Creating or Updating a Build Project

Issue: When you try to create or update a build project, you receive the following error: "Code:Invalid-InputException, Message:CodeBuild is not authorized to perform: sts:AssumeRole on arn:aws:iam::*account-ID*:role/*service-role-name*".

Possible causes:

- The AWS Security Token Service (AWS STS) has been deactivated for the AWS region where you are attempting to create or update the build project.
- The AWS CodeBuild service role associated with the build project does not exist or does not have sufficient permissions to trust AWS CodeBuild.

Recommended solutions:

- Make sure AWS STS is activated for the AWS region where you are attempting to create or update the build project. For more information, see Activating and Deactivating AWS STS in an AWS Region in the *IAM User Guide.*
- Make sure the target AWS CodeBuild service role exists in your AWS account. If you are not using the console, make sure you did not misspell the Amazon Resource Name (ARN) of the service role when you created or updated the build project.
- Make sure the target AWS CodeBuild service role has sufficient permissions to trust AWS CodeBuild. For more information, see the trust relationship policy statement in Create an AWS CodeBuild Service Role.

Error: "The bucket you are attempting to access must be addressed using the specified endpoint..." When Running a Build

Issue: When you run a build, the `DOWNLOAD_SOURCE` build phase fails with the error "The bucket you are attempting to access must be addressed using the specified endpoint. Please send all future requests to this endpoint."

Possible cause: Your pre-built source code is stored in an Amazon S3 bucket, and that bucket is in a different AWS region than the AWS CodeBuild build project.

Recommended solution: Update the build project's settings to point to a bucket that contains your pre-built source code, and that bucket is in the same region as the build project.

Error: "Failed to upload artifacts: Invalid arn" When Running a Build

Issue: When you run a build, the `UPLOAD_ARTIFACTS` build phase fails with the error "Failed to upload artifacts: Invalid arn".

Possible cause: Your Amazon S3 output bucket (the bucket where AWS CodeBuild stores its output from the build) is in a different AWS region than the AWS CodeBuild build project.

Recommended solution: Update the build project's settings to point to an output bucket that is in the same region as the build project.

Error: "Unable to Locate Credentials"

Issue: When you try to run the AWS CLI, use an AWS SDK, or call another similar component as part of a build, you get build errors that are directly related to the AWS CLI, AWS SDK, or component. For example, you may get a build error such as "unable to locate credentials."

Possible causes:

- The version of the AWS CLI, AWS SDK, or component in the build environment is incompatible with AWS CodeBuild.
- You are running a Docker container within a build environment that uses Docker, and that Docker container does not have access to the necessary AWS credentials by default.

Recommended solutions:

- Make sure your build environment has the following version or higher of the AWS CLI, AWS SDK, or component.
  - AWS CLI: 1.10.47
  - AWS SDK for C++: 0.2.19
  - AWS SDK for Go: 1.2.5
  - AWS SDK for Java: 1.11.16
  - AWS SDK for JavaScript: 2.4.7
  - AWS SDK for PHP: 3.18.28
  - AWS SDK for Python (Boto3): 1.4.0
  - AWS SDK for Ruby: 2.3.22
  - Botocore: 1.4.37
  - CoreCLR: 3.2.6-beta
  - Node.js: 2.4.7
- If you need to run a Docker container in a build environment and that container requires AWS credentials, you must pass through the credentials from the build environment to the container. In your build spec, include a Docker `run` command such as the following, which in this example uses the `aws s3 ls` command

to list your available Amazon S3 buckets. The `-e` option passes through the necessary environment variables for your container to access AWS credentials.

```
1 docker run -e AWS_DEFAULT_REGION -e AWS_CONTAINER_CREDENTIALS_RELATIVE_URI your-image-tag
    aws s3 ls
```

- If you are building a Docker image and the build requires AWS credentials (for example, to download a file from Amazon S3), you must pass through the credentials from the build environment to the Docker build process as follows.

  1. In your source code's Dockerfile for the Docker image, specify the following `ARG` instructions.

```
1 ARG AWS_DEFAULT_REGION
2 ARG AWS_CONTAINER_CREDENTIALS_RELATIVE_URI
```

  2. In your build spec, include a Docker `build` command such as the following. The `--build-arg` options will set the necessary environment variables for your Docker build process to access the AWS credentials.

```
1 docker build --build-arg AWS_DEFAULT_REGION=$AWS_DEFAULT_REGION --build-arg
    AWS_CONTAINER_CREDENTIALS_RELATIVE_URI=$AWS_CONTAINER_CREDENTIALS_RELATIVE_URI -t
    your-image-tag .
```

Earlier Commands in Build Specs Are Not Recognized by Later Commands

Issue: The results of one or more commands in your build spec are not recognized by later commands in the same build spec. For example, a command might set a local environment variable, but a command run later might fail to get the value of that local environment variable.

Possible cause: In build spec version 0.1, AWS CodeBuild runs each command in a separate instance of the default shell in the build environment. This means that each command runs in isolation from all other commands. By default, then, you cannot run a single command that relies on the state of any previous commands.

Recommended solutions: We recommend you use build spec version 0.2, which solves this issue. If you must use build spec version 0.1 for some reason, we recommend using the shell command chaining operator (for example, `&&` in Linux) to combine multiple commands into a single command. Or include a shell script in your source code that contains multiple commands, and then call that shell script from a single command in the build spec. For more information, see Shells and Commands in Build Environments and Environment Variables in Build Environments.

Apache Maven Builds Reference Artifacts from the Wrong Repository

Issue: When you use Maven with an AWS CodeBuild provided Java build environment, Maven pulls build and plugin dependencies from the secure central Maven repository at https://repo1.maven.org/maven2. This happens even if your build project's `pom.xml` file explicitly declares other locations to use instead.

Possible cause: AWS CodeBuild provided Java build environments include a file named `settings.xml` that is preinstalled in the build environment's `/root/.m2` directory. This `settings.xml` file contains the following declarations, which instruct Maven to always pull build and plugin dependencies from the secure central Maven repository at https://repo1.maven.org/maven2.

```
1 <settings>
2   <activeProfiles>
3     <activeProfile>securecentral</activeProfile>
4   </activeProfiles>
5   <profiles>
6     <profile>
```

```
 7        <id>securecentral</id>
 8        <repositories>
 9          <repository>
10            <id>central</id>
11            <url>https://repo1.maven.org/maven2</url>
12            <releases>
13              <enabled>true</enabled>
14            </releases>
15          </repository>
16        </repositories>
17        <pluginRepositories>
18          <pluginRepository>
19            <id>central</id>
20            <url>https://repo1.maven.org/maven2</url>
21            <releases>
22              <enabled>true</enabled>
23            </releases>
24          </pluginRepository>
25        </pluginRepositories>
26      </profile>
27    </profiles>
28 </settings>
```

Recommended solution: Do the following:

1. Add a `settings.xml` file to your source code.

2. In this `settings.xml` file, use the preceding `settings.xml` format as a guide to declare the repositories you want Maven to pull the build and plugin dependencies from instead.

3. In the `install` phase of your build project, instruct AWS CodeBuild to copy your `settings.xml` file to the build environment's `/root/.m2` directory. For example, consider the following snippet from a `buildspec.yml` file that demonstrates this behavior.

```
1 version 0.2
2
3 phases:
4   install:
5     commands:
6       - cp ./settings.xml /root/.m2/settings.xml
```

Build Commands Run as root by Default

Issue: AWS CodeBuild runs your build commands as the root user. This happens even if your related build image's Dockerfile sets the `USER` instruction to a different user.

Cause: AWS CodeBuild runs all build commands as the root user by default.

Recommended solution: None.

The Bourne Shell (sh) Must Exist in Build Images

Issue: You are using a build image that is not provided by AWS CodeBuild, and your builds fail with the message "build container found dead before completing the build."

Possible cause: The Bourne shell (`sh`) is not included in your build image. AWS CodeBuild needs `sh` to run build commands and scripts.

Recommended solution: If `sh` in not present in your build image, be sure to include it before you start any more builds that use your image. (AWS CodeBuild already includes `sh` in its build images.)

Error: "AWS CodeBuild is experiencing an issue" When Running a Build

Issue: When you try to run a build project, you receive the following error during the build's `PROVISIONING` phase: "AWS CodeBuild is experiencing an issue."

Possible cause: Your build is using environment variables that are too large for AWS CodeBuild. AWS CodeBuild can raise errors once the length of all environment variables (all names and values added together) reach a combined maximum of around 5,500 characters.

Recommended solution: Use Amazon EC2 Systems Manager Parameter Store to store large environment variables and then retrieve them from your build spec. Amazon EC2 Systems Manager Parameter Store can store an individual environment variable (name and value added together) that is a combined 4,096 characters or less. To store large environment variables, see Systems Manager Parameter Store and Systems Manager Parameter Store Console Walkthrough in the *Amazon EC2 Systems Manager User Guide*. To retrieve them, see the `parameter-store` mapping in Build Spec Syntax.

Error: "BUILD_CONTAINER_UNABLE_TO_PULL_IMAGE" When Using a Custom Build Image

Issue: When you try to run a build that uses a custom build image, the build fails with the error `BUILD_CONTAINER_UNABLE_TO_PULL_IMAGE`.

Possible causes:

- The build image's overall uncompressed size is larger than the build environment compute type's available disk space. To check your build image's size, use Docker to run the `docker images REPOSITORY:TAG` command. For a list of available disk space by compute type, see Build Environment Compute Types.
- AWS CodeBuild does not have permission to pull the build image from your Amazon Elastic Container Registry (Amazon ECR).

Recommended solutions:

- Use a larger compute type with more available disk space, or reduce the size of your custom build image.
- Update the permissions in your repository in Amazon ECR so that AWS CodeBuild can pull your custom build image into the build environment. For more information, see the Amazon ECR Sample.

Builds May Fail When File Names Have Non-US English Characters

Issue: When you run a build that uses files with file names containing non-US English characters (for example, Chinese characters), the build fails.

Possible cause : : Build environments provided by AWS CodeBuild have their default locale set to `POSIX`. `POSIX` localization settings are less compatible with AWS CodeBuild and file names that contain non-US English characters and can cause related builds to fail.

Recommended solution: Add the following commands to the `pre_build` section of your build specification. These commands make the build environment use US English UTF-8 for its localization settings, which is more compatible with AWS CodeBuild and file names that contain non-US English characters.

For build environments based on Ubuntu:

```
1 pre_build:
2   commands:
3     - export LC_ALL="en_US.UTF-8"
4     - locale-gen en_US en_US.UTF-8
5     - dpkg-reconfigure locales
```

For build environments based on Amazon Linux:

```
1 pre_build:
2   commands:
3     - export LC_ALL="en_US.utf8"
```

Builds May Fail When Getting Parameters from Amazon EC2 Parameter Store

Issue: When a build tries to get the value of one or more parameters stored in Amazon EC2 Parameter Store, the build fails in the DOWNLOAD_SOURCE phase with the following error: "Parameter does not exist."

Possible causes: The service role the build project relies on does not have permission to call the ssm:GetParameters action or the build project uses a service role that is generated by AWS CodeBuild and allows calling the ssm:GetParameters action, but the parameters have names that do not start with /CodeBuild/.

Recommended solutions:

- If the service role was not generated by AWS CodeBuild, update its definition to allow AWS CodeBuild to call the ssm:GetParameters action. For example, the following policy statement allows calling the ssm:GetParameters action to get parameters with names starting with /CodeBuild/:

```
1  {
2    "Version": "2012-10-17",
3    "Statement": [
4      {
5        "Action": "ssm:GetParameters",
6        "Effect": "Allow",
7        "Resource": "arn:aws:ssm:REGION_ID:ACCOUNT_ID:parameter/CodeBuild/*"
8      }
9    ]
10 }
```

- If the service role was generated by AWS CodeBuild, update its definition to allow AWS CodeBuild to access parameters in Amazon EC2 Parameter Store with names other than those starting with /CodeBuild/. For example, the following policy statement allows calling the ssm:GetParameters action to get parameters with the specified name:

```
1  {
2    "Version": "2012-10-17",
3    "Statement": [
4      {
5        "Action": "ssm:GetParameters",
6        "Effect": "Allow",
7        "Resource": "arn:aws:ssm:REGION_ID:ACCOUNT_ID:parameter/PARAMETER_NAME"
8      }
9    ]
10 }
```

"Access denied" Error Message When Attempting to Download Cache

Issue: When attempting to download the cache on a build project that has cache enabled, you receive the following generic error: "Access denied".

Possible causes:

- You have just configured caching as part of your build project.
- The cache has recently been invalidated via the `InvalidateProjectCache` API.
- The service role being used by CodeBuild does not have `s3:GetObject` and `s3:PutObject` permissions to the Amazon S3 bucket that is holding the cache.

Recommended solutions: For first time use, it's normal to see this immediately after updating the cache configuration. If this error persists, then you should check to see if your service role has `s3:GetObject` and `s3:PutObject` permissions to the Amazon S3 bucket that is holding the cache. For more information, see Specifying S3 permissions.

Error: "Unable to download cache: RequestError: send request failed caused by: x509: failed to load system roots and no roots provided"

Issue: When you try to run a build project, the build fails with the error: "RequestError: send request failed caused by: x509: failed to load system roots and no roots provided."

Possible causes:

- You have configured caching as part of your build project and are using an older Docker image that includes an expired root certificate.

Recommended solutions:

- Update the Docker image that is being used in your AWS CodeBuild the project. For more information, see Docker Images Provided by AWS CodeBuild.

Error: "Unable to download certificate from S3. AccessDenied"

Issue: When you try to run a build project, the build fails with the error "Unable to download certificate from S3. AccessDenied".

Possible causes:

- You have chosen the wrong S3 bucket for your certificate.
- You have entered the wrong object key for your certificate.

Recommended solutions:

- Edit your project. For **Bucket of certificate**, choose the S3 bucket where your SSL certificate is stored.
- Edit your project. For **Object key of certificate**, type the name of your S3 object key.

Error: "Git Clone Failed: unable to access 'your-repository-URL': SSL certificate problem: self signed certificate"

Issue: When you try to run a build project, the build fails with the error "Git Clone Failed: unable to access 'your-repository-URL': SSL certificate problem: self signed certificate."

Possible causes:

- Your source repository has a self-signed certificate, but you have not chosen to install the certificate from your S3 bucket as part of your build project.

Recommended solutions:

- Edit your project. For **Certificate**, choose **Install certificate from S3**. For **Bucket of certificate**, choose the S3 bucket where your SSL certificate is stored. For **Object key of certificate**, type the name of your S3 object key.
- Edit your project. Select **Insecure SSL** to ignore SSL warnings while connecting to your GitHub Enterprise project repository. **Note**
  We recommend that you use **Insecure SSL** for testing only. It should not be used in a production environment.

Error: "The policy's default version was not created by enhanced zero click role creation or was not the most recent version created by enhanced zero click role creation."

Issue: When you try to update a project in the console, the update failed with the error: "The policy's default version was not created by enhanced zero click role creation or was not the most recent version created by enhanced zero click role creation."

Possible causes:

- You have manually updated the policies attached to the target AWS CodeBuild service role.
- You have selected a previous version of a policy attached to the target AWS CodeBuild service role.

Recommended solutions:

- Edit your AWS CodeBuild project, and deselect **Allow AWS CodeBuild to modify this service role so it can be used with this build project**. Manually update the target AWS CodeBuild service role to have sufficient permissions. For more information, see Create an AWS CodeBuild Service Role.
- Edit your AWS CodeBuild project, and select **Create a role**.

Limits for AWS CodeBuild

The following tables list the current limits in AWS CodeBuild. These limits are for each supported AWS region for each AWS account, unless otherwise specified.

Build Projects

Resource	Default limit
Maximum number of build projects	1,000
Length of a build project name	2 to 255 characters, inclusive
Allowed characters in a build project name	The letters A-Z and a-z, the numbers 0-9, and the special characters - and _
Maximum length of a build project description	255 characters
Allowed characters in a build project description	Any
Maximum number of build projects you can request information about at any one time by using the AWS CLI, or AWS SDKs	100
Maximum number of tags you can associate with a build project	50
Number of minutes you can specify in a build project for the build timeout of all related builds	5 to 480 (8 hours)
Number of subnets you can add under VPC configuration	1 to 16
Number of security groups you can add under VPC configuration	1 to 5

Builds

Resource	Default limit
Maximum number of concurrent running builds *	20
Maximum number of builds you can request information about at any one time by using the AWS CLI, AWS SDKs	100
Number of minutes you can specify for the build timeout of a single build	5 to 480 (8 hours)

* Limits for the maximum number of concurrent running builds vary, depending on the compute type. For some compute types, the default is 20. For a new account, the limit can be between 1 and 5. To request a higher concurrent build limit or if you get a "Cannot have more than X active builds for the account" error, contact AWS support.

AWS CodeBuild for Windows—Third Party Notices

When you use AWS CodeBuild for Windows builds, you have the option to use some third party packages/modules to enable your built application to run on Microsoft Windows operating systems and to interoperate with some third party products. The following list contains the applicable third-party legal terms that govern your use of the specified third-party packages/modules.

Topics

- 1) Base Docker Image—windowsservercore
- 2) windows-base Docker Image—Choco
- 3) windows-base Docker Image—git --version 2.16.2
- 4) windows-base Docker Image—microsoft-build-tools --version 15.0.26320.2
- 5) windows-base Docker Image—nuget.commandline --version 4.5.1
- 7) windows-base Docker Image—netfx-4.6.2-devpack
- 8) windows-base Docker Image—visualfsharptools, v 4.0
- 9) windows-base Docker Image—netfx-pcl-reference-assemblies-4.6
- 10) windows-base Docker Image—visualcppbuildtools v 14.0.25420.1
- 11) windows-base Docker Image—microsoft-windows-netfx3-ondemand-package.cab
- 12) windows-base Docker Image—dotnet-sdk

1) Base Docker Image—windowsservercore

(license terms available at: https://hub.docker.com/r/microsoft/windowsservercore/)

License: By requesting and using this Container OS Image for Windows containers, you acknowledge, understand, and consent to the following Supplemental License Terms:

MICROSOFT SOFTWARE SUPPLEMENTAL LICENSE TERMS

CONTAINER OS IMAGE

Microsoft Corporation (or based on where you live, one of its affiliates) (referenced as "us," "we," or "Microsoft") licenses this Container OS Image supplement to you ("Supplement"). You are licensed to use this Supplement in conjunction with the underlying host operating system software ("Host Software") solely to assist running the containers feature in the Host Software. The Host Software license terms apply to your use of the Supplement. You may not use it if you do not have a license for the Host Software. You may use this Supplement with each validly licensed copy of the Host Software.

ADDITIONAL LICENSING REQUIREMENTS AND/OR USE RIGHTS

Your use of the Supplement as specified in the preceding paragraph may result in the creation or modification of a container image ("Container Image") that includes certain Supplement components. For clarity, a Container Image is separate and distinct from a virtual machine or virtual appliance image. Pursuant to these license terms, we grant you a restricted right to redistribute such Supplement components under the following conditions:

(i) you may use the Supplement components only as used in, and as a part of your Container Image,

(ii) you may use such Supplement components in your Container Image as long as you have significant primary functionality in your Container Image that is materially separate and distinct from the Supplement; and

(iii) you agree to include these license terms (or similar terms required by us or a hoster) with your Container Image to properly license the possible use of the Supplement components by your end-users.

We reserve all other rights not expressly granted herein.

By using this Supplement, you accept these terms. If you do not accept them, do not use this Supplement.

As part of the Supplemental License Terms for this Container OS Image for Windows containers, you are also subject to the underlying Windows Server host software license terms, which are located at: https://www.microsoft.com/en-us/useterms.

2) windows-base Docker Image—Choco

(license terms available at: https://github.com/chocolatey/chocolatey.org/blob/master/LICENSE.txt)

Copyright 2011 - Present RealDimensions Software, LLC

Licensed under the Apache License, version 2.0 (the "License"); you may not use these files except in compliance with the License. You may obtain a copy of the License at

http://www.apache.org/licenses/LICENSE-2.0

Unless required by applicable law or as agreed to in writing, software distributed under the License is distributed on an "AS IS" BASIS, WITHOUT WARRANTIES OR CONDITIONS OF ANY KIND, either express or implied. See the License for the specific language governing permissions and limitations under the License.

3) windows-base Docker Image—git --version 2.16.2

(license terms available at: https://chocolatey.org/packages/git/2.16.2)

Licensed under GNU General Public License, version 2, available at: https://www.gnu.org/licenses/old-licenses/gpl-2.0.html

4) windows-base Docker Image—microsoft-build-tools --version 15.0.26320.2

(license terms available at: https://www.visualstudio.com/license-terms/mt171552/)

MICROSOFT VISUAL STUDIO 2015 EXTENSIONS, VISUAL STUDIO SHELLS and C++ REDISTRIBUTABLE

These license terms are an agreement between Microsoft Corporation (or based on where you live, one of its affiliates) and you. They apply to the software named above. The terms also apply to any Microsoft services or updates for the software, except to the extent those have additional terms.

IF YOU COMPLY WITH THESE LICENSE TERMS, YOU HAVE THE RIGHTS BELOW.

1. **INSTALLATION AND USE RIGHTS**. You may install and use any number of copies of the software.

2. **TERMS FOR SPECIFIC COMPONENTS**.

    1. **Utilities**. The software may contain some items on the Utilities List at http://go.microsoft.com/fwlink/?LinkId=523763&clcid=0x409. You may copy and install those items, if included with the software, on to yours or other third party machines, to debug and deploy your applications and databases you developed with the software. Please note that Utilities are designed for temporary use, that Microsoft may not be able to patch or update Utilities separately from the rest of the software, and that some Utilities by their nature may make it possible for others to access machines on which they are installed. As a result, you should delete all Utilities you have installed after you finish debugging or deploying your applications and databases. Microsoft is not responsible for any third party use or access of Utilities you install on any machine.

2. **Microsoft Platforms.** The software may include components from Microsoft Windows; Microsoft Windows Server; Microsoft SQL Server; Microsoft Exchange; Microsoft Office; and Microsoft SharePoint. These components are governed by separate agreements and their own product support policies, as described in the license terms found in the installation directory for that component or in the "Licenses" folder accompanying the software.

3. **Third Party Components.** The software may include third party components with separate legal notices or governed by other agreements, as described in the ThirdPartyNotices file accompanying the software. Even if such components are governed by other agreements, the disclaimers and the limitations on and exclusions of damages below also apply. The software may also include components licensed under open source licenses with source code availability obligations. Copies of those licenses, if applicable, are included in the ThirdPartyNotices file. You may obtain this source code from us, if and as required under the relevant open source licenses, by sending a money order or check for $5.00 to: Source Code Compliance Team, Microsoft Corporation, 1 Microsoft Way, Redmond, WA 98052. Please write source code for one or more of the components listed below in the memo line of your payment:

   - Remote Tools for Visual Studio 2015;
   - Standalone Profiler for Visual Studio 2015;
   - IntelliTraceCollector for Visual Studio 2015;
   - Microsoft VC++ Redistributable 2015;
   - Multibyte MFC Library for Visual Studio 2015;
   - Microsoft Build Tools 2015;
   - Feedback Client;
   - Visual Studio 2015 Integrated Shell; or
   - Visual Studio 2015 Isolated Shell.

   We may also make a copy of the source code available at http://thirdpartysource.microsoft.com.

3. **DATA.** The software may collect information about you and your use of the software, and send that to Microsoft. Microsoft may use this information to provide services and improve our products and services. You may opt-out of many of these scenarios, but not all, as described in the product documentation. There are also some features in the software that may enable you to collect data from users of your applications. If you use these features to enable data collection in your applications, you must comply with applicable law, including providing appropriate notices to users of your applications. You can learn more about data collection and use in the help documentation and the privacy statement at http://go.microsoft.com/fwlink/?LinkId=528096&clcid=0x409. Your use of the software operates as your consent to these practices.

4. **SCOPE OF LICENSE.** The software is licensed, not sold. This agreement only gives you some rights to use the software. Microsoft reserves all other rights. Unless applicable law gives you more rights despite this limitation, you may use the software only as expressly permitted in this agreement. In doing so, you must comply with any technical limitations in the software that only allow you to use it in certain ways. You may not

   - work around any technical limitations in the software;
   - reverse engineer, decompile or disassemble the software, or attempt to do so, except and only to the extent required by third party licensing terms governing the use of certain open-source components that may be included with the software;
   - remove, minimize, block or modify any notices of Microsoft or its suppliers in the software;
   - use the software in any way that is against the law; or
   - share, publish, rent or lease the software, or provide the software as a stand-alone hosted as solution for others to use.

5. **EXPORT RESTRICTIONS.** You must comply with all domestic and international export laws and regulations that apply to the software, which include restrictions on destinations, end users, and end use. For further information on export restrictions, visit (aka.ms/exporting).

6. **SUPPORT SERVICES**. Because this software is "as is," we may not provide support services for it.

7. **ENTIRE AGREEMENT**. This agreement, and the terms for supplements, updates, Internet-based services and support services that you use, are the entire agreement for the software and support services.

8. **APPLICABLE LAW**. If you acquired the software in the United States, Washington law applies to interpretation of and claims for breach of this agreement, and the laws of the state where you live apply to all other claims. If you acquired the software in any other country, its laws apply.

9. **CONSUMER RIGHTS; REGIONAL VARIATIONS**. This agreement describes certain legal rights. You may have other rights, including consumer rights, under the laws of your state or country. Separate and apart from your relationship with Microsoft, you may also have rights with respect to the party from which you acquired the software. This agreement does not change those other rights if the laws of your state or country do not permit it to do so. For example, if you acquired the software in one of the below regions, or mandatory country law applies, then the following provisions apply to you:

    1. **Australia**. You have statutory guarantees under the Australian Consumer Law and nothing in this agreement is intended to affect those rights.

    2. **Canada**. If you acquired this software in Canada, you may stop receiving updates by turning off the automatic update feature, disconnecting your device from the Internet (if and when you re-connect to the Internet, however, the software will resume checking for and installing updates), or uninstalling the software. The product documentation, if any, may also specify how to turn off updates for your specific device or software.

    3. **Germany and Austria**.

        1. **Warranty**. The properly licensed software will perform substantially as described in any Microsoft materials that accompany the software. However, Microsoft gives no contractual guarantee in relation to the licensed software.

        2. **Limitation of Liability**. In case of intentional conduct, gross negligence, claims based on the Product Liability Act, as well as, in case of death or personal or physical injury, Microsoft is liable according to the statutory law.Subject to the foregoing clause (ii), Microsoft will only be liable for slight negligence if Microsoft is in breach of such material contractual obligations, the fulfillment of which facilitate the due performance of this agreement, the breach of which would endanger the purpose of this agreement and the compliance with which a party may constantly trust in (so-called "cardinal obligations"). In other cases of slight negligence, Microsoft will not be liable for slight negligence.

10. **DISCLAIMER OF WARRANTY. THE SOFTWARE IS LICENSED "AS-IS." YOU BEAR THE RISK OF USING IT. MICROSOFT GIVES NO EXPRESS WARRANTIES, GUARANTEES OR CONDITIONS. TO THE EXTENT PERMITTED UNDER YOUR LOCAL LAWS, MICROSOFT EXCLUDES THE IMPLIED WARRANTIES OF MERCHANTABILITY, FITNESS FOR A PARTICULAR PURPOSE AND NON-INFRINGEMENT.**

11. **LIMITATION ON AND EXCLUSION OF DAMAGES. YOU CAN RECOVER FROM MICROSOFT AND ITS SUPPLIERS ONLY DIRECT DAMAGES UP TO U.S. $5.00. YOU CANNOT RECOVER ANY OTHER DAMAGES, INCLUDING CONSEQUENTIAL, LOST PROFITS, SPECIAL, INDIRECT OR INCIDENTAL DAMAGES.** This limitation applies to (a) anything related to the software, services, content (including code) on third party Internet sites, or third party applications; and (b) claims for breach of contract, breach of warranty, guarantee or condition, strict liability, negligence, or other tort to the extent permitted by applicable law.

    It also applies even if Microsoft knew or should have known about the possibility of the damages. The above limitation or exclusion may not apply to you because your country may not allow the exclusion or limitation of incidental, consequential or other damages.

EULA ID: VS2015_Update3_ShellsRedist_

5) windows-base Docker Image—nuget.commandline --version 4.5.1

(license terms available at: https://github.com/NuGet/Home/blob/dev/LICENSE.txt)

Copyright (c) .NET Foundation. All rights reserved.

Licensed under the Apache License, version 2.0 (the "License"); you may not use these files except in compliance with the License. You may obtain a copy of the License at

http://www.apache.org/licenses/LICENSE-2.0

Unless required by applicable law or as agreed to in writing, software distributed under the License is distributed on an "AS IS" BASIS, WITHOUT WARRANTIES OR CONDITIONS OF ANY KIND, either express or implied. See the License for the specific language governing permissions and limitations under the License.

7) windows-base Docker Image—netfx-4.6.2-devpack

MICROSOFT SOFTWARE SUPPLEMENTAL LICENSE TERMS

.NET FRAMEWORK AND ASSOCIATED LANGUAGE PACKS FOR MICROSOFT WINDOWS OPERATING SYSTEM

Microsoft Corporation (or based on where you live, one of its affiliates) licenses this supplement to you. If you are licensed to use Microsoft Windows operating system software (the "software"), you may use this supplement. You may not use it if you do not have a license for the software. You may use this supplement with each validly licensed copy of the software.

The following license terms describe additional use terms for this supplement. These terms and the license terms for the software apply to your use of the supplement. If there is a conflict, these supplemental license terms apply.

BY USING THIS SUPPLEMENT, YOU ACCEPT THESE TERMS. IF YOU DO NOT ACCEPT THEM, DO NOT USE THIS SUPPLEMENT.

If you comply with these license terms, you have the rights below.

1. **DISTRIBUTABLE CODE.** The supplement is comprised of Distributable Code. "Distributable Code" is code that you are permitted to distribute in programs you develop if you comply with the terms below.

    1. **Right to Use and Distribute**.

        - You may copy and distribute the object code form of the supplement.
        - *Third Party Distribution.* You may permit distributors of your programs to copy and distribute the Distributable Code as part of those programs.

    2. **Distribution Requirements. For any Distributable Code you distribute, you must**

        - add significant primary functionality to it in your programs;
        - for any Distributable Code having a filename extension of .lib, distribute only the results of running such Distributable Code through a linker with your program;
        - distribute Distributable Code included in a setup program only as part of that setup program without modification;
        - require distributors and external end users to agree to terms that protect it at least as much as this agreement;
        - display your valid copyright notice on your programs; and
        - indemnify, defend, and hold harmless Microsoft from any claims, including attorneys' fees, related to the distribution or use of your programs.

3. **Distribution Restrictions. You may not**

- alter any copyright, trademark or patent notice in the Distributable Code;
- use Microsoft's trademarks in your programs' names or in a way that suggests your programs come from or are endorsed by Microsoft;
- distribute Distributable Code to run on a platform other than the Windows platform;
- include Distributable Code in malicious, deceptive or unlawful programs; or
- modify or distribute the source code of any Distributable Code so that any part of it becomes subject to an Excluded License. An Excluded License is one that requires, as a condition of use, modification or distribution, that
  - the code be disclosed or distributed in source code form; or
  - others have the right to modify it.

2. **SUPPORT SERVICES FOR SUPPLEMENT**. Microsoft provides support services for this software as described at www.support.microsoft.com/common/international.aspx.

8) windows-base Docker Image—visualfsharptools, v 4.0

(license terms available at: https://raw.githubusercontent.com/Microsoft/visualfsharp/master/License.txt)

Copyright (c) Microsoft Corporation. All rights reserved.

Licensed under the Apache License, version 2.0 (the "License"); you may not use these files except in compliance with the License. You may obtain a copy of the License at

http://www.apache.org/licenses/LICENSE-2.0

Unless required by applicable law or as agreed to in writing, software distributed under the License is distributed on an "AS IS" BASIS, WITHOUT WARRANTIES OR CONDITIONS OF ANY KIND, either express or implied. See the License for the specific language governing permissions and limitations under the License.

9) windows-base Docker Image—netfx-pcl-reference-assemblies-4.6

MICROSOFT SOFTWARE LICENSE TERMS

MICROSOFT .NET PORTABLE CLASS LIBRARY REFERENCE ASSEMBLIES – 4.6

These license terms are an agreement between Microsoft Corporation (or based on where you live, one of its affiliates) and you. Please read them. They apply to the software named above. The terms also apply to any Microsoft

- updates,
- supplements,
- Internet-based services, and
- support services

for this software, unless other terms accompany those items. If so, those terms apply.

BY USING THE SOFTWARE, YOU ACCEPT THESE TERMS. IF YOU DO NOT ACCEPT THEM, DO NOT USE THE SOFTWARE.

IF YOU COMPLY WITH THESE LICENSE TERMS, YOU HAVE THE PERPETUAL RIGHTS BELOW.

1. **INSTALLATION AND USE RIGHTS.** You may install and use any number of copies of the software to design, develop and test your programs.

2. **ADDITIONAL LICENSING REQUIREMENTS AND/OR USE RIGHTS.**

   1. **Distributable Code.** You may distribute the software in developer tool programs you develop, to enable customers of your programs to develop portable libraries for use with any device or operating system, if you comply with the terms below.

      1. **Right to Use and Distribute. The software is "Distributable Code."**

         * *Distributable Code.* You may copy and distribute the object code form of the software.
         * *Third Party Distribution.* You may permit distributors of your programs to copy and distribute the Distributable Code as part of those programs.

      2. **Distribution Requirements. For any Distributable Code you distribute, you must**

         * add significant primary functionality to it in your programs;
         * require distributors and your customers to agree to terms that protect it at least as much as this agreement;
         * display your valid copyright notice on your programs; and
         * indemnify, defend, and hold harmless Microsoft from any claims, including attorneys' fees, related to the distribution or use of your programs.

      3. **Distribution Restrictions. You may not**

         * alter any copyright, trademark or patent notice in the Distributable Code;
         * use Microsoft's trademarks in your programs' names or in a way that suggests your programs come from or are endorsed by Microsoft;
         * include Distributable Code in malicious, deceptive or unlawful programs; or
         * modify or distribute the Distributable Code so that any part of it becomes subject to an Excluded License. An Excluded License is one that requires, as a condition of use, modification or distribution, that
           * the code be disclosed or distributed in source code form; or
           * others have the right to modify it.

3. **SCOPE OF LICENSE.** The software is licensed, not sold. This agreement only gives you some rights to use the software. Microsoft reserves all other rights. Unless applicable law gives you more rights despite this limitation, you may use the software only as expressly permitted in this agreement. In doing so, you must comply with any technical limitations in the software that only allow you to use it in certain ways. You may not

   * work around any technical limitations in the software;
   * reverse engineer, decompile or disassemble the software, except and only to the extent that applicable law expressly permits, despite this limitation;
   * publish the software for others to copy; or
   * rent, lease or lend the software.

4. **FEEDBACK.** You may provide feedback about the software. If you give feedback about the software to Microsoft, you give to Microsoft, without charge, the right to use, share and commercialize your feedback in any way and for any purpose. You also give to third parties, without charge, any patent rights needed for their products, technologies and services to use or interface with any specific parts of a Microsoft software or service that includes the feedback. You will not give feedback that is subject to a license that requires Microsoft to license its software or documentation to third parties because we include your feedback in them. These rights survive this agreement.

5. **TRANSFER TO A THIRD PARTY.** The first user of the software may transfer it, and this agreement, directly to a third party. Before the transfer, that party must agree that this agreement applies to the transfer and use of the software. The first user must uninstall the software before transferring it separately from the device. The first user may not retain any copies.

6. **EXPORT RESTRICTIONS.** The software is subject to United States export laws and regulations. You must comply with all domestic and international export laws and regulations that apply to the software.

These laws include restrictions on destinations, end users and end use. For additional information, see www.microsoft.com/exporting.

7. **SUPPORT SERVICES.** Because this software is "as is," we may not provide support services for it.

8. **ENTIRE AGREEMENT.** This agreement, and the terms for supplements, updates, Internet-based services and support services that you use, are the entire agreement for the software and any support services we provide.

9. **APPLICABLE LAW.**

   1. **United States.** If you acquired the software in the United States, Washington state law governs the interpretation of this agreement and applies to claims for breach of it, regardless of conflict of laws principles. The laws of the state where you live govern all other claims, including claims under state consumer protection laws, unfair competition laws, and in tort.

   2. **Outside the United States.** If you acquired the software in any other country, the laws of that country apply.

10. **LEGAL EFFECT.** This agreement describes certain legal rights. You may have other rights under the laws of your country. You may also have rights with respect to the party from whom you acquired the software. This agreement does not change your rights under the laws of your country if the laws of your country do not permit it to do so.

11. **DISCLAIMER OF WARRANTY. THE SOFTWARE IS LICENSED "AS-IS." YOU BEAR THE RISK OF USING IT. MICROSOFT GIVES NO EXPRESS WARRANTIES, GUARANTEES OR CONDITIONS. YOU MAY HAVE ADDITIONAL CONSUMER RIGHTS OR STATUTORY GUARANTEES UNDER YOUR LOCAL LAWS WHICH THIS AGREEMENT CANNOT CHANGE. TO THE EXTENT PERMITTED UNDER YOUR LOCAL LAWS, MICROSOFT EXCLUDES THE IMPLIED WARRANTIES OF MERCHANTABILITY, FITNESS FOR A PARTICULAR PURPOSE AND NON-INFRINGEMENT.**

    FOR AUSTRALIA—YOU HAVE STATUTORY GUARANTEES UNDER THE AUSTRALIAN CONSUMER LAW AND NOTHING IN THESE TERMS IS INTENDED TO AFFECT THOSE RIGHTS.

12. **LIMITATION ON AND EXCLUSION OF REMEDIES AND DAMAGES. YOU CAN RECOVER FROM MICROSOFT AND ITS SUPPLIERS ONLY DIRECT DAMAGES UP TO U.S. $5.00. YOU CANNOT RECOVER ANY OTHER DAMAGES, INCLUDING CONSEQUENTIAL, LOST PROFITS, SPECIAL, INDIRECT OR INCIDENTAL DAMAGES.**

    This limitation applies to

    - anything related to the software, services, content (including code) on third party Internet sites, or third party programs; and
    - claims for breach of contract, breach of warranty, guarantee or condition, strict liability, negligence, or other tort to the extent permitted by applicable law.

    It also applies even if Microsoft knew or should have known about the possibility of the damages. The above limitation or exclusion may not apply to you because your country may not allow the exclusion or limitation of incidental, consequential or other damages.

10) windows-base Docker Image—visualcppbuildtools v 14.0.25420.1

(license terms available at: https://www.visualstudio.com/license-terms/mt644918/)

MICROSOFT VISUAL C++ BUILD TOOLS

MICROSOFT SOFTWARE LICENSE TERMS

MICROSOFT VISUAL C++ BUILD TOOLS

These license terms are an agreement between Microsoft Corporation (or based on where you live, one of its affiliates) and you. They apply to the software named above. The terms also apply to any Microsoft services or updates for the software, except to the extent those have different terms.

IF YOU COMPLY WITH THESE LICENSE TERMS, YOU HAVE THE RIGHTS BELOW.

1. **INSTALLATION AND USE RIGHTS**.

   1. One user may use copies of the software to develop and test their applications.

2. **DATA**. The software may collect information about you and your use of the software, and send that to Microsoft. Microsoft may use this information to provide services and improve our products and services. You may opt-out of many of these scenarios, but not all, as described in the product documentation. There are also some features in the software that may enable you to collect data from users of your applications. If you use these features to enable data collection in your applications, you must comply with applicable law, including providing appropriate notices to users of your applications. You can learn more about data collection and use in the help documentation and the privacy statement at http://go.microsoft.com/fwlink/?LinkID=528096. Your use of the software operates as your consent to these practices.

3. **TERMS FOR SPECIFIC COMPONENTS**.

   1. **Build Server**. The software may contain some Build Server components listed in BuildServer.TXT files, and/or any files listed on the BuildeServer list located following this Microsoft Software License Terms. You may copy and install those items, if included in the software, onto your build machines. You and others in your organization may use these items on your build machines solely for the purpose of compiling, building, verifying and archiving your applications or running quality or performance tests as part of the build process.

   2. **Microsoft Platforms**. The software may include components from Microsoft Windows; Microsoft Windows Server; Microsoft SQL Server; Microsoft Exchange; Microsoft Office; and Microsoft Share-Point. These components are governed by separate agreements and their own product support policies, as described in the license terms found in the installation directory for that component or in the "Licenses" folder accompanying the software.

   3. **Third Party Components**. The software may include third party components with separate legal notices or governed by other agreements, as described in the ThirdPartyNotices file accompanying the software. Even if such components are governed by other agreements, the disclaimers and the limitations on and exclusions of damages below also apply.

   4. **Package Managers**. The software may include package managers, like Nuget, that give you the option to download other Microsoft and third party software packages to use with your application. Those packages are under their own licenses, and not this agreement. Microsoft does not distribute, license or provide any warranties for any of the third party packages.

4. **SCOPE OF LICENSE**. The software is licensed, not sold. This agreement only gives you some rights to use the software. Microsoft reserves all other rights. Unless applicable law gives you more rights despite this limitation, you may use the software only as expressly permitted in this agreement. In doing so, you must comply with any technical limitations in the software that only allow you to use it in certain ways. For more information, see http://www.microsoft.com/licensing/userights. You may not

   - work around any technical limitations in the software;
   - reverse engineer, decompile or disassemble the software, or attempt to do so, except and only to the extent required by third party licensing terms governing use of certain open source components that may be included with the software;

- remove, minimize, block or modify any notices of Microsoft or its suppliers;
- use the software in any way that is against the law; or
- share, publish, rent or lease the software, or provide the software as a stand-alone hosted as solution for others to use.

5. **EXPORT RESTRICTIONS**. You must comply with all domestic and international export laws and regulations that apply to the software, which include restrictions on destinations, end users and end use. For further information on export restrictions, visit (aka.ms/exporting).

6. **SUPPORT SERVICES**. Because this software is "as is," we may not provide support services for it.

7. **ENTIRE AGREEMENT**. This agreement, and the terms for supplements, updates, Internet-based services and support services that you use, are the entire agreement for the software and support services.

8. **APPLICABLE LAW**. If you acquired the software in the United States, Washington law applies to interpretation of and claims for breach of this agreement, and the laws of the state where you live apply to all other claims. If you acquired the software in any other country, its laws apply.

9. **CONSUMER RIGHTS; REGIONAL VARIATIONS**. This agreement describes certain legal rights. You may have other rights, including consumer rights, under the laws of your state or country. Separate and apart from your relationship with Microsoft, you may also have rights with respect to the party from which you acquired the software. This agreement does not change those other rights if the laws of your state or country do not permit it to do so. For example, if you acquired the software in one of the below regions, or mandatory country law applies, then the following provisions apply to you:

   - **Australia**. You have statutory guarantees under the Australian Consumer Law and nothing in this agreement is intended to affect those rights.
   - **Canada**. If you acquired this software in Canada, you may stop receiving updates by turning off the automatic update feature, disconnecting your device from the Internet (if and when you re-connect to the Internet, however, the software will resume checking for and installing updates), or uninstalling the software. The product documentation, if any, may also specify how to turn off updates for your specific device or software.
   - **Germany and Austria**.
     - **Warranty**. The properly licensed software will perform substantially as described in any Microsoft materials that accompany the software. However, Microsoft gives no contractual guarantee in relation to the licensed software.
     - *Limitation of Liability*. In case of intentional conduct, gross negligence, claims based on the Product Liability Act, as well as, in case of death or personal or physical injury, Microsoft is liable according to the statutory law.
       Subject to the foregoing clause (ii), Microsoft will only be liable for slight negligence if Microsoft is in breach of such material contractual obligations, the fulfillment of which facilitate the due performance of this agreement, the breach of which would endanger the purpose of this agreement and the compliance with which a party may constantly trust in (so-called "cardinal obligations"). In other cases of slight negligence, Microsoft will not be liable for slight negligence.

10. **LEGAL EFFECT**. This agreement describes certain legal rights. You may have other rights under the laws of your state or country. This agreement does not change your rights under the laws of your state or country if the laws of your state or country do not permit it to do so. Without limitation of the foregoing, for Australia, **YOU HAVE STATUTORY GUARANTEES UNDER THE AUSTRALIAN CONSUMER LAW AND NOTHING IN THESE TERMS IS INTENDED TO AFFECT THOSE RIGHTS**

11. **DISCLAIMER OF WARRANTY. THE SOFTWARE IS LICENSED "AS-IS." YOU BEAR THE RISK OF USING IT. MICROSOFT GIVES NO EXPRESS WARRANTIES, GUARANTEES OR CONDITIONS. TO THE EXTENT PERMITTED UNDER YOUR LOCAL LAWS, MICROSOFT EXCLUDES THE IMPLIED WARRANTIES OF MERCHANTABILITY, FITNESS FOR A PARTICULAR PURPOSE AND NON-INFRINGEMENT.**

12. **LIMITATION ON AND EXCLUSION OF DAMAGES. YOU CAN RECOVER FROM**

MICROSOFT AND ITS SUPPLIERS ONLY DIRECT DAMAGES UP TO U.S. $5.00. YOU CANNOT RECOVER ANY OTHER DAMAGES, INCLUDING CONSEQUENTIAL, LOST PROFITS, SPECIAL, INDIRECT OR INCIDENTAL DAMAGES.

This limitation applies to (a) anything related to the software, services, content (including code) on third party Internet sites, or third party applications; and (b) claims for breach of contract, breach of warranty, guarantee or condition, strict liability, negligence, or other tort to the extent permitted by applicable law.

It also applies even if Microsoft knew or should have known about the possibility of the damages. The above limitation or exclusion may not apply to you because your country may not allow the exclusion or limitation of incidental, consequential or other damages.

11) windows-base Docker Image—microsoft-windows-netfx3-ondemand-package.cab

MICROSOFT SOFTWARE SUPPLEMENTAL LICENSE TERMS

MICROSOFT .NET FRAMEWORK 3.5 SP1 FOR MICROSOFT WINDOWS OPERATING SYSTEM

Microsoft Corporation (or based on where you live, one of its affiliates) licenses this supplement to you. If you are licensed to use Microsoft Windows operating system software (for which this supplement is applicable) (the "software"), you may use this supplement. You may not use it if you do not have a license for the software. You may use a copy of this supplement with each validly licensed copy of the software.

The following license terms describe additional use terms for this supplement. These terms and the license terms for the software apply to your use of the supplement. If there is a conflict, these supplemental license terms apply.

BY USING THIS SUPPLEMENT, YOU ACCEPT THESE TERMS. IF YOU DO NOT ACCEPT THEM, DO NOT USE THIS SUPPLEMENT.

If you comply with these license terms, you have the rights below.

1. **SUPPORT SERVICES FOR SUPPLEMENT**. Microsoft provides support services for this software as described at www.support.microsoft.com/common/international.aspx.

2. **MICROSOFT .NET BENCHMARK TESTING**. The software includes the .NET Framework, Windows Communication Foundation, Windows Presentation Foundation, and Windows Workflow Foundation components of the Windows operating systems (.NET Components). You may conduct internal benchmark testing of the .NET Components. You may disclose the results of any benchmark test of the .NET Components, provided that you comply with the conditions set forth at http://go.microsoft.com/fwlink/?LinkID=66406.

   Notwithstanding any other agreement you may have with Microsoft, if you disclose such benchmark test results, Microsoft shall have the right to disclose the results of benchmark tests it conducts of your products that compete with the applicable .NET Component, provided it complies with the same conditions set forth at http://go.microsoft.com/fwlink/?LinkID=66406.

12) windows-base Docker Image—dotnet-sdk

(available at https://github.com/dotnet/core/blob/master/LICENSE)

The MIT License (MIT)

Copyright (c) Microsoft Corporation

AWS CodeBuild User Guide Document History

Here is a list of important changes to the *AWS CodeBuild User Guide*.

- **Latest API version:** 2016-10-06
- **Latest documentation update:** January 25, 2018

Change	Description	Date Changed
AWS CodeBuild available in Asia Pacific (Mumbai), EU (Paris), and South America (São Paulo)	AWS CodeBuild is now available in the Asia Pacific (Mumbai), EU (Paris), and South America (São Paulo) regions. For more information, see the AWS CodeBuild section of the "AWS Regions and Endpoints" topic in the Amazon Web Services General Reference.	March 28, 2018
GitHub Enterprise support	AWS CodeBuild can now build from source code stored in a GitHub Enterprise repository. For more information, see GitHub Enterprise Sample.	January, 25, 2018
Git clone depth support	AWS CodeBuild now supports the creation of a shallow clone with a history truncated to the specified number of commits. For more information, see Create a Build Project.	January, 25, 2018
VPC support	VPC-enabled builds are now able to access resources inside your VPC. For more information, see VPC Support.	November, 27, 2017
Dependency caching support	AWS CodeBuild now supports the dependency caching. This allows AWS CodeBuild to save certain reusable pieces of the build environment in the cache and use this across builds.	November, 27, 2017
Build badges support	AWS CodeBuild now supports the use of build badges, which provide an embeddable, dynamically generated image (badge) that displays the status of the latest build for a project. For more information, see Build Badges Sample.	November 27, 2017

Change	Description	Date Changed
AWS Config integration	AWS Config now supports AWS CodeBuild as an AWS resource, which means the service can track your AWS CodeBuild projects. For more information about AWS Config, see Use AWS Config with AWS CodeBuild Sample.	October 20, 2017
Automatically rebuild updated source code in GitHub repositories	If your source code is stored in a GitHub repository, you can enable AWS CodeBuild to rebuild your source code whenever a code change is pushed to the repository. For more information, see GitHub Pull Request Sample.	September 21, 2017
New ways for storing and retrieving sensitive or large environment variables in Amazon EC2 Systems Manager Parameter Store	You can now use the AWS CodeBuild console or the AWS CLI to retrieve sensitive or large environment variables stored in Amazon EC2 Systems Manager Parameter Store. You can also now use the AWS CodeBuild console to store these types of environment variables in Amazon EC2 Systems Manager Parameter Store. Previously, you could only retrieve these types of environment variables by including them in a build spec or by running build commands to automate the AWS CLI. You could only store these types of environment variables by using the Amazon EC2 Systems Manager Parameter Store console. For more information, see Create a Build Project, Change a Build Project's Settings, and Run a Build.	September 14, 2017
Build deletion support	You can now delete builds in AWS CodeBuild. For more information, see Delete Builds.	August 31, 2017

Change	Description	Date Changed
Updated way to retrieve sensitive or large environment variables stored in Amazon EC2 Systems Manager Parameter Store by using a build spec	AWS CodeBuild now makes it easier to use a build spec to retrieve sensitive or large environment variables stored in Amazon EC2 Systems Manager Parameter Store. Previously, you could only retrieve these types of environment variables by running build commands to automate the AWS CLI. For more information, see the parameter-store mapping in Build Spec Syntax.	August 10, 2017
AWS CodeBuild supports Bitbucket	AWS CodeBuild can now build from source code stored in a Bitbucket repository. For more information, see Create a Build Project and Run a Build.	August 10, 2017
AWS CodeBuild available in US West (N. California), EU (London), and Canada (Central)	AWS CodeBuild is now available in the US West (N. California), EU (London), and Canada (Central) regions. For more information, see the AWS CodeBuild section of the "AWS Regions and Endpoints" topic in the Amazon Web Services General Reference.	June 29, 2017
.NET Core in Linux sample	A sample showing how to use AWS CodeBuild and .NET Core to build an executable file out of code written in C# has been added. For more information, see the .NET Core in Linux Sample.	June 29, 2017
Alternate build spec file names and locations supported	You can now specify an alternate file name or location of a build spec file to use for a build project, instead of a default build spec file named buildspec.yml at the root of the source code. For more information, see Build Spec File Name and Storage Location.	June 27, 2017

Change	Description	Date Changed
Updated build notifications sample	AWS CodeBuild now provides built-in support for build notifications through Amazon CloudWatch Events and Amazon Simple Notification Service (Amazon SNS). The previous Build Notifications Sample has been updated to demonstrate this new behavior.	June 22, 2017
Docker in custom image sample added	A sample showing how to use AWS CodeBuild and a custom Docker build image to build and run a Docker image has been added. For more information, see the Docker in Custom Image Sample.	June 7, 2017
Fetch source code for GitHub pull requests	When you run a build with AWS CodeBuild that relies on source code stored in a GitHub repository, you can now specify a GitHub pull request ID to build. You can also specify a commit ID, a branch name, or a tag name instead. For more information, see the **Source version** value in Run a Build (Console) or the `sourceVersion` value in Run a Build (AWS CLI).	June 6, 2017
Build specification version updated	A new version of the build spec format has been released. Version 0.2 addresses the issue of AWS CodeBuild running each build command in a separate instance of the default shell. Also in version 0.2, environment_variables is renamed to env, and plaintext is renamed to variables. For more information, see Build Specification Reference for AWS CodeBuild.	May 9, 2017
Dockerfiles for build images available in GitHub	Definitions for many of the build images provided by AWS CodeBuild are available as Dockerfiles in GitHub. For more information, see the "Definition" column of the table in Docker Images Provided by AWS CodeBuild.	May 2, 2017

Change	Description	Date Changed
AWS CodeBuild available in EU (Frankfurt), Asia Pacific (Singapore), Asia Pacific (Sydney), and Asia Pacific (Tokyo)	AWS CodeBuild is now available in the EU (Frankfurt), Asia Pacific (Singapore), Asia Pacific (Sydney), and Asia Pacific (Tokyo) regions. For more information, see the AWS CodeBuild section of the "AWS Regions and Endpoints" topic in the Amazon Web Services General Reference.	March 21, 2017
AWS CodePipeline test action support for AWS CodeBuild	You can now add to a pipeline in AWS CodePipeline a test action that uses AWS CodeBuild. For more information, see Add an AWS CodeBuild Test Action to a Pipeline (AWS CodePipeline Console).	March 8, 2017
Build specs support fetching build output from within selected top-level directories	Build specs now enable you to specify individual top-level directories whose contents you can instruct AWS CodeBuild to include in build output artifacts. You do this by using the base-directory mapping. For more information, see Build Spec Syntax.	February 8, 2017
Built-in environment variables	AWS CodeBuild provides additional built-in environment variables for your builds to use. These include environment variables describing the entity that started the build, the URL to the source code repository, the source code's version ID, and more. For more information, see Environment Variables in Build Environments.	January 30, 2017
AWS CodeBuild available in US East (Ohio)	AWS CodeBuild is now available in the US East (Ohio) region. For more information, see the AWS CodeBuild section of the "AWS Regions and Endpoints" topic in the Amazon Web Services General Reference.	January 19, 2017

Change	Description	Date Changed
AWS Lambda sample	A reference was added to a sample showing how to use AWS CodeBuild along with Lambda, AWS CloudFormation, and AWS CodePipeline to build and deploy a serverless application that follows the AWS Serverless Application Model (AWS SAM) standard. For more information, see the AWS Lambda Sample.	December 20, 2016
C++ and Go samples	Samples showing how to use AWS CodeBuild to build C++ and Go output artifacts have been added. For more information, see the C++ Sample and the Go Sample.	December 9, 2016
Shell and command behaviors information	AWS CodeBuild runs each command you specify in a separate instance of a build environment's default shell. This default behavior can produce some unexpected side effects for your commands. We recommend some approaches to work around this default behavior if needed. For more information, see Shells and Commands in Build Environments.	December 9, 2016
Environment variables information	AWS CodeBuild provides several environment variables that you can use in your build commands. You can also define your own environment variables. For more information, see Environment Variables in Build Environments.	December 7, 2016
Troubleshooting topic	Troubleshooting information is now available. For more information, see Troubleshooting AWS CodeBuild.	December 5, 2016
Jenkins plugin initial release	This is the initial release of the AWS CodeBuild Jenkins Plugin. For more information, see Use AWS CodeBuild with Jenkins.	December 5, 2016
User Guide initial release	This is the initial release of the AWS CodeBuild User Guide.	December 1, 2016

AWS Glossary

For the latest AWS terminology, see the AWS Glossary in the *AWS General Reference*.